HELPING PEOPLE GROW

Understanding the Five Conditions
for Life Change

JOHN DEHNERT

credo
house publishers

Helping People Grow
Copyright © 2021 by John Dehnert
All rights reserved.

Published in the United States of America by Credo House Publishers,
a division of Credo Communications, LLC, Grand Rapids, Michigan
credohousepublishers.com

Unless otherwise noted, Scripture quotations are from the Holy Bible, New International Version®, NIV® Copyright ©1973, 1978, 1984, 2011 by Biblica, Inc.®. Used by permission. All rights reserved worldwide.

ISBN: 978-1-62586-189-4

Cover and interior design by Frank Gutbrod
Editing by Mike Vander Klipp

Printed in the United States of America

First edition

For Coleene.

And for Joey, Jilly, Zach, and Timmy.

*And for all the family I don't know yet,
or those I may never know.*

I've been thinking of you this whole time.

CONTENTS

" WHEN WAS THE TIME YOU MOST NEEDED GOD? "

INTRODUCTION

Personal growth is a journey often born of need, or of outright desperation. When we stop getting what we think we need, that place of deprivation has a way of getting us on our feet and moving.

That's how it was for me when I realized I could no longer handle life on my own. It was shocking, actually, to come face to face with that reality.

How did I get there? It all started with a simple question:

"When was the time you most needed God?"

I've come to love this question. I've asked it hundreds of times—usually in small groups or with a close friend. It's valuable when it connects us to our most relevant need, and beautiful when we normalize that need with people we love.

I first heard this question years ago, gathered in a small beach house in Oxnard, California with my new boss, John Ortberg, and the other pastors on our staff team. The five of us had gotten away to be together, pray for wisdom, and simply become friends. We had a daunting job ahead of us, so we prayed for wisdom and talked about how to lead our established—and entrenched—church through some very big changes. Since we needed God so badly, John began our first morning together asking that simple question.

Even now, many years later, I remember the rush of fear in my heart when I heard John's words. It felt something like an emotional ambush. Most distressing was the size of my heart response compared to the size of the question. In a word, I felt panic. Why panic? What was so severe about that simple question to kick up such a big emotional response? I didn't know, but I couldn't seem to calm my heart.

"What is happening to me? Can everyone see what this question is doing in my heart?" Those were the questions I cycled through over the next few moments as I struggled back to my feet emotionally. After the tiniest recovery I leapt to damage control, racing through ways I might get out of answering the question out loud.

In my core, in the deep hidden parts of my heart—a place I rarely visited and knew little about, in that place I could see I was in trouble. In that one simple question—perfectly timed by the Holy Spirit, I collided with a part of my story I had never seriously considered before—not one single time.

The Weight of My Life

Back in the day, it was popular to talk about the challenge of stress in terms of "life-change units." Anybody remember that? The big idea with this is that new events—events that cause life change— add stress to our lives in various amounts. The death of a spouse adds the most, while a parking ticket adds the least.

What I didn't realize that morning at the beach house was the massive weight I carried from all the life change of the previous year and a half. For starters, I had lost both my grandfather and father within six months of each other. I also moved my family five times: one of those times, four hundred miles from my sleepy hometown of Sacramento to chaotic Los Angeles. I resigned my first ministry position quite badly—my fault all the way—and left my entire community of friends. I took on a new ministry that was both struggling and dysfunctional. On top of all that, we welcomed our second son to our young family, and I started a new undergrad program. Other than that, everything was a piece of cake.

Taken one at a time, each of these is a manageable life event, but taken all together, one after another, they were too much for me. I collected enough life-change units during that stretch to bring down a village. But at the time, the idea of being needy was a complete mystery to me. And then John mercifully spoke the words I desperately needed, *"When was the time you most needed God?"*

It wasn't so much the question that stunned me; it was the massive need that burst through the surface all at once. That was the sucker-punch that knocked me off my feet emotionally.

The idea of "need" was like cuneiform to me; I had heard of it and I knew it existed a long time ago in a faraway land, but it was irrelevant in my personal life, so I never considered it seriously. I mean that literally. Naively, need was not something I concerned myself with, because I thought I could do anything through sheer willpower. I was living the perpetual Nike commercial: "Just Do It!"

In the end, on that day at the beach house, I couldn't avoid the question—that terrifying intruder in the night. I stayed quiet as long as I could until it was my turn to respond, and then I couldn't hold it in. I broke open as completely as one can imagine. It was as shameful an event as I had ever experienced at the time. I simply began to cry uncontrollably as my new friends gave me the unbelievable gift of "presence." They leaned in, slid their chairs closer and whispered prayers of comfort. To be honest, it was hard to believe their generous care.

My reaction to that question was almost more than I could handle, but their response was absolutely scandalous, at least in the world I knew at the time. The messages I had internalized over the years were incongruent with their response to my "outlandish" show of emotion. For years I had wrapped my heart tightly in the "no pain" rule that says, "If it hurts, suck it up and walk it off." But not one of those dear friends confirmed that rule on that day. On the contrary, they violated it completely and flagrantly, disregarding a revered family rule I assumed was true everywhere.

Growth Began for Me

And so it began . . . all those years ago. Through one question and a collection of kind friends, I began a growth journey I never could have imagined—one that continues to this very day.

As I sit here in my tiny office, writing these words, I'm moved to tears thinking about that day; in fact I'm often moved to tears, but they no longer feel unpardonable. Come to find out, I'm quite an emotional man, but now my authentic emotions feel entirely appropriate to me. I feel like I am being precisely the person God made me to be. I feel joy, relief, and peace, knowing that who I am on the outside increasingly reflects who I am on the inside.

For decades now, it's been one step after another, fighting for and seeking to cooperate with the work of the Holy Spirit in my life. Jesus promised he would send the Holy Spirit as a counselor who leads us to the truth. In fact, in John's gospel Jesus calls the Holy Spirit the "Spirit of truth." I have come to know the best thing I can do is yield to the Counselor who is always doing an internal work in me, helping me recognize and follow his plans for my life.

In the spirit of full disclosure, I've not experienced a straight line of growth in my life; I've suffered setbacks over the years—times I wondered when I would see forward progress again. In fact, after that day at the beach house, things got darker for me for some time before it felt like the sun came out again. But that's my story, and I came to know that my darkness was part of God's growth process for me.

Not only did growth begin in me, but I also came to know growth was both necessary and possible. The need for growth wasn't for feeble people who couldn't stand on their own; it was for me—and come to find out, instability is a part of everyone's life.

Who Do You Love?

You picked up this book for a reason. If leading comes naturally to you, maybe you're drawn to this big idea of developing others. Whether or not you're a leader, chances are there is someone who matters to you, and deep in your heart you hope for some life change on their behalf.

So here's my question: "Who do you love?" Who matters most to you? What person would you gladly sacrifice for, so she might become the person God intends for her to be? In your quiet thoughts, who are the important people you contemplate? If you're like me, in less cluttered moments your mind drifts to those you love the most, and in those moments you are drawn to a kind of concern best described as "holy aspiration."

Who stirs that in you? Is it a young son with a reckless streak who feels comfortable living on the edge, walking close to trouble? Maybe you see a pensive mood in your child and you worry he may be drifting into isolation. Do you think of a young daughter whose identity is more defined by "looks" and "likes" than her inherent, eternal value? How about a lifelong friend who has always struggled to string together healthy decisions? Or maybe you think of a troubled family member who is locked in a cycle of addiction. Most of us have people who matter to us deeply and for whom the Holy Spirit stirs his aspirations in our hearts. Who is that for you?

Is there a group of people who "belong" to you? Are you a teacher or a coach? Maybe you are a small-group leader in your church. If you're single, maybe you think of your friend group, the ones you do life with week in and week out—your unofficial family. If you're married, especially married with kids, your family probably comes to mind immediately. Maybe you plead with God daily for your children to grow up to become healthy, independent men or women who follow Jesus with their whole hearts. It could be, like me, that your heart bursts with love and concern for a group of people whom Jesus has asked you to shepherd. And in quiet, holy moments you simply daydream over how the Holy Spirit may be leading them to their next point of growth.

Many of us feel a sense of accountability for someone else, as though they belong to us in some way. Sometimes that belonging is official, like with family; at other times it's the less defined belonging of friendship or mentoring. Either way, we often take some responsibility for others and then hope, on their behalf, for a bright future and healthy wholeness. Bottom line, there are people who matter to us; we long for them to become the best version of themselves.

Growth Is Possible

Since that morning in the beach house with my friends, I've become borderline obsessed with the growth process. My wife Coleene would say, "Nope. He's *fully* obsessed with it." Fair enough. I find it hard not to be preoccupied with the hope and contentment that comes from seeing the Holy Spirit actively work in my heart and in the hearts of others. It's not perfection that excites me; it's the reality of progress.

As I pay attention to the Holy Spirit, cooperate, and keep my feet moving, I actually see forward progress that yields healing and wholeness. This is no longer theory for me; it's a reality I get to live in all the time. I simply love growing because I've come to know it is possible—for me and for everyone I know. It's not often easy, but it absolutely can happen. And again, I'm not talking about perfection—that is never an option in this life. I am really clear that Jesus is our perfection and it's only through his sacrifice on the cross that growing is available at all.

Over the last two decades I've worked at some of the largest, most innovative churches in America. Because of that, I've led many hundreds of leaders and thousands of small group members through the filter of personal growth and transformation. That whole time, I continually asked, "How does growth happen?" and more to the point, *"How can I help people grow?"*

What an audacious question to ask, let alone answer—but it can be answered. Bottom line, there is a legitimate response to that growth question, and I think the answer works anywhere with anyone. (I'll admit, I cringed a little when I wrote that last sentence. I'm actually tempted to delete it or rewrite it to soften its edges, but I won't because I believe it's absolutely true.) Growth is normal, all we have to do is remove the barriers. It's not only available to us and to everyone we know, but there is actually a way to cooperate with it naturally.

The truth is you have a heavenly Father who wants you to grow, and he also wants everyone you know to grow and thrive. Those are his aspirations for you as his child. He wants you to grow up and become like his Son Jesus.

I have three adult sons and I loved when they were really small—I mean tiny. I remember lying on the coach and watching TV with them resting on my chest—they fit perfectly between my chin and waist. I still have such fond and warm feelings about that time. They were so small and fragile, and they were mine to care for. But I can honestly say there was never a single moment during that time when I thought, "I wish they would always be babies just like this." Not one moment! Ever!

My aspirations for my sons have always been for them to become healthy, strong men who love God and love people, and that will never change. Well guess what? That desire doesn't change with our heavenly Father either. As the most loving Father ever, he is always helping us mature into our best selves.

Growth Is the Great Adventure

My wife and I are part of a small church in the North Park neighborhood of San Diego. It is an extraordinary church of mostly young people led by my gifted friend Andy Rodgers. I've noticed something about these young friends of ours.

The most recently arriving generation of adults love travel—it's actually a really big deal for them. When I hear them talk about travel plans or previous trips, they focus on seeing new things, visiting isolated locations, experiencing a new people group or culture, and ultimately living some form of big adventure. Honestly, I believe this millennial sentiment for adventure reveals what has been true of us from the beginning: we humans love adventure. We are actually created to be a part of God's grand kingdom-adventure here on earth.

I'm not an adrenaline junkie—not even close—but I actually know something about adventure: big adventures, some planned and some not, most connected either to the Pacific Ocean or Mexico or both.

I've swum with dolphins, sea lions, whale sharks, and pilot whales. Freediving in Baja, my friend Zach and I dropped into a gigantic school of barracuda, all darting and slashing through the water, gorging on a swirling school of sardines the size of my house.

My Baja fishing buddies and I have caught thousands of game fish: Dorado, yellowtail, and sailfish, to name a few. One time we landed a massive striped marlin on light fishing tackle, and it only took three and a half hours. (I've got the pictures to prove it). That, my friends, is a big adventure.

We've been stranded in the Sea of Cortez on a sixteen-foot aluminum boat, the sun setting behind the horizon. We've also taken "big water" over the top of our little pilot-house boat, crawling through wind waves back to the beach where we launched. On other heart-pumping days we've fished in swells twice the height of our boat, so that much of the day we never saw the horizon.

I've caught spiny lobster by hand, spearfished off of remote islands, and cruised through kelp with 300-pound giant sea bass. I even know the fear of being circled by sharks while solo scuba diving in San Diego, sans shark cage.

These are undeniably big adventures, but for me they pale in comparison to the bigger adventure of life-change and growth. In fact, it's not even close. None of those adventures is enough for me, and honestly I don't think they are enough for the human soul. Are they fun? Yes. Enough? No. Worth doing? Absolutely. Life sustaining? Not at all.

In Ecclesiastes 1:14, Solomon summarized his collection of big adventures as "chasing after the wind," and now I think I know what he means.

The great adventure begins when we invite the God of creation—the God of marlin and lobster and giant black sea bass— into our lives to help us become the people he made us to be. The even greater adventure, though, is helping others cooperate with that same loving heavenly Father. That is partnering with the One who made it all, and that adventure is satisfying in a way no other kind of experience can match.

More than that, I believe this kind of life change is a thrilling fulfillment of who we are as people. We are made to "give birth" to the next generation. We are made to create and care for life in others, and when we do that it's like the currents come together and carry us to a part of life we would never find on our own. *That is the big adventure of helping people change and grow.*

I still love our Baja excursions to the Sea of Cortez, but I don't fish as much as I used to, and I'm pretty sure my pilot-whale days are over. Why? Because there is something I love more than my own adventures: I find way more satisfaction in helping others experience the adventures I've lived. These days I love driving the boat on our trips or setting up gear for my sons and friends. Come to find out, the biggest adventures in life aren't enough unless I can pass them on to someone else. And the greatest adventure of all, the one we were all made to live, is loving Jesus with all we are, and then helping others love him too.

Growth Can Be Your Adventure . . . and Theirs

You and I don't know each other, but I'm thrilled for you, from a distance. As you read through this book you will get a flavor for my heart, because I am no longer willing to keep it to myself. (Thank you for that, Jesus.)

Right now I feel joy as I ponder how the Holy Spirit will guide you on your growth adventure. I imagine times when you will be absolutely convinced of your value to God because you experience his active care in your heart: leading, nudging, encouraging, and clarifying. That is authentic evidence that God is paying attention to you—that he's interested in you, and that you matter to him.

I also imagine hope taking hold in your heart as you come to know you're not left to your own limited ideas and efforts. I envision a contentment in your soul that comes from relying on the pure wisdom and truth of the Holy Spirit—the kind of contentment Jesus spells out in the beatitudes: one blessing after another.

Why do I imagine these things? Because I've seen them take shape in my own life and in the lives of hundreds of others. I'm a believer; it's as simple as that. I believe that when we actively surrender to Jesus' aspirations, we come to experience a deeply satisfying—even wild—adventure of growth and transformation. The ultimate beauty in all of this is that you can offer that adventure to everyone you hold dear.

So, one last time: *Who do you love?* The journey of growth is real and available. I'm praying this very moment that you will go "all in" on what Jesus has for you, *but also for those you love.*

This book is all about helping others see and cooperate with what God wants to do in their lives. Maybe that seems like an impossible task to you, but I'm telling you it's not. Helping others grow is not just way more possible than you might imagine; it's reasonable. When you understand the parts and pieces of the growth environment, I think you will agree it makes a lot of sense.

The Five Life-Changing Conditions for Growth

Throughout this book I will break down the five conditions that lead naturally to life change. All together, these conditions create an environment where growth happens best. Here is a quick preview of these conditions.

1. **Safety:** It must be okay to be less than perfect. We need to know that our weaknesses and imperfections are not going to be used against us. *Safety is always the place to start, or restart, with someone you lead.* This is the fuel that empowers your relationship with loved ones. The gospel story is the ultimate message of safety.

2. **Truth:** After safety has been established in a relationship, people are ready to look at what is true of themselves. Truth is the keystone to growth and maturity; you cannot grow without it. It is the raw material used by the Holy Spirit in our transformation. So we need to look at the truth of our lives through the truth of God's Word.

3. **Vulnerability:** Transformation is not a solo sport. We cannot know what is true of ourselves by ourselves; we need others. In the mechanics of the growth process, vulnerability is the actual way we show up in any life-changing relationship or community.

4. **Words of Affirmation:** All of us have collected messages in life; both good messages and bad messages. Those messages turn into our beliefs, and some of those beliefs, if they are misguided, are massive barriers in our growth process. In life-changing environments, we affirm the right messages and dispute the wrong ones.

5. **Caregiving:** Often, the human heart is suspicious. Caregiving is proof of real love in a relationship or community. When we are generous with care we are a lot like Jesus, providing "evidence" of our love to those we lead.

Finally . . .

I hope you will go and visit amazing places and see breathtaking sights for the rest of your life. But know that you don't have to go anywhere to live an amazing adventure, because it's waiting for you in the life you're living right now. You can know the thrill of seeing people say "yes" to Jesus and then live in the life transforming gospel adventure God intends for them. That's where we're headed.

PART ONE

Leading for Life Change

RELATIONSHIP IS YOUR TICKET TO LASTING INFLUENCE

My greatest leadership challenge of the last decade or so has been with my son Tim.

Before he hit his teen years, we really struggled with each other. Truth be told, we just didn't like each other very much. I was an overwhelmed, easily threatened father, and he was an articulate and demanding son. The mixing of his quick wit and verbal skills with my insecurity and impatience created a big wall between us. In other words, he was mouthy and I was insecure—and that was a big problem for both of us. At times I felt like our relationship was my Kryptonite: I could not figure it out. I actually began to wonder if this whole "life-changing conditions" thing was fiction.

At the heart of our conflict was a woman—my wife, his mother. We fought over Coleene in ways I'm a little embarrassed to admit. In fact, we had a running joke for years that started when he was about seven years old. The three of us were together somewhere and Timmy walked up between Coleene and me, looked me in the eyes, smiled, and said, "She's my woman!"

"Oh no, you did not just say that!" That was my response . . . and then I laughed out loud, but there was some truth in what he said. We both wanted to be first in her life, so we squared off against each other. There is a ton of complexity I've left out, but essentially I felt like I was locked in a battle of wills with my son, whom I loved deeply.

And then Tim turned thirteen.

Apparently that's the age, some say, when parents and kids officially stop liking each other. I had a friend actually tell me that, kind of like advice, or a parenting "pro-tip," so that I would see it coming and know it would pass eventually. She said, "You know he's not going to like now you for a while, right? But it's okay, before you know it, he'll be twenty and things will be fine again."

Hold up there. I was not okay with that, and I decided right then I wasn't going to surrender to that advice. I must admit, I actually felt it though. I could sense not only the relational distance growing between us, but an increase in disrespect and dishonor on both sides. So I came out with it.

One day we were driving in the car and I said, "Timmy, apparently we're not supposed to like each other anymore. We aren't supposed to be friends. Are you good with that? I'm actually not okay with it." It was quiet for a long moment and then he said, "That's awkward!" But then he told me he wasn't okay with it either, finally landing us on the same page.

That mini-agreement was a first plank in the bridge back to each other–a plank I could use to rebuild my place in his life. So I asked him if we could pay attention to our friendship together. He said yes and that's what we've done, together, since that day. I know parenting isn't all about friendship; I get that, but the way he and I felt about each other was a massive barrier keeping us apart, and I had to do something about it. If I wanted to have influence in my son's life, something needed to change.

That episode with Tim confirmed one of my key life-lessons about how everyday people create conditions for change and growth. There is a way it happens, and setting up those conditions requires us to love and lead people intentionally.

In a sentence, the core of this is all about *"Leading . . . those who belong to you . . . where they need to go."* Let's unpack that now matching those elements with three big ideas: (1) Shepherding, (2) span of care, and (3) a picture of maturity. We will look at the first element in this chapter and the last two elements in the next.

1. "Leading . . .": Shepherding and Spiritual Leadership

Shepherding is all about paying attention and helping people choose what is next. The Holy Spirit is doing an internal work in us all the time. Great spiritual leaders know this about the Holy Spirit, and they help others look for his leading. That is the core of spiritual leadership, and that's what shepherding is all about.

As a shepherd, I always start with one simple question of the Holy Spirit: "What are you shining your spotlight on in our lives and how can we see it together?" In other words, I want to help others discern growth areas that the Holy Spirit intends to shape and change. Sometimes he reveals something obvious, like a lack of patience with a family member. Other times he may surface something more profound, such as deep shame that has kept someone in emotional chains for years.

Either way, the natural follow up to that first question is: "Holy Spirit, how do you want us to respond to what you are helping us see?" Shepherding is all about recognizing, together, what the Holy Spirit is illuminating in a follower's life and then helping them cooperate with next steps.

That's an easy idea to put in a sentence, but it's as complex as the human heart, and that's why the Holy Spirit is the key player in the growth process. I am not smart enough to know what someone needs next. I can't see the truest condition of their heart. I am massively limited by all that is swirling around in my own heart. *I am simply not enough.* And guess what? All those things are true of you too. Human shepherds aren't equipped to lead human sheep *by themselves;* we need the great Shepherd to guide the entire process. The beautiful thing is that, as followers of Jesus, we have him! God sent the great Counselor as our teacher and guide.[1]

If you're not convinced of this yet, spend a little time in Paul's first letter to the Corinthian church. In chapter one, he admonishes the Christians there for divisively following human leaders, "I follow Paul" . . . "I follow Apollos" . . . "I follow Cephas." Some were also following Jesus, of course.

Paul's point in this passage is that human leadership is insufficient, and we must unite around the wisdom of God, centering on Jesus and the cross.[2] He then spends the last half of the chapter contrasting human wisdom with God's wisdom. His big conclusion is, "the foolishness of God is wiser than man's wisdom, and the weakness of God is stronger than man's strength."[3]

That's when Paul begins to personalize his message. In chapter two, he reminds the Corinthians of his own weakness and trembling as their leader. He points out that his ministry in the church doesn't come from his own wisdom and persuasion, but from the power of the Holy Spirit.[4]

So let me summarize the big-picture process of shepherding for clarity and emphasis. The core practice of shepherding is recognizing and cooperating with the work of the Holy Spirit in the lives of those you lead, helping them take their next step of growth in order to become more like Jesus.

This is the kind of spiritual leadership that turns the five life-changing conditions into an irresistible force for transformation and growth.

Positional Leaders and Shepherding

When I first heard John Maxwell speak about relational leaders, I knew immediately I wanted to become one. Not only did it make sense intuitively, I could also see that the best leaders in my own life had led out of deep relationship. Through those shepherds, I discovered there is a kind of leader who can create life-changing conditions . . . *but there is another kind of leader who can't, or won't.* And this is where many of us get tripped up.

What most of us stumble over, at some point in our lives, is positional leadership.[5] Just like it sounds, this is about the official role or position of a leader. If you've ever been given a title—like boss, parent, officer, supervisor, president, pastor, coach, judge, teacher, or referee—then you've been a positional leader. It is extremely common and entry-level leadership at best.

A good way to understand positional leadership is that people *have to follow you* because you hold the position above them in the org chart. This is "top heavy" leadership, focused mostly on the leader's mission, goals, or agenda.

Many years ago I had a boss just like this. He called his developmental process "motivation through failure." I'm actually not joking. He intentionally threw us into situations where we were over our heads so we would fail miserably. His point, he told us, was that failure would motivate us to learn what he had to teach us. I remember telling him, "I'm ready now, I want to learn. What do I need to know?" But he was in charge and we weren't, and that was obvious to everybody.

Just to be clear, positional leadership is absolutely essential at times. When my sons were teenagers, they had curfews and weren't allowed to drive with friends in the car. I had to require of them what I knew was the best thing for them. End of story. Similarly, in an emergency, I want trained professionals in charge and calling the shots. On the battlefield, soldiers don't brainstorm options and take votes. Even in sports, we know the coach is the one who calls the plays.

But there are certain downside realities that show up when we rely exclusively on positional leadership in everyday life. People will do what a positional leader says only as long as they have to. The second a positional leader turns his back, all bets are off. People will only do what he requires and not a single thing more. And they won't do what he says if they can get away with it. So positional leadership is the least effective kind of influence if you want to elevate things like buy-in, alignment, or ownership.

Jesus was hardest on these kinds of shepherds. In Matthew chapter twenty-three he delivered maybe his harshest words ever to the consummate positional leaders of the day. Here we read that Jesus was sparring with the Jewish religious leaders—back and forth they went. Then at some point Jesus turned away from the sparing, spoke directly to the crowd, and confronted the leaders publicly, calling them hypocrites, frauds, and blind fools, among other things. By shining a light on their motives, Jesus revealed that those leaders simply wanted to appear good and be honored by others.

Relational Leaders Make the Best Shepherds

With relational leaders, people don't follow because they have to, *they follow because they want to.* Likely the most famous quote credited to John Maxwell is: "People don't care how much you know, until they know how much you care."[6] I can start that quote with just about any group of leaders in the church and they will nod and finish my sentence.

Have you ever heard the rest of his quote though? "Leadership begins with the heart," Maxwell continues, "not the head. It flourishes with a meaningful relationship, not more regulations." Then he gives the essential ingredient: "People who are unable to build solid, lasting relationships will soon discover that they are unable to sustain long, effective leadership. Needless to say, you can love people without leading them . . . *but you cannot lead people without loving them.*"[7]

For relational leaders, the agenda isn't obedience or compliance; it's growth and transformation. That's where these leaders begin, and that starting point makes all the difference. They exist for the benefit of the followers, not the other way around. When people are led this way, they soon believe that the goal of the relationship is their own transformation. They come to believe, in the very best way, that *they* are the agenda. Over time, their hearts are convinced the shepherd is all about the care and well-being of those he leads. When that happens, cynical hearts soften, suspicious hearts are persuaded, and anxious hearts turn peaceful—all because the followers come to know they are loved first and most, and led second.

This is actually a really big deal because people often start with a completely different view of leaders. I once had a leader who told me he didn't care what I did, just as long as I didn't embarrass him. I was crushed by those words. I immediately thought, "So this whole thing is about whether or not I'm an embarrassment to you? That's all we are to each other?" Sadly, yes, that was what our working relationship was all about.

I know parents who emphasize image as a family value. Their goal is to have a family that looks and acts perfectly, so they heap expectations on their children to become obedient, successful, thin, competent, and problem-free. The pressure is on for sons and daughters in families like that because the family image trumps the actual growth and maturity of the children. Rule-keeping gets elevated over relationship as hiding and shame become the emotional habits of the family.

Relational leadership refutes all that. In fact, the first goal of relational leadership is—no surprise—connecting relationally with those you lead, because relationship is the foundation of influence.

Relationship is your ticket to influence others. It is your "license" to lead, and you only get one of those from the people who follow you. Without it, they may obey, they may comply . . . but they won't follow. Not for long. I had been my son's father for thirteen long years before I actually got my ticket into Tim's life, and it changed everything.

The apostle Paul writes, "I am again in the pains of childbirth until Christ is formed in you."[8] The longer I work at shepherding, the more relevant those words are to me. Just work that metaphor a bit.

Giving birth is all about the child; the baby is the crescendo of the birthing experience. Certainly, nothing happens without the mother, she carries the baby and she, alone, feels the deep pain of childbirth, yet the process is truly all about that new life coming into the world. The mother endures the struggle and pain because of who is coming.

This is the urgency Paul is getting at. His metaphor embodies what the relational shepherd is willing to endure for the sake of those he leads. This kind of shepherding is hard—really hard. It's often slower than we like. The leader generally carries the weight of the relationship. There is a ton of downside for the leader and a ton of upside for the follower. But the crescendo of the shepherding process is what gets birthed in the heart of a follower when she senses the direction of the Holy Spirit in her life and says "yes" to his leading.

This is what I am willing to go through for those I love and lead. As a relational leader, I start with them and I stay with them. I don't move on to myself. They are the point of our shepherding relationship, and I am the one helping them see the work of the great Shepherd in their hearts. It is hard to help people change and grow. It would be way easier if I just told you what to do and then enforced that. But that won't change your heart; barking orders only makes my life easier.

So there is a message I often rehearse in my heart, and occasionally I speak it to those I lead. It goes like this: "I don't deserve to lead you until you say so. I don't deserve to be trusted until you say I'm trustworthy. I am willing to earn my influence and trust with you, or not have it at all."

You can act like that message isn't true, but it doesn't change reality. If you haven't *earned* your ticket into someone's life through genuine love and authentic relationship, you will not be trusted and followed for long. You may be obeyed, but remember, that's something completely different.

This kind of leadership doesn't exist naturally in the wild, so you will need to birth it in your heart and raise it on your own. I can't give you mine either; it's only for me. The fantastic news, though, is you can come to love this kind of shepherding. When you see what it yields in children, students, group members, employees, soldiers, and others, you will wonder why you ever led any other way.

Shaping the Hands or the Heart

Positional leadership yields shallow change, but the relational version leads to deep change. Another way to say this is positional leadership is all about the hands—*what you do,* but relational leadership shapes the heart—*what you love.*

Years ago I was sitting in a conference listening to Erwin McManus when he said, "It's more important to shape what people care about than what they believe." I was so gripped by the implication of his words, I don't think I heard another thing the rest of his session.

Sometime later I ran across a quote attributed to the French author Antoine de Saint-Exupery who wrote, "If you want to build a ship, don't herd people together to collect wood and don't assign them tasks and work, but rather *teach them to long for* the endless immensity of the sea."[9] [Emphasis mine.] There is that heart-shaping idea again.

Most recently, I heard Tim Keller say, "What you really are, basically, is what you love the most. It's not your beliefs, at least what you subscribe to, that make you what you are. It's what your heart trusts in; what your heart loves the most that makes you who you are."

Theologian and philosopher James K. A. Smith is immensely helpful in all this. He points out that each of our hearts long for some version of an ideal "kingdom," a world that seems just right to us. He writes, "This is true for any human being; it is a structural feature of human creatureliness. You can't not love. It's why the heart is the seat and fulcrum of the human person, the engine that drives our existence. We are lovers first and foremost."[10] So the question isn't *whether* we will love, but *what* will we love.

This is the big idea behind helping people change and grow. Relational leaders are most interested in what their followers love, because that's the driving force behind life change. When someone's heart is changed, their life changes too, because behavior follows affection, not the other way around. In fact, affection resists behavior if that behavior is not aligned with the heart.

I know this is oversimplifying, but I've often thought that all I need to do as a leader and a shepherd is help people fall deeply in love with Jesus and with other people, and then let them do what comes naturally. In reality, what we know and think has huge impact on what we love, so there is a bigger process in play. But still, the bullseye of transformation is the heart.

At some point this became clear to me. I realized that I can focus the bulk of my shepherding influence on what a follower does and what they know, or I can help them pay attention to what they love. We are what we love, and that's why Jesus said the most important thing in life is loving God and loving people.

The human heart is our steering wheel and we follow wherever it leads. Smith tells us, "To be human is to be on a quest. To live is to be embarked on a kind of unconscious journey toward a destination of your dreams. You can't *not* bet your life on something. You can't *not* be headed somewhere. We live leaning forward, bent on arriving at the place we long for."[11] My friend Brad Sarian says, "We are not 'thinking-things,' we are lovers. Until someone's heart longs for Jesus, there is no hope that they will think their way into following him."

My point exactly.

The Heart of a Shepherd

If shaping the hearts of followers is important, it is absolutely essential for shepherds. This means the first priority of relational shepherding is falling in love with those you lead (the platonic version), because just like followers, shepherds are both propelled and guided by what they love.

When we love those we lead, our hearts turn toward them in the same way the needle of a compass aims north. When that happens, we'll be amazed by the care we deliver naturally, and by the quality of our leadership. Loving those we lead solves a ton of leadership challenges ahead of time, simply because our hearts are fully awake and aiming in the right direction.

When shepherds love their followers, they lead at higher levels. They just do. They engage more deeply, and longer, when conflict arises. They are unwilling to resort to habits of self-protection when misunderstood or resisted. They "start" with the needs of their followers, instead of their own preferences. They feed their leadership resolve from the fuel of a devoted heart, becoming fully present and current with their followers. Bottom line, they reach beyond self-interest and shepherd based upon what's best for the ones they lead.

I think I can offer you a bunch of techniques so that you can *act* like a loving shepherd, but that's not *being* one. This isn't something you just do, because this can't be conjured up if your heart is unchanged by Jesus' love for you.

There is a common catchphrase these days that says, "Fake it 'til you make it." That does not work when it comes to leading and loving. If you don't actually love those you lead, but you're trying to act like you do, they will sniff out your emotional dishonesty a mile away.

The truth is, you . . . are . . . pursued . . . by a heavenly Father who wants you. Jesus climbed into your world not to get you to obey, but to get *you*. The heart of the Father is to have you as his child and, out of that love, he pursues you. That reality can become the foundation of our shepherding relationships with those we lead.[12] It can also be the reality that places your followers where they belong in your heart.

So consider starting there. Contemplate your worth to your heavenly Father and his massive love for you—allow that reality to fill up in your heart. Then from that awareness, ask him to grow your love for those he's asking you to lead.

We will circle back to this later, but it's critical you begin to reach for this big idea right away, and never let it go. Shepherding from a loving heart is where all of this starts; it's the foundation for creating life-changing conditions.

BECOMING MORE LIKE JESUS IS THE POINT

2. "... those who belong to you ...": Span of Care

Who Belongs to You?

If shepherding is going to work, you need to be clear about who "belongs" to you and who doesn't. Jesus is the great overseer[1] and he asks his shepherds to care for his people.[2] Good shepherding happens when we lead those whom Jesus has given us to lead. *It also happens when we do not lead those he hasn't given us to lead.* Knowing the difference between the two is crucial.

This is, likely, the most violated reality among leaders today! Nearly every leader I know, paid or unpaid, is caring for more people than they can handle effectively and paying the price for it in exhaustion, anxiety, and ineffectiveness.

The rationale I hear most from overloaded leaders usually has something to do with hospitality and inclusiveness. They want to create a spot for "just one more," and they have space in the room, so they say yes to adding yet another. It's funny though, because eventually even "limitless" leaders reach the end of their resources and must ultimately say "no" to someone. Why does that have to happen after they've said "yes" to too many, leaving themselves depleted, ineffective and heading for burnout? Shepherding too many people poorly means that the leader ends up not shepherding anyone well. And that's where all of this breaks down.

For the sake of absolute clarity, and because this is such a hard issue for most of us, let me be ruthlessly direct. Jesus is not asking you to shepherd everyone that you like. He isn't asking you to shepherd everyone you know who is in need or in crisis. He isn't even asking you to shepherd everyone you can actually help. Bottom line, he is not asking you to shepherd anyone based on the needs, opportunities, or circumstances in their lives. If he were, nearly everyone would become your responsibility. But he is asking us to shepherd a few—only a few.

Jesus modeled giving most of himself to a few, and some of himself to many. We read this all throughout the Gospels, but we see it clearly when he himself picked his own "few."[3] In Luke's Gospel we read that Jesus prayed through the night, and then in the morning selected twelve of his disciples to become his inner circle.

Try to place yourself in that event for a moment. Jesus gathers his larger group of followers, and then calls out twelve men to himself, naming them apostles. Imagine the pressure you would have felt in Jesus' sandals. Imagine what was going through the minds of those in the crowd of followers. Some were chosen publicly, but the majority of them remained unchosen. I have to admit, that's not even close to how I would have done it. I would have set up one-on-one meetings, cast vision, and then called each person individually. But not Jesus; he spotlighted his selection process by assembling a crowd and then calling specific people.

However that went down, we have to conclude from that point on the twelve disciples "belonged" to Jesus in a way that no others did. As a group, they became the main focus of his attention, instruction, correction, and caregiving. They comprised his span of care, and before long they would change the world, *because of his focused impact in their lives.*

I'm not saying that Jesus didn't have a wider public ministry to hundreds and thousands. But I am saying that he gave the bulk of his shepherding to a select few, and in doing that, he also accomplished his wider gospel plans. In current language, we might say the disciples were his "ministry delivery system." Peter Scazzero would say Jesus accepted "the gift of limits."[4] Being fully human— and also fully God—Jesus knew he had limited personal resources and chose how to spend them most wisely.

Jesus actually walked past sick, hungry, and demon-possessed people without healing, feeding, or freeing them. At times he withdrew from the crowds and willingly allowed people to walk away from him. But he was crystal clear about his plan for those twelve who belonged to him.

Just about everyone has to lead others in one way or another. If you are a leader—if you have that certainty—then there are people who "belong" to you, and these people make up your span of care. There are *some* you are meant to lead personally . . . and there are *many others* (read: everyone else) you are meant not to lead. If you want to truly influence those you love—those in your span of care—then start right here and accept this. Become okay with the limited number of people God places in your care.

How Span of Care Works

I first heard the phrase "span of care" in the mid-1990's, and it changed everything for me.[5] The big idea behind span of care is that *everyone should be cared for, but no one should care for more than they can handle.*

Structurally, span of care comes from Exodus 18 where Moses is confronted by his father-in-law, Jethro, for handling all the disputes of the people of Israel by himself.[6] Jethro is astonished that Moses sits before the people from morning until evening, hearing one dispute after another. He knows this is not only bad for the people; it also exceeds Moses' capacity to lead well.

So Jethro delivers straight talk to Moses, saying, "What you are doing is not good." He goes on to point out that Moses is the bottleneck in the whole scenario and he's going to wear everyone out because the load is too heavy for any one person.

Jethro's solution seems obvious now, but it must have been cutting-edge at the time. He essentially says, "Spread the load around, Moses." Jethro advises him to appoint leaders to oversee groups of thousands, hundreds, fifties and, tens. Roughly speaking, that's the structure—that is span of care.

"Too Much" Is a Real Thing

If span of care is going to work for you, you must come to grips with your limits as a leader—and really as a person. It's built on the belief that "too much" is a real thing and that we're prone to take on more than we can handle.

For me, I had to accept the fact that I have a specific capacity as a shepherd, my capacity may be different than someone else's, and that is totally okay. It's a silly metaphor, but when I talk about this with leaders I tell them that, as a shepherd, I am a "quart jug," not a "gallon jug." The problem I run into is when I try to fit a gallon of shepherding into my life, because at that point, I exceed my capacity and my leadership gets really messy.

Another way I explain this is with "touches." Since shepherding is relational, I tell leaders we can think of our capacity in terms of "relational touches" with people. For me, I know that I have roughly twelve to fifteen quality "touches" to give out. That means that I can only handle twelve to fifteen shepherding relationships in my life at any given moment. Sometimes my number of touches is on the low end of the range, sometimes it's on the high end—it depends on what else is drawing away my energy. But I get to decide how I use those touches.

I cannot tell you who should be in your span of care, but with conviction I can say you should have one. If you want to shepherd your loved ones well, whoever they are, you need to pay attention to your capacity. For Jesus, his primary span of care was the twelve disciples. What should yours be? Only you can decide this for yourself.

Span of Care Reaches Farther Than You Think

I once heard John Maxwell talk about his span of care while he was the Senior Pastor of Skyline church in San Diego. During his sermon, he stopped at one point and said, "If you have been discipled by me, I'd like you to stand up." About a dozen men stood to their feet. Then he said, "If you've been discipled by them, I'd like you to stand up." About a hundred men rose from their chairs. You probably see what's coming: he said it one more time and the room was filled with hundreds of men standing among friends and family. It was stunning, and I've never forgotten that moment.

In that huge urban church, span of care was normal, and soon it would become normal for me. Through the reach of one intentional leader, many hundreds of families were transformed in the struggling community surrounding Skyline church.

Making Room for Your Span of Care

When we get this wrong as a culture it is like no one "belongs" to anyone and relational shepherding happens nowhere. If I am being totally honest, that's how it seems in too many of our churches today. The current version of the "Big C" church isn't set up for the kind of shepherding Jesus lived out.

If you feel like you're entangled in too many demands, your life probably isn't set up to lead a healthy span of care. "Life" these days is not aligned to help us with this either—life is aligned on speed and volume. In today's culture we are increasingly compelled to go faster and do more, so you may need to trim away some of your life in order to go all-in on leading just a few people.

I have a dear friend, Denny, who is one of the most devoted leaders I've ever known. Years ago, though, I thought I saw an alarming flaw begin to show up in his life. In a nutshell, he had his hands in too many things and I thought I could see burnout for him just over the horizon. Since he was in my span of care, I shared my concern with him.

I said, "Denny can I tell you one thing that worries me? I think you're doing too much and you're spending the best of yourself on assignments that don't belong to you." He thought and prayed about it, and later agreed he needed to focus and make changes. Over the next year or so, he scaled back his ministry roles, actually quit his day job, and launched a 501c3 ministry called Men of Resolution, targeted at helping men become faithful followers of Jesus.

Since that time, many hundreds of men have "resolved" to lead well in their homes, at work and in their churches—all because Denny decided to *set up his life* to give most of himself to a few and some of himself to many.

You can absolutely do that too. You may not want to do it the way Denny did, but change is an option. You could quietly close out responsibilities over time and simply say no to new assignments when others come to an end. You could then allow margin to open up in your life, without refilling it, to give more and more of yourself to the care of the select few God brings you. Or you could just rip off the Band-Aid and overcome the inertia of your life with some big moves toward simplicity.

But know this: doing any version of that starts with asking the Holy Spirit to align your heart on his kingdom plans. When you start with the Spirit's direction, a deep love for the group of people that he leads you to will begin growing in you, compelling you to help them walk closer to Jesus. And that's when the fun begins.

3. *". . . where they need to go.":* A Picture of Maturity

If your shepherding is going to work, you must have a picture of what it looks like to be fully mature. To be effective, growth needs a target: a desired destination or a picture of maturity. If we aren't leading toward something positive, the growth process becomes random, subjective, frustrating, and unproductive. The good news is that *God isn't going for nothing, or just for anything*—he has someone in mind when he thinks of who we can become.

Over the years, leaders have talked about this in a bunch of different ways. One prominent church asks the question, "What would a fully devoted follower of Jesus look like?" Their answer is, "Daily progress toward "The Five Gs": Grace, Growth, Group, Gifts, and Good Stewardship." That's their picture of maturity; it's what they're going for as they grow disciples.

Saddleback Church is known for being "Purpose Driven," focusing their followers on what they classify as the five purposes of the Christian life: fellowship, discipleship, worship, ministry, and evangelism.

In one of my favorite books, *Primal Leadership*, the authors write about the difference between the "ought self" and the "ideal self," contrasting who we are with who we might become.[7]

I could go on and on with the different maturity pictures I've seen over the years, and in all honesty I can't improve on any of them. Trust me, I've tried. However, I think there's a fresh approach we need to take if we are going to shepherd our loved ones well.

Jesus Is Our Picture of Maturity

Simply put, the picture of maturity God has for us is his son Jesus.[8] This isn't the fresh part yet, but it's the essential truth we need to build upon—a truth that's too easy to overlook. In Jesus, we have a perfect picture of what it means to be a human follower of God.

The apostle Peter describes Jesus as sinless and without deceit, even in suffering.[9] The apostle John tells us Jesus not only came to remedy our sin, but also there is no sin in him.[10] The writer of Hebrews describes Jesus as a high priest who knows all about our weaknesses because he faced all the temptations we face and still lived perfectly, without sin.[11] We read in the Gospels that God the Father publicly endorses Jesus as his Son and declares his deep pleasure with him.[12] *So plain and simple, Jesus is who we are going for in the growth process.* It doesn't need to be any more complicated than that.

As disciples of Jesus, we can hold up the picture of our lives next to the picture of his life and always have a sense of direction and progress.

Now here's the fresh part; here's where it gets immensely helpful for shepherding others. Jesus is not only our picture of maturity, there's actually a way to query his life as a guide for the way we live.

Since the Holy Spirit is always speaking into our hearts and aiming us at becoming more like Jesus, we can live *dependently* on the Holy Spirit's guidance. That means our relationship with the Holy Spirit is our querying process for becoming like Jesus—we simply need to understand how it works.

God doesn't hand us an alliterated list of Jesus' characteristics for us to imitate. He gives us the Bible and then reaches out to shape and guide us relationally. In relationship, the Holy Spirit helps us see the truth of our lives—our upside and downside—and then aims us back to the truth of the Bible to shape our hearts over time. In the most beautiful way possible, the Holy Spirit is actually guiding our unique spiritual growth plan—that is, if we will let him and if we will cooperate.

That cooperation is the core of our shepherding relationship with followers, and it happens through three simple practices: (1) Asking, (2) Paying Attention and (3) Following. Let's take a look at how these work.

1. Asking . . .

With Jesus as our picture of maturity, the question we must always ask is, "How would Jesus live my life if he were me?"[13] A couple years ago, Grant Clark, a gifted pastor and friend from South Africa, actually posed that question to our church family here in San Diego: "Imagine Jesus moving into North Park; what would that look like? How would he show up in our world today?"

This is the nature of our query with the Holy Spirit, and it's unique to each of us. Imagine Jesus moving into your neighborhood, your home, your family, your vocation—*how would he live your life if he were you?* Here's the comforting reveal: The Holy Spirit actually knows the answer to that question, and he is guiding you and those you love toward that answer all the time.

When we ask that question over and over we're naturally driven back to the gospels to understand how Jesus thought, lived, and related to imperfect people. In doing that, we begin to understand Jesus' motivation, and the Holy Spirit kindles in us a desire to become more like him.

Through this spiritual growth mechanism—this simple question—we become students of Jesus' life; he truly becomes our rabbi and we follow him deeper into the details of our lives, under the power and direction of the Holy Spirit.

How would Jesus work as an IT analyst in a large company that lacks direction and devalues employees? How would Jesus love a neighbor who yells at him because of where he parks on their street? How would Jesus teach English to a classroom of disrespectful high school students? How would Jesus sell copiers in a profit-obsessed company that chews up its sales people with unrealistic revenue goals? How would Jesus shop at Costco around rude people who lack awareness and block aisles? How would Jesus navigate the loneliness of singleness in a world filled with families? How would Jesus respond to the fear and uncertainty of older age and physical decline? How would Jesus pastor church members who misunderstand him and resist his leadership?

All of those scenarios actually exist in the real world, along with billions of others. Whatever situation you face, Jesus is your picture of how to live in it, and you'll begin to see your way through that situation when you dependently query the Holy Spirit for clarity and next steps.[14]

As shepherds, this is the place it all starts as we lead those in our span of care. The Holy Spirit is kind of like our transformational search engine, always coming back with ways that followers can become more like Jesus. But we have to help them stay eager to ask the question.

This metaphor breaks down for some of us because we rarely get responses from the Holy Spirit like a file download. Remember, God's plan for our growth is rooted in relationship; he walks with us as we live our lives, relating and informing all along the way. So when he points us toward answers to that big question—*How would Jesus live if he were me?*—it's way more conversational than informational, because he desires relationship more than the transfer of data.

Think of it like this: in your mind you have an internal voice always weighing in on what you encounter throughout the day. The name for this is "inner speech" or the "inner narrator"—the voice of your mind always speaking beneath the surface of your external world. And this is where the Holy Spirit often meets us and guides us along the way. He actually enters into our internal conversation.[15] We can help our loved ones meet the Holy Spirit in that place, ready to be guided by him. For this to work, though, they will need to do what I suggest next.

2. Paying Attention . . .

It is not enough to ask the big question; we must also slow down, still our hearts and turn toward the Holy Spirit as he moves and speaks.

But let's be real, paying attention to anything these days is an increasing challenge because of the "decibel level" of our world. Life is simply "loud," and the "noise" of culture is nonstop. It's kind of like being tapped on the shoulder every day, all day long, and hearing, "Hey check this out." "Here's the scoop." "Have you heard about this?" "You need to know that." "Don't miss this."

Because our attention has literally become monetized, companies and individuals will do just about anything to get you to look up from your life and "e-focus" on their message with a click or a like. They get paid when you pay them some of your attention, so it's like living in a world filled with five-year-olds, all screaming, "lookit me! Lookit me! Lookit me!"

The Holy Spirit, on the other hand, has never raised his voice with me. I don't think it's like that with him. He doesn't shout or push us around or throw a tantrum to get our attention. In fact, his voice is often compared to a whisper, and we will never hear him over the clamor of the world *unless we intend to.*

Professor and author Elizabeth Dryer writes that, "In a profound way, our intentionality is a key ingredient determining whether we notice God everywhere or only in church or only in suffering *or nowhere.* It all depends on how we choose to fashion our world."[16] [Emphasis mine.]

This reminds me of one of my early complaints as a scuba diver. Starting out, I went on dozens of dives and I never seemed to see all the cool stuff my dive buddies saw. At the time, I thought that diving was all about covering as much of the sea floor as possible on a single cylinder of air. One of my dive buddies finally clued me in though. He said, "Dude, you need to slow way down and look around. You won't ever see a thing until you're willing to notice all that you're swimming past."

How true that turned out to be. I actually began to do "stationary dives," where I would descend to the sea floor, find an interesting spot and stay put. Amazingly, I began to notice the sea life that had been there all the time, and it was thrilling, all because I opted for something other than speed and volume. That's how it works in the real world too. It is amazing what God leads us to when we pause and pay attention in order to notice his direction.

Ruth Haley Barton writes, "Many of us are choosing to live lives that do not set us up to pay attention, to notice those places where God is at work and to ask ourselves what these things mean. We long for a word from the Lord, but somehow we have been suckered into believing that the pace we keep is what leadership requires."[17] Forget leading for a moment, most of us think the speed-and-volume formula is what we need just to keep up in our everyday lives.

Then Barton delivers just the right question: "Do I even have *mechanisms in my life* that create space for paying attention, so that I don't miss the places where God himself is trying to communicate with me?"[18] [Emphasis mine.]

Shepherding can be the life-mechanism that makes paying attention possible for those you lead, and frankly for you as well. Just like my stationary dives, we can help people come to a full stop—as a life habit—in order to become more "mind-full" of the Holy Spirit all around them.

Creating the "Holy Pause"

In the sixth century, Saint Benedict established the practice of *statio* in his monastic community.[19] Instead of running from one task to the next, they simply began to pause between the activities that filled their lives and become present with God. Get this: they viewed *statio*—"the holy pause"—as one of the essential solutions for dealing with their too-busy lives. They felt they were losing a sense of the presence of Jesus because of the demands and distractions *of sixth century life.* Anybody else get the irony of that, in light of our lives?

From the word *statio* we get our words "station" and "stationary." It can also carry the idea of "standing," in the sense of standing at a post or an anchorage. In the Roman military it was the word used for placing guards in locations that needed surveillance. So it carries the idea of stopping, firming up your feet, and looking around.

To be clear, shepherding isn't *statio*, but in the shepherding relationship we help followers hit the pause button on their busy lives and look up to regain eye contact with Jesus. The rhythm of shepherding is, quite literally, the "holy pause" we need because it helps us interrupt our obsession to run mindlessly from one activity to another—nonstop, in perpetual motion, driven by a relentless and unending internal to-do list.

If our loved ones are going to become more like Jesus, they must see him in their lives and they must hear him speak. It is the shepherding relationship that creates what Joan Chittister attributes to *statio*, "the time between times."[20] Similar to *statio*, this divine relationship causes followers to come to a full stop and pay attention to the Holy Spirit before running off to the next thing. And before you know it, this stop-and-listen rhythm gets woven into the routine of our lives. That's when paying attention becomes as normal as food and rest.

3. Following . . .

Paying attention makes following possible. As we become more aware of the Holy Spirit, we begin to see how he wants to help us change and grow. Simply put, he calls us to take next steps. The way

I've explained this over the years is, "Sometimes his next steps are something I do, and sometimes they're something I do *in* me." So whether he starts with a piece of truth to believe or an action to take, it all comes down to responding.

Following always requires a step from the follower. If I am backpacking with a friend who is blazing a trail, I must take actual steps in order to keep up. That's the way it works with Jesus too. Following doesn't work without stepping. So when the Holy Spirit reveals growth areas, nudging and guiding, we have to actually "move our feet" in response. It is this response—the step we take— that starts the lifelong process of placing one foot in front of the other as we focus on Jesus ahead of us.

Just the Next Step, Not All the Steps

In the Sierras, east of Sacramento, there is a rugged wooded area called Emigrant Gap, named for the many people who crossed it heading west during the gold rush in the 1800s. It was such a challenging route that the pioneers who came upon it were forced to disassemble their wagons and lower them on ropes down sheer cliffs in order to keep going.

I've crossed much of Emigrant Gap on foot, not knowing ahead of time how hard it was going to be. Truth be told, I'm not sure I would have made that trek had I known how punishing it would be. That's how it is for many of us—probably even most of us—when we know the road ahead is severe.

Every one of us has a gap in our lives—a vast open area representing the distance between the current version of ourselves and the "Jesus version" of who we can become. The journey across that gap is an amazing adventure, but it's also painful and exhausting, even daunting at times.

I don't have a ton of confidence that many of us would sign up for this journey if we knew how hard it was going to be ahead of time, which is where the mercy and wisdom of the Holy Spirit comes in. I can't think of a single time God has laid out "the map" in front of me, or someone I know, and said, "Here's where we're going and here's how to get there." Instead of the big picture, the Holy Spirit offers his hand and helps us watch our step. Much of our process, then, is all about this connection, our trust . . . *and simply taking the next step.*

Andy Stanley writes, "One gets to the place one wants to be the same way one got to the place one didn't want to be—by putting one foot in front of the other and moving in a specific direction."[21]

My shepherding friends love this part of the growth process because it's where we see much of the forward progress in followers. I love this part of shepherding too!

I love this part because I love using tools. I mean actual tools, like sawzalls and impact guns. Well, this is the time in the growth process when we get to use a lot of our shepherding tools. I'm referring to things like searching the Bible, pursuing spiritual disciplines, taking assessments, asking diagnostic questions, reading assignments, and following spiritual practices, to name a few. It is likely you've learned some very helpful practices along the way, and this "following phase" is the time to break those out and offer them to others.

Finally . . .

This process—*Asking, Paying Attention, and Following*—has been the guiding construct for my shepherding for as long as I can remember now. Its beauty is its simplicity and the way it overlays the complexity of our lives. It is so simple, in fact, that we can locate ourselves in the process at any time, but it also accommodates the complexity of the human heart, and then naturally propels us forward, through life's distractions, toward Jesus.

Looking Forward

So there they are, the bigger parts of the process for helping others grow. With this big-picture fly-by, I intend for you to see the relational context for the five life-changing conditions. The premise of this book is that there are conditions that make transformation possible. Those conditions exist in a process; a context; a *relationship*, actually. That context is what we've been looking at in the last two chapters.

However, none of the big ideas I've mentioned so far are possible if the conditions aren't right. In other words, you can understand all that we've looked at so far and still remain unable to influence others . . . *if you miss what comes next.*

PART TWO

The Five Life-Changing Conditions

" SAFETY IS THE DOORWAY TO ALL THE CONDITIONS. "

SAFETY HEALS
THE HUMAN HEART

There is an entire genre in film and television about the struggle for survival in a suddenly dangerous world. It's called "post-apocalyptic," and it's everywhere. Zombie herds wander the world mindlessly attacking the living. Pandemic breaks out, decimating the human population. Spontaneously sentient machines rise up against their human creators. Aliens from space arrive to wipe out humanity and loot the Earth's natural resources. It's not necessarily the feel-good entertainment of the day, but as a genre it is wildly popular.

However these stories go, in this genre something terrible has happened and everything has changed. Something has "broken the world," leaving survivors to fight and struggle to recreate a tiny patch of safety in a fallen and dangerous world.

I actually really like this genre. (I'm pretty sure you just judged me in your heart right there.) It feels like our story really: the story of humankind. For me, this is more than a metaphor; it's actually a picture of the world we were all born into. Something went wrong; everything has changed; the world is broken, and threats are normal. The Bible describes it this way: "Cursed is the ground because of you; through painful toil you will eat of it all the days of your life. It will produce thorns and thistles for you."[1]

Though our story began under God's good pleasure and full approval, humankind chose to live a different story and the safe life God intended for his creation is gone, replaced by life under the curse. Threat has become our default mode, plunging us into the struggle to find peace and safety once again.

So it's not unreasonable to say there actually is something post-apocalyptic about the world we live in. We are born into danger . . . but that's not the end of the story.

Feelin' good yet?

Created for Safety

Can you imagine a world where safety was common and danger was rare? Changing lanes on the freeway would feel more like a door held open and less like kicking that door in. Telemarketers would call while you're *not* eating dinner just to find out where to send the check. Cart-bumping would be a thing of the past in Costco and Walmart. Opinions online would be laced with thoughtfulness and humility. Conservatives would tell progressives, "You've got a good point there." Progressives would say to conservatives, "You know, I never thought of it like that." Raider fans would shout encouragement to opposing quarterbacks, "You can do it Tom Brady, we believe in you!" That would be a crazy world for sure.

Now imagine for a moment *your actual life without relational threats.* I recently asked the social media universe to help me imagine such a thing, and I loved the thoughtful responses:

"You don't have to watch your back because nobody's trying to get one over on you."

"Conversations would be free and easy, motivated by generous curiosity."

"You wouldn't have to worry about people's motivation or worry about being misunderstood."

"People would be transparent with their strengths and *their weaknesses."*

"We would start out believing the best about each other, not the worst."

"People would feel cared for and paid attention to."

"All touch would be appropriate and loving."

However we describe life without relational danger, it's the kind of world we were intended to live in. It really was our natural habitat before the world was broken. In Genesis we get a curious snapshot from that first world: "The man and his wife were both naked, and they felt no shame."[2] I guess you could say Adam and Eve were *naked and unafraid.*

Let's be real though, this is probably not the picture most of us would use to describe safety—not today anyway. We're fine with the private "husband and wife" version of this picture, but those aren't the limits in this verse. No, this verse actually describes the natural state of humankind when we were at our best.

Nonetheless, we are way more comfortable with the "fully clothed and feel no shame" version of the world. In fact, many of us say the fear of finding ourselves naked in public is our worst nightmare. There is even an endurance reality TV show called *Naked and Afraid* where one man and one woman, total strangers and completely naked, get paired up and then survive together in the wild for twenty-one days. Kind of an anti-Garden of Eden scenario. The novelty of the show is the obvious horror of having to do all that without clothes—it's just unfathomable for most of us. "Naked" and "no shame" don't automatically go together in our minds.

But again, that's how it was when the world was just right. For Adam and Eve there was nothing obstructing the truth about the other. They needed no cover because there was no jeopardy in life at this point. In some uses of the Hebrew phrase "no shame," it actually means to "have no barrier." Adam and Eve had no barrier in the most literal sense, because there was no need to conceal or hide anything. They each had complete, intimate knowledge of the other, and total acceptance of one another.

This is what you and your loved ones were made for: *to thrive in a world where you are fully known and fully loved.* It is simply the consummate human experience, and that's what this snapshot really shows us.

The Divine "Change Order"

What you may not realize is that it took something like a divine "change order" for this to happen. Seven times in Genesis chapter one we read that God created and then saw his creation was either "good" or "very good."

Chapter two, however, is not a continuation of the creation account; rather, it's something like a second camera angle on the same event—a focused shot on the formation of man and woman. In this shot we see the streak of "goods" come to an end when God himself points out something that's wrong in Paradise: "It is *not good* for the man to be alone."[3] [Emphasis mine.] John Ortberg writes, "God creates a man in his own image. God looks at this man, who bears his likeness, and he says, 'Not good.'"[4]

What is truly striking, Ortberg points out, is that this all happens prior to the Fall. "There is no sin, no disobedience, nothing to mar the relationship between God and man."[5] And yet God says, "Not good." The stunning truth is that in spite of this one-of-a-kind relationship, God still describes Adam as "alone."

But God has a solution to Adam's aloneness and a change is on the way. God says the remedy is coming in the form of a "helper." A useful way to understand this is that a helper supplies what is needed by another, and in this case what's needed is the opposite of isolation. That's what is "suitable" about the relationship between Adam and Eve. It was not good for Adam to be alone—it was good for him to have a "helper." And that unspoiled helping relationship was to be marked by total transparency and perfect love.

So life, as God created it, was the safest place ever; but that was life before the apocalypse—before the world was broken.

Danger Comes to Paradise

Years ago I wrote in my journal, "Fear and danger were my natural habitat growing up." As I came into thoughtful consciousness as a young boy, I realized my little world was unpredictable, precarious, angry, hostile, and painful in many ways. Because that's what it was like to grow up as the only son in my alcoholic father's house.

At some point early on, my father realized I wasn't going to be the son he longed for, and that's when the relational danger spiked for me. I'm sure we had pleasant times in our family, but I can't conjure a single memory related to my dad that isn't connected to some form of ridicule, disappointment, or physical pain—those are simply my dominant emotional memories of him. In fact, most of my childhood memories are connected to a deep fear that something would happen that would cause him to pay attention to me. With my dad I learned it was safest to be invisible and forgotten.

I drew conclusions about myself because of my father. It was always risky to be me around him, so I decided to become someone else—at least on the outside. With his message of disappointment playing on loop in my mind, I buried my real self and became aggressive, mean, and violent. I also became a black-belt at observation, constantly cycling through the same set of questions: What's the emotional temperature here? How do people view me? What gets celebrated and condemned in this place? What gets rewarded and what gets punished?

Guided by my answers, I hid my true self away and mastered the fine arts of self-protection and performance. I learned to become whomever I needed to be, wherever I was. It just felt too risky not to put on some made up version of myself.

Sadly, I carried all of that pathology with me into adulthood. Even today I push back against what feels like an emotional allergy, stemming from a soul-conflict between who I "should be" and who I really am. It's exhausting to compete against the anxiety of a fake life.

That's how danger flooded into my small world—life under "the curse" had begun for me.

Safety Lost

We don't know how long Adam and Eve enjoyed the ecstasy of pure safety, but we do know it came to an end.[6] It shouldn't surprise us that the emotional bond of our relationship with God is precisely where Satan focused his assault on humanity.

In Genesis three we read that Satan placed his crosshairs on this perfect new community, poisoning it with mistrust, selfish ambition, and pride.[7] Through deception, exaggeration, and grandiosity the devil convinced Adam and Eve things weren't as they appeared to be.

As a result, the first humans not only questioned God's goodness, they mistrusted his motives and came to believe living in his perfect love was not in their best interests. Somehow they were convinced that God was withholding his best from them. Blinded to the truth, they actually turned and walked away from the deepest longing of the human heart.

Danger then flooded into creation and humanity was washed out of Paradise in a torrent of shame and sinfulness. And because of this ancient rebellion, we no longer default toward the symbiosis of "fully known and fully loved." Our new norm is *caution*, driven by the assumption there are those in the world out to get us; *protection*, raising our fists against those who might hurt us; and *performance*, straining to earn our worth and value from those around us.

This garden story is the beginning of the great "current" always drawing us away from our heavenly Father and from his original plans for us. Because of this story, we've been looking for fig leaves ever since.

Feelin' better yet? Hang in there, you will.

Danger is the Human Experience

I probably don't have to ask you to imagine your life *with* relational threats; no one lives free of those. Sometimes a lack of safety can be slight and benign; even ambient. You might have a talkative friend who never seems to ask how you're doing, so you keep those conversations light and safely at the surface, since he doesn't seem to care anyway. Maybe you feel uncomfortable walking into new settings, like being the new person on the job or joining a cycling club. I have a few friends who experience low-grade fear when they're out in public and they can't seem to pinpoint why. Sometimes I feel a dip in safety around my mechanic, like my "man card" is in jeopardy. For the life of me, I have no idea what a throttle body is or how it gets clogged, or where you'd even find one on a car.

These are fairly minor, run-of-the-mill, low-safety scenarios. Most of us just shake them off and keep moving—kind of like responding to the weather when it's a bit too hot or too cold.

But there are other times when violations of safety reach deeply into our hearts. Just think this through a bit: When have you felt like it's not okay to be yourself around someone, or around a group of people? When have you been outright mistreated or hurt? How about those times when you decided it was best not to let someone in on a risky aspiration, a personal celebration, or a painful memory? Maybe you've been tempted to live behind a propped-up version of yourself to keep people from seeing who you really are.

If you relate to any of this, it's because deep relational threats are common in life.

Some know danger through *betrayal* by family or close friends. This is the terrible "switch-out" that happens when loyalty and love are suddenly replaced with deceit, unfaithfulness, or outright hurtfulness. When this goes down it's easy to think, "I must never allow this to happen again!"

Nearly everyone I know has felt some form of *disapproval* from others. It might come from a parent, a lifelong friend, or a group of coworkers. Many even confess feeling judged and condemned in faith communities like the churches we belong to.

Quite often the underlying message passed along in all this is, "You're not enough." You're not tough enough, responsible enough, smart enough, ladylike enough, faith-full enough, pretty enough, strong enough, orthodox enough . . . whatever. If that message had a voice it would say, "You are incomplete in your current version and I wish you were different. You disappoint me."

I have a friend who has lived her entire adult life under the weight of her parents' indifference. They never seemed to care who she was becoming, what she was doing, or where she was headed. She has carried the weight of that apathy through life like thick iron chains around her neck. Though she's always busy with family and friends, she rarely allows others access to her internal world, because her heart is convinced no one is truly interested and she's on her own.

There are many more examples I could give—as many as there are people. We could talk about conditional acceptance, abandonment, shaming, public humiliation or correction, transactional relationships, bullying, neglect, rejection, or outright issues of abuse in all its forms and degrees of severity.

But now a moment of severe honesty: the danger I released into relationships for decades was sarcasm. One way to think about sarcasm is that it's a way to say whatever you want, especially angry and hurtful things, and get away with it through humor.

"I'm being sarcastic. It's a joke. I'm kidding." That was how I responded when people called me on my toxic sarcasm. I wanted them to believe the problem was their inability to take a joke, not the hurtful words I had just spoken. The atrocity of my sarcasm, though, was that I could dump really awful messages on people without being held responsible. I spoke the hurtful words, people received them, and then I walked away without taking damage because I got a laugh.

A number of years ago I was in a counseling session with two of my adult sons. I was being my normal sarcastic self and the counselor noticed it, casually, skillfully: "Wow, you've got quite a sarcastic wit."

I took it as a complement and said, "Yeah, I guess so. It's kind of worked for me in life." *And then the bottom fell out.*

One of my sons looked me in the eyes and said, "Yeah? Well your sarcasm has never worked for me." My other son took it further, "Your sarcasm has always hurt me, my whole life." Then we talked about the deep wounds I had inflicted on my boys and what we all wanted to do about it.

I realized in that moment one of the "life skills" I had relied on my whole life had flooded my family with threat and risk. It was dangerous for my sons to be themselves because of the awful sarcastic messages I spoke into their lives.

Can you see that the list of relational threats is vast and common to us all? Do you understand that every single person you love feels the historical sum of the vulnerabilities they've suffered in life? Can you fathom the reality that, in some way, we store those experiences within us as a primitive, autonomic reality? And then we live our lives in response to all that history.

Making Sense of Danger

Openings and Closings

Life is risky for everyone, and that risk comes from somewhere. A helpful way to think about this is that each of us experience "openings" and "closings" in life. Generally speaking, how we feel about the world we live in—and the people in that world—comes from the way we've responded to those openings and closings.

Openings are specific moments when important people treat us with love, care, respect, and dignity. In doing this, they call us out of ourselves into the safety they create. When we experience these openings we end up feeling valued and pursued, believing we can be loved without having to earn it in spite of our flaws.

Closings, on the other hand, are episodes when we're deeply hurt by people who are important to us. In those times we walk away feeling shamed, criticized, judged, devalued, or unacceptable. The general message from such closings is, "You're not okay the way you are—you're flawed, incomplete, and unacceptable." Because of these closings, some of us live as fists tightly clenched. When that happens, it's easy to view the world of people as hostile and unsafe, causing us to walk through life with our guard up, closed off to deep relationships with family and friends.

It is no exaggeration to say everyone you've ever met has lived through openings and closings, and they carry those emotional memories with them through life. None of us shows up anywhere alone. We bring with us—consciously or not—our entire history of human relationships—healthy and harmful, pleasant and painful, joyous and tragic. Some of us have paid attention to that history to understand and heal the wounds we've received. Some of us have not. Some of us are still in the process of understanding and healing.

Wherever we land on that continuum, *relational safety and danger have massive impact on whether or not we will become like Jesus*. This is true of you and of everyone you know and love.

Danger and the Human Soul

One of the fascinating exercises I do with leaders is to describe relational danger, and then ask them to share how they've experienced it in their own lives. Think about that for yourself for a moment. Maybe imagine someone you feel unsafe with right now, or a social setting in which you feel vulnerable and exposed. At those times, how does your heart tell you to behave? How are you compelled to show up in those settings? How has that gone for you historically?

Relational danger is the great threat of the human soul. Many years ago I discovered a little book, *The Diving Bell and the Butterfly*—a memoir by Jean-Dominique Bauby.[8] In his prologue, Bauby describes his body as a diving bell after a cerebrovascular accident—a massive stroke—rendered his brain stem useless. The result for Bauby was a condition called "locked-in syndrome"—total paralysis from head to toe, with no ability to speak and complete loss of motor function.

Mercifully though, his one lifeline to the world was his ability to blink his left eye. So one blink at a time, he dictated letters, wrote words, composed sentences, crafted paragraphs, and ultimately finished this amazing gift of a book. In doing that, Bauby gave us a glimpse into his life, but he also gave us a metaphor that reached beyond his malady.

Locked-in syndrome isn't just a physical condition, it's also an affliction of the human heart. Becoming unsafe in the world of people can lock us into a kind of isolation that feels like an iron chamber at the bottom of the sea. We were never meant to live isolated from others, and that is the great tragedy that occurs when relational safety is lost.

After they chose to sin, Adam and Eve felt the shame of their sinfulness, covered themselves, and fled from God. They ran from perfect love in the perfect community, straight toward the isolation of the very first diving bell. Without safety, fear becomes our iron barrier as we attempt to shield ourselves against perceived judgement, condemnation, rejection, punishment, and any number of other relational penalties. We begin to believe it's safest to stay locked inside our internal world and keep who we are to ourselves.

When we live long enough under that threat, our "emotional-flinch" keeps us hidden and unknown, and our focus turns to survival and pain management. John Ortberg writes, "Every human being carries hurts or scars or wounds. Our tendency since the Fall is to hide as if our life depended on it. This is exactly wrong. Our life depends on getting found. There is no healing in hiding."[9]

This has been a global epidemic for as long as we've walked the earth. The shame and jeopardy that took root in Adam and Eve passed genetically to the hearts of their boys, Cain and Abel. That second generation was infected with insecurity, jealousy, and anger as Cain gave in to sibling rivalry and murdered Abel in calculated rage. The outbreak had begun.

The emotional pandemic then traced its way through recorded history from one human heart to another, even to my own. I not only lived fearfully under the threat of a disappointed alcoholic father, I passed that fear along to my own sons in the form of cruel sarcasm.

That, my friends, is how emotional threat works. Infected by fear and worries of vulnerability, we resort to self-protective behavior and, unwittingly or not, spread relational risk to those around us. The pathogen Satan used to drive us from perfect love and perfect community has infected the human heart, and now we pass it back and forth to each other.

Safety Heals the Human Heart

Ready for some good news? I bet you are. *Safety heals the human heart*. Or at the very least, it is the essential first ingredient in that healing process.

Safety is what we feel when we believe we are known and understood and then loved and accepted without conditions or judgment. When our hearts are convinced of that, we move toward trust and openness with those who create safety and away from those who jeopardize it. Our healthy tendency is always to choose safety if that option is open to us.

You can be the one who creates safety for those you love, and it makes all the difference. That's what we will look at next.

CREATING CIRCLES OF SAFETY 04

H ere in San Diego we have the "World Famous San Diego Zoo," located next to our downtown. Lesser known, but equally amazing, is the San Diego Zoo Safari Park in rural East County. What I love about the Safari Park is that park designers have created massive open areas to replicate, as best they can, the natural habitat of the animals. In one attraction, guests ride a tram around the entire perimeter of those habitats as a guide describes the animals and their behaviors.

As I visited the park and rode the tram, what stood out to me, over and over again, was the phrase, "circles of safety," used by our guide to describe groupings of animals.[1] "On your left, down by the watering hole, our oryx graze in a circle of safety." "On top of the next hill you see a herd of gerenuk resting in their circle of safety." "In the next valley, a pack of lowland dachshunds cluster in a circle of safety." Just kidding about the dachshunds, but not kidding about the circles of safety.

Nearly every species we saw that day settled naturally in vigilant, outwardly facing circles to create a collective environment of safety for all. They do this in the Safari Park because that's how they behave in the wild where their lives depend on each other.

Humans were made to live in circles of safety as well. These circles are a necessity, not a luxury. Every one of us has a vulnerable side—a side we can't see or defend. If we feel threatened, we can turn and face that threat, but all we're really doing is pointing our vulnerability away from danger.

We cannot be our own refuge because we can't have our own backs. To be human is to be vulnerable. So it's no wonder we feel disoriented and out of sorts when we feel isolated, because on our own we spin endlessly through life trying to keep our vulnerable side away from the threats that make up our world.

What makes us different from the animal world is that our threats are mostly relational, hence emotional; and even though they originate externally, we feel them internally. So we still need circles of safety, but in our circles—in our safe communities— we face our threats best when we turn *toward* each other. Unlike the Safari Park animals, we find safety in vigilant, *inwardly-facing* circles where we become known and loved. These are the communities where we place our vulnerabilities in the hands of safe people who then watch our backs for us while we also watch theirs. Safety is the connective tissue of the relationships that make these circles work.

Transformed by Circles of Safety

Amazing things happen in the human soul when we settle into these kinds of safe communities. Author and social architect Simon Sinek says, "We always confront danger every day, in life and in business. [But when] we feel safe, remarkable things start to happen."[2]

In 2014, Sinek delivered a wildly popular TED Talk—at this writing, it has nearly thirteen million views—on the social impact of people who create safety for others.[3] In his talk he tells the story of Army Captain William Swenson, who repeatedly rushed into enemy fire to save wounded soldiers. In a YouTube video, which Sinek mentions, you can actually watch Captain Swenson load one of his wounded friends on a helicopter and then kiss the soldier before the chopper flies off under fire. Sinek asks the question, "Where do people like that [Captain Swenson] come from?" In other words, what happened in that man's life to transform him into such a self-giving, empathetic defender of his people?

At first, Sinek assumed soldiers like Captain Swenson do heroic acts because they are just better people—that's why they volunteer for the armed forces and others don't. But he looked closer and discovered that selfless action is actually related more to the surrounding conditions. He said, "If you get the environment right, every single one of us has the capacity to do . . . remarkable things, and more importantly, others have that capacity too."[4] We do remarkable things in the right conditions because we become remarkable people.

When we stand in circles of safety, we become more free to change, grow, and reach for healing. We take the time and energy we would otherwise use to protect ourselves and focus those resources on becoming better versions of ourselves. We actually want those better versions of ourselves when we're not preoccupied with threats in our environment.

As I said earlier in this book, growth is normal; all we have to do is remove the barriers. *Fear may be the great barrier to growth.* It shuts down functions of the brain that naturally move us toward creativity, transparency, courage, curiosity, and healthy risk—all functions of forward progress. When we're fearful, we retreat behind internal walls erected for self-protection—we pull up the drawbridge, fill the moat, and post guards in the towers.

But all of that changes when the threat is gone. Gary Smalley says this is simply the way it works: "When people feel safe in our presence, they naturally open up. And when they open up, connection naturally occurs. You don't have to force it. You don't have to coax it. You don't even have to encourage it. It just happens."[5]

When we feel safe, our souls come out of hiding. We switch out of crisis mode and start believing that personal hope and change is reasonable again. That's not simply a function of social training; it's an outcome of God's original design for our souls.

The Physiology of Safety

For generations now we have known about our three basic responses to danger: fight, flight, or fright (freezing). When we feel threatened, the most primitive part of our brain—the part that forms first in the womb—sends lightning-fast signals throughout our body to prepare us for action. Through a process called neuroception[6] our nervous system receives data and signals a response to our body before the rational part of our brain has a chance to weigh in.

Consider the classic "stranger in the dark" scenario: Imagine you're walking alone at night on a dark city street, and suddenly a stranger steps around the corner. Maybe he's just a dad heading home to his family after a long day of work. Or it could be the Uber Eats guy dropping off a late-night meal. Neither of those options matter to the early warning system in your brain.

Before you give conscious thought to what might be happening, your physiology snaps into action, preparing you to survive this "threat." Your pupils dilate. Your heart beats faster. Adrenaline begins to flow. Your muscles tighten. All of that happens simply to help you fight better and run faster. And get this: it doesn't matter if the threat is real or imagined.

What you may not know, however, is the autonomic system that signals the alarm is the same system that returns us to "normal" when the threat ends. In 2011, research scientist Stephen Porges published *The Polyvagal Theory*, explaining in part how this de-escalation happens.

When the "all clear" safety cues are received in the brain, our "social engagement system"[7] responds and our bodies begin to produce the hormone oxytocin, essentially changing our biology to a peacetime state. Simon Sinek calls oxytocin "chemical love" because of the way it increases our connection to others.[8] He also calls it the "safety hormone," explaining that the more time we spend with people, the more willing we are to become vulnerable. If that goes well, the vulnerability then triggers the flow of more oxytocin, and in no time we develop deep bonds with friends in that community.[9]

The essential takeaway from all this is that safety is the preferred state for our bodies. In fact, our physiology is always moving us in that direction if the conditions are right. In a recent blog post, therapist Ellen Boeder explains, "We have an imperative for safety deeply wired into our minds and bodies."[10]

When that imperative is met, our bodies de-escalate from "just survive" mode and settle into thrive mode. Our ability to figure things out and make forward progress comes alive in our neural wiring when we are safe. We become biologically free to think and feel without concern for protection and security.

In safety, our bodies actually align on growth as we open ourselves to options and possibilities, risk and calculation. Ellen Boeder tells us, "Emotional safety enables us the freedom to . . . dream, be wildly creative, share bold ideas, feel increased compassion, and express ourselves freely with one another."[11] Later she says that when we feel safe in our hearts and in our bodies, "our social engagement system enables us to collaborate, listen, empathize, and connect, as well as be creative, innovative, and bold in our thinking and ideas."[12] So we're not just hardwired for safety; we're also hardwired for growth. *All we need are the right conditions.*

We are simply at our best when we feel safe. But none of that is available when we feel threatened. Without safety our bodies want to fight better, run faster, or simply play dead. When we feel threatened, it always goes back to fight, flight, or fright.

Here's the punchline: as leaders, we cooperate with this biological imperative in the body when we create safe conditions for people. This is a massive leadership advantage, and all we have to do is get behind the physiology of those we love and lead. When we do that, we help followers learn how to cooperate with their own design, deploying their inner resources that only come online when the proper conditions allow.

If Safety Had a Voice

Ultimately, safety is about anticipation. It happens when someone reveals a weakness, flaw, sin, brokenness, or hurt, and they anticipate receiving love and acceptance in return. If we keep this rhythm going, before long that anticipation turns into a belief.

Safety heals the human heart because of what we come to believe about ourselves and others under benevolent conditions. There is an embedded message in every safe environment. So when we create safety, people draw new conclusions about themselves and about life simply because of their new environment.

For many years now I've told leaders that "safety has a voice" and that it communicates undeniable messages. When you create a circle of safety for others, it tells them . . .

> **"You are worth a big effort."** You have such value to me I will make sacrifices to arrange my life around creating an environment that allows you to grow and thrive.

> **"You are not on your own."** I will be a fully present, fully participating, and healthy player in your life. You can count on me to be available and helpful. I'm not perfect and I don't have all the answers, but we can look for them together. You have partners in this caring community.

"We are in this together." The Holy Spirit is doing an internal work in us to help us become more like Jesus. He is doing that in you and he is doing that in me. Together, we can cooperate with his work in our lives.

"I am interested in you." I want to see you, understand you, know you, and love you. You fascinate me. Jesus created you with undeniable beauty and complexity, just like the rest of creation. I can't wait to know you better. Count on me to initiate.

"I 'start' with you and not with me." I choose your interests before I choose my own. I exist to serve you, not the other way around. I am here for your benefit, not to benefit from you. I don't want something from you, but I want many things for you. This circle exists for your sake first, not for mine. I'm not in this for me, I'm in it for you. *This a powerful—I would say essential—core message of safety that preempts the doubt and skepticism common in human hearts.*[13]

"I am not leaving." I won't force you to stay, but I won't abandon you either. We may not remain in the same circle of safety forever, but I won't reject you and walk away. You can count on my acceptance and love because it is unconditional—you don't get to earn it or lose it. Your worth, and my love, are settled.

It is nearly impossible for me to read those messages without tears welling in my eyes, because they touch a universal need in the human heart. That need is connected to a latent question we ask of every significant relationship: "Will my heart be safe in your hands?"[14]

When safety is released in the community long enough, people believe their weaknesses and imperfections will not be used against them. They believe it's okay to be needy, because that's simply a part of the human condition. They come to know that sin and brokenness are a part of us all, and that holiness and healing are a genuine option. They find out there is a strength in community that no individual can experience on his or her own.

Safety Isn't Pain-Free

Safety has nothing to do with creating a bubble-wrap world for people too fragile to care for themselves. It is not like that at all! Many critical messages have been written recently about "helicopter parents" who live to create offense-free "safe-zones" for their over-trophied "snowflakes." That's not what this is. (And by the way, it's unproductive and hurtful to disparage every newly arriving generation of adults.)

Safe does not mean easy or pain-free. But it does mean secure. In a safe environment it is okay being your imperfect self as you struggle toward developing into the person God designed you to be.

The reason this is such a big deal is because *the pathway to competence runs through incompetence.* Do you get that? In order to become good at something you have to start out doing that thing badly. The pathway to holiness—to becoming more like Jesus—runs through wickedness—living only for ourselves.

This is the way sanctification works. We *slowly learn* to forgive mean people when all we really want to do is hit back. We get better *over time* at saying no to our "me-first" demands. Kindness and generosity *grow in us* as we discover the joy of giving. And ultimately, loving becomes our driving motivation as empathy *gradually displaces* criticism and judgment from our hearts.

None of that happens overnight, and it is incredibly helpful to work on these things in the open, with other people, in an environment that both allows imperfect progress and celebrates genuine growth. We can be both training partners and cheering fans for each other.

Trust me, there is nothing simple or easy about this process. If there is anything "snowflakey" about you, a circle of safety will change that, and you'll be happy for it. These kinds of communities require effort, stamina, and courage you'd never experience otherwise. But the net result is change and growth you'd never think was possible, leading naturally to rich contentment and joy.

In his letter to the Philippians, Paul tells us to, "continue to work out [our] salvation."[15] For the record, he doesn't tell us to work *for* our salvation. He is pointing us back to the practice of aligning our attitudes—our thoughtful plans in life—with Jesus' attitude.[16] That is a growth imperative Jesus-followers can obey only because of God's work in us. In fact, in the very next verse he contrasts our "work" with God's partnership with us: "for it is God *who works in you* to will and to act according to his good purpose."[17] [Emphasis mine.]

Safe communities are the places we can actually live out Paul's imperative. In those communities, people come to believe it makes sense to be transparent with their growth process. Circles of safety become "life labs" where we practice our Jesus-following skills together in the open, and it's okay to do that because going public with our lives doesn't require perfection. On the contrary, pulling back the curtain on our messy, sinful lives and asking for help gets celebrated and championed. In those communities, that kind of vulnerable transparency is simply what we do.

And then transformation begins. I'm getting ahead of myself, but when we add truth to safety, change is on the way. I'm telling you, that's the way it works. We will take a closer look at this in the next chapter, but now is a good time to start making that connection.

Safety Restored

The current version of our world is not what God was going for when he created the heavens and the earth. His plan included pure intimacy with his people. Out of that relationship, we were to enjoy a mysterious partnership with him that is hard to imagine—something, in part, like a sub-regency. God created, and then he handed over part of that creation to our care and supervision.[18] He literally commanded us to thrive, fill the earth, and take charge.

The perfect family. Wildly fulfilling and creative work, the kind of stuff we dream of doing. Love from a Father captivated with his children. *We lost all of that.* We picked a different plan, our own plan, and broke the world.

Can you even begin to imagine the horrific shock, the absolute terror, that Adam and Eve must have felt when they realized what they had done, what they had given up, and what they got in return? At times I wonder if there was some kind of mad scramble to get a do-over.

It makes sense to me, in my flawed view, that God would simply wash his hands of humanity and move on. In fact, why doesn't he? Why doesn't he just turn away from our know-it-all petulance and willful independence? For goodness' sake, who do we think we are anyway? Why doesn't he give us what we chose in the garden: life without him? I'll tell you why: because love doesn't do that. Love scans the horizon. Love comes alongside. Love reaches out. Love retrieves. Love welcomes back. *Love restores.*

God is not okay with the broken world we live in, and he is less okay with living estranged from his children. The heart of the Father is to have us, and out of his pure love he reaches into this mess we've made of ourselves.

Our creator came for us; he came for you and for me and for everyone we know and love. In the purest form of empathy,

Jesus entered our world in the flesh and lived a fully human life (and a fully divine one) to offer us our spot back in his divine family.

In Galatians, the apostle Paul refers to Jesus' life on earth as something like a divine rescue mission. "Jesus gave his life for our sins," Paul writes, "just as God our Father planned, in order to *rescue us from this evil world* in which we live."[19] [Emphasis mine.] It's all there: our willful disobedience, a loving Father, Jesus' work on earth, and rescue from an evil and broken world. But this isn't just a rescue *from* something, he's rescuing us *for* something.

Later in Paul's letter, he tells us the Father sent Jesus to buy us out of slavery so he could adopt us into his family.[20] That's the restoration part. He wants us back in the family and he will make the ultimate sacrifice to make that a possibility. By dying on the cross to pay for our disobedience, Jesus offers to substitute his perfect holiness for our willful depravity.[21]

When we accept Jesus' offer by choosing to follow him, our identity changes. We are no longer slaves, chained to the flawed systems, strategies, appetites, and ambitions of our broken world. We become sons and daughters of the Father, restoring us to the best circle of safety ever.

That is the gospel; that's in part the good news Jesus came to deliver. He brought God's kingdom to earth, and we now have the option to live in it as family members and citizens. The ultimate circle of safety is available again to anyone who wants it.

Leaders Create Safety First

Jesus created safety first. He laid aside his divine privilege, became a servant, and humbled himself, dying on the cross to make sure our ultimate safety was secure.[22] In doing that, he simply lived out his identity as the good shepherd, saying "yes" to his love for all of us.[23]

Jesus is the perfect leader. He went first. It was his life for ours. He stood between us and our ultimate threat, and now he calls us to lead the same way, telling us to "Love each other as I have loved you."[24]

He even contrasts his perfect leadership with the self-serving leadership of the day. In a confrontation with his disciples, he reminds them that they know what bad leadership looks like, because they see it every day in the leaders who rule their world.[25]

These flawed leaders start with themselves, push people around, and pound on their chests in self-importance. Jesus, however, brings a different kind of leadership, and the negative, self-centered version stops with him. Then he calls the disciples to follow his lead: take a step down, lay aside your interests first, and serve those who belong to you before you serve yourselves.

What the disciples don't know at this point is this kind of shepherding will change the world.

Followers-First Leadership

Simon Sinek famously says, "Leaders Eat Last."[26] With those three words, he establishes both a priority and an order for caregiving. If I choose to live out those words, I decide to value loved ones above myself and tend to their needs before my own. This is a decision all real leaders face: meet your own interests first or give your best to those you lead. Sinek's response is unwavering: "Leaders are the ones who are willing to give up something of their own for us. Their time, their energy, their money, maybe even the food off their plate. When it matters, leaders choose to eat last."[27]

Sinek's message comes from his work with the Marine Corps. He tells the story of officers in the field who make sure their soldiers eat before they do.[28] The officers literally eat last. This, in fact, is what they believe makes the Marine Corps so great. The officers set aside their own interests to make sure those in their care get what they need. It's a classic "you" before "I," "we" before "me" scenario.

For Sinek, the broader message these leaders deliver is, "I will give what we all need, the very essence of life, to the ones I love so that they may live and thrive; even if it means I eat less."[29] The way Jesus said it was, "I am the good shepherd. The good shepherd lays down his life for the sheep."[30]

In everyday life, this is about more than who gets to eat what, and when. It's about the normal behavior of shepherds when they establish and maintain the circle of safety, and it's ultimately guided by the core value of "followers first." These kinds of shepherds . . .[31]

> . . . *go first.* They walk into the unknown and uncertain before others do. When something hard has to be done, they are in line to do it before anyone else. They're on their feet. They initiate. They investigate. They move off to cover new ground, and only then call others to follow.

> . . . *sacrifice themselves.* They are willing to have less so loved ones can have more. They aren't primarily about the bottom line, the goal, the mission, the agenda, or their own personal success. Before all that, they focus on the health and growth of loved ones. They yield their individual aspirations for the well-being of followers. Bottom line, they choose caregiving over their own comfort.

> . . . *control the perimeter.* Conditions may be sketchy and precarious in the world, but these leaders work to keep that danger from touching those inside the perimeter. They ensure the circle of safety extends all the way around those they lead, not just around themselves or a select few. In a way they create their own world of conditions, and in that world threats from the larger context aren't allowed in. Real leaders don't ignore the outside threats; they may even talk about them, but followers don't have

to spend precious time and energy on them because the perimeter is secure.

. . . scan the horizon. You could call this hopeful caution, as opposed to distracted paranoia. They pay attention. They look for potential threats, but equally important, they look for opportunities, advantages, and resources that will benefit the community. Bad things don't spring up and good things aren't missed. All leadership happens in a given context. Caring leaders aren't so focused on that context that they wander into trouble or walk by opportunities. Their eyes are up and focused on what is coming over the horizon, whether good or bad.

. . . run toward threats. We really only have three options to danger in our world: run toward it, run away from it, or act like it isn't there. Caring leaders do not ignore trouble. They face threats and then take intentional steps to neutralize them. They stand between their followers and danger the way a father stands between his children and an angry dog. They are the buffer, the fixer and the protector when conditions threaten the community.

. . . correct mistakes. Shepherds don't lead perfectly, and they don't pretend like they do. They make mistakes like the rest of us, but they don't then cover them up or deny them. We don't require perfection of our leaders, but we need transparent responsibility if we're going to trust them. We feel safe when leaders come clean about flaws and mistakes. It not only humanizes them in our eyes, it leads us to believe they can be trusted with the truth, even when that truth is hard.

I'll admit, this kind of leadership is a tough sell in our world today. We live in an "eat first" culture that often ridicules "followers-first" leadership. But remember, the crowd ridiculed Jesus too, and he saved the world.

So much of our culture elevates the worst kind of human greed and pride, but that's not what Jesus modeled. He showed us that leadership is not a "step up," it's a "step down" into the lives of followers. Healthy, generous leading is not someone's chance to get more, it's a chance to give people what they need most. And this spotlights the core struggle in the human heart, because creating the right conditions requires sacrifice, work, time, and energy. If you work to be this kind of a leader, it will cost you something. Retired Marine Corps Lieutenant General George Flynn says, "The cost of leadership is self-interest."[32]

This is absolutely the right thing to live out if you want to help others change and grow. If Jesus matters to you, and if you've committed your life to follow him, then you are most like him as a leader when you create safety first. If there are people who matter to you, you give them the best chance at transformation when you lead like Jesus.

Finally—Safety Is the Doorway to Everything Else

Ranger the "rez dog" came to live with us a few weeks ago. Years ago, he was rescued from a Native American reservation in the south valley of Albuquerque—hence, the title "rez dog." We're not sure of his breed, but we see in him some cattle dog and maybe a little pit bull around the jaw—both highly courageous breeds.

One thing we're certain of, though, is that he was abused as a puppy—maybe severely abused, most likely by men. Spend any time with Ranger and you'll see he lives with his own unique list of fears, such as men with facial hair, being around tall people, and walking toward water.

One of his greatest fears is a door-not-fully-opened. Yep, you read that right. If a door is fully open he is happy to walk through it on his own, but to Ranger a door-not-fully-opened might as well be the Great Wall of China.

Last week I decided to measure his fear of these terrifying not-fully-opened doors. He and I were in my office and I walked out, intentionally leaving the door partially opened. I knew he wanted to follow me (he always does), but that half-opened door locked him tightly in my office.

I decided to up the ante and get his jar of "Chicken Chips," treats that are normally irresistible to that guy. I stood at the end of the hallway and told him I had his chicken chips; I even shook the jar. Usually that turns him into a hunch-backed, tail-wagging wiggle machine. But I got nothing, not even a peek.

Then I walked down the hall so he could see with his own eyes what I was holding. No movement at all. Finally, I pulled out one of the chicken chips and held it out. Ranger didn't budge, not an inch. He sat, staring at his chicken chip, locked inside his invisible cage of fear.

Here's the happy ending. I walked into my office, turned toward the door and said, "Ranger, let's go." And then he walked with me right out through that door-not-fully-open and snagged his chicken chip off the floor. You should have seen how happy he was.

I was the solution to his entire dilemma. He needed safe conditions, in the form of a safe person, to go and get what he wanted really badly. I'm not sure how hungry he would have had to get to push through his fear, but I do know the safety of having me walk with him was enough to get him moving. No question, Ranger is really scared of completely irrational things, but just add me and he's courageous enough to push through all his fears, at least so far.

Ranger is just like all of us, in a way. He's kind of a picture of the human condition I've mentioned throughout this chapter. Something went wrong, his world was broken, and now his default state is danger and fear.

Those you love and lead have great potential to live immobilized by their fears. Even when Jesus opens growth paths for them, and the Holy Spirit illuminates those paths, they can remain unwilling to take next steps.

You can change all that. You can come alongside them and simply say, "Let's go together," and that can be enough to get them moving. Even a tasty and appealing future can feel terrifying when we have to walk that journey alone. But then again, we were never supposed to.

I cannot overstate this. I cannot make a big enough deal out of this. Safety is almost always the place to start—or restart—with any kind of life-changing community. It is only through relational safety that we get anywhere near the other life-changing conditions: truth, vulnerability, words of affirmation, and caregiving.

Safety is the doorway to everything else. It's not enough on its own, but it makes all the other life-changing conditions come alive and work. I don't know this just because of the way I've led others; I know it because of the way I have been led.

Once I felt safe enough with certain people, I felt free to look at the parts of me that were less than perfect—the parts that needed both healing and transformation. Then I allowed those safe people access to those parts of my life. And that's when everything changed—the healing began, and growth finally became an option. I've also witnessed this same process hundreds of times with others.

This is what we offer through circles of safety. When we do this, we become partners with Jesus and push back against the dangers of our broken world.

"TRUTH IS THE RAW MATERIAL OF LIFE-CHANGE."

TRUTH-CHALLENGED LIVING IN A TRUTH-OPTIONAL WORLD

Have you ever run into a friend and known immediately there was something big going on in his life? He didn't have to say a word; you just knew by the look on his face or the angle of his shoulders or the skip in his step. The signs might even be so subtle only close friends or family would notice.

When Flynn walked into church last week, I knew immediately something good had just happened. I'm pretty sure all of his friends saw it. I couldn't say exactly what I thought I saw, but I knew he was acting a little differently. It wasn't exactly a swagger, but he clearly had a bounce in his step I hadn't seen in a while. Was it confidence? Was it good news? Did he just have a fantastic breakfast? What was going on?

A few of our friends reached to him for high-fives, which then turned into full-body bear hugs. Flynn tipped his head back, smiled big and held eye contact with family and friends. He was obviously in a very happy place, surrounded by his own personal "fun bunch," and together they were celebrating a big win.

And then I saw it clearly—yep, it happened. The day had finally arrived, and Flynn was wearing his brand-new big-boy pants.

Oh, by the way, Flynn is three years old, and he had a sticker taped to his back that read, "I'm potty training." It's a sticker we use at our church to help our little friends stay on track with their growth plan. Way to go Flynn!

I love that sticker! I smile every time I see it.

Forget for a moment what it says, and think about what it means. That sticker is way more than informational; it has a confessional quality to it. It tells us there's an aspect of Flynn's life he needs to work on. He is unfinished, a work in progress, and you could even say life gets a little messy for Flynn when he forgets that. It's like he is telling everyone, "I'm working on my life, and it might require us to get our hands dirty from time to time."

Flynn's sticker is also an implied request for help. There is no explicit ask and it doesn't provide instructions. It doesn't say, "Hey will you keep an eye on me and if I get a little squirmy, will you help me get to the bathroom?" But we all get the basic message, "I'm Flynn, and I'm going to need occasional help." I admire that about Flynn. He knows he doesn't have it all together, and he's not going to act like he does.

What I love most about his sticker is that it activates all of us—his family and friends—and now we are all in on his growth process. There will be times when Flynn forgets about his own next steps, or times when he tries to white-knuckle it and just get by. But that's where we come in, because we see his sticker and we know his success depends, in part, on our help. His sticker—his request for help—keeps us alert and dialed in. You might say there are times we are more aware of Flynn's growth area than he is; times when we see what's true of Flynn better than he sees it himself. But we love our little friend and we intend to be a supportive and helpful part of his process. His little sticker has turned us into "Team Flynn," and we've rallied around this new truth in his life.[1]

I Wish Everybody Had a Sticker

I think life would be better if we all had stickers. Way better!

Can you imagine living in a sticker-wearing world where it was normal for people to know the truth about each other? Actual stickers on our backs wouldn't work; they wouldn't be enough. But what if we lived leaning into the truth about ourselves, and then welcomed safe and helpful people into that process with us? If they feel safe enough, those we lead can come to believe it's okay and reasonable to turn around and show their "stickers" to the right people.

Think of a sticker as something that is true of you. It's certainly not your whole truth, but it represents a substantial reality in your life. Flynn doesn't wear his sticker to tell us about a big win he is celebrating; it's about a challenge he's trying to overcome. That's the way it works for us as well. Your sticker is a declaration to others— not just that you have some growing to do, but that your growing is about a specific part of your life. *Essentially, your sticker says, "Here's what is true of me. Will you help?"*

If that's what our stickers say to the people around us, then it means they represent the parts of us that are less than perfect. When we "wear our stickers"—when we reveal what's true about ourselves to safe people—we're ultimately admitting our downside. We are telling some of the people around us we've got work to do, and that work might include any number of things the Holy Spirit highlights. He might reveal something wide-ranging, like a growing darkness in our mood or a general sense of impatience with people. He might also pinpoint issues like signature sins, fears, or compulsions. But common to any growth area is our follow-up request for help. Again, that's how stickers work: "Here's where I need to grow; will you help me take a next step?"

"I'm Screwed Up!"

Back in the late 90s I was a division leader—think "front-line pastor"—at Willow Creek Church in Chicago. My job was to develop leaders and help unconnected people find their way into small-group communities. Those were my core tasks, but my mission was to help people become more like Jesus—the church leadership asked that from all of us. That meant we were all in the growth and transformation business.

One of our strategies with that task centered on creating "transitional events" for the thousands of people who came to our weekend services. Since we believed "life change happens best in small groups," we wanted to place those groups close enough to our services that people could walk from their seats in the auditorium right into one of our small-group events.

The demographic I led was single adults in their 40s and 50s. To me, that meant the vast majority of those who came to our events would be coming alone, without the safety net of a spouse. I felt like the relational stakes would be sky-high for most of them, so I needed to level the playing field for everyone, turn up the safety in the room, and put on my sticker.

On night one, with hundreds of brand-new people in the room, I made the case for "doing life together" instead of doing life on our own. I talked about the value of connecting with new friends and laid out some of the barriers that might keep them locked in isolation. At one point I even confessed my own temptation to manage their impressions of me. "I want you to like me," I said, "I want you to think I'm good at what I do. I want you to approve." I confessed I had some messed-up messages in my heart that made those desires too important to me.

Finally, I told them the only way I knew to push back against all those messages was to come clean about myself. I said, "I want to stand up here, on our first week together, and get something out of the way." And after a short pause, I declared, *"I . . . am . . . screwed . . . up!"* It was a pin-drop moment for sure, but I kept going . . .

"That's right. I am screwed up!"

"I did not get through life unscathed . . . and neither did you. I did not get through life unhurt by important people in my life. I took damage along the way."

"Telling all of you this truth lets me off the hook, and now I no longer need to manage your impressions of me. I am now freer to be myself and continue my journey of growth."

But I didn't stop there. I told the crowd I wanted to let them off the hook too. Then I led them in a public declaration—a group confession really. On the count of three, they shouted back to me, *"I'm screwed up too, John!"* It was glorious—one of my favorite belly-laugh moments ever—and it was the beginning of a kind of big-group vulnerability every one of them could use to start their growth process.

To this day, I know transformation is always preceded by the truth. I knew it all those years ago with my new friends, and I know it now. So what I really did, way back then, was turn my back toward everyone in the room and show them my sticker. I told everybody I have downside; I have work to do, and I really need help from others. I wish it was more like that everywhere.

Side note, for months after that event, people walked up to me in public and said, "Hey John, I'm still a little screwed up. But things are really changing for me . . . and I love my new group of friends." Growth had begun for them.

Each of the people you love and lead carry the knowledge of their own flaws, sins, and growth areas, but unlike Flynn, they may choose to keep those things hidden from the helpful people in their lives. You'll come to see that this type of hiding actually locks your loved ones out of their own growth process. We cannot change what we cannot see or refuse to look at. The good news is that you can make seeing reality a legitimate option for those you shepherd. More on this shortly.

What's Your Sticker?

As a shepherd, it feels right for me to lead with my sticker. I know we all have them, so it makes sense to start out being transparent with the parts of me that need growing. I don't hand out a list of my flaws and failures, but I don't hide them in conversation either. I live and talk as though downside is a part of all of our lives, especially mine.

One of my life habits is journaling and then talking with safe friends about what I write. Two questions I ask all the time are, "What is true of me?" and "What is my downside?" I usually grab a cup of coffee, settle into my study, and simply start a conversation with Jesus about those open-ended questions.

Lately, he has been highlighting some uncomfortable clarity. For one, I am prone to actual violence, not just angry thoughts. I grew up putting my hands on people, mostly because I gave in to my father's message: "You're going to be a fighter, not a lover." Those were his actual words my whole life. No surprise, then, that I grew up loving combat sports like boxing and wrestling. Unfortunately those spilled over into my real life as I came to view aggression and violence as a reasonable option under certain circumstances.

Violence still feels like a reasonable option for me today, maybe in the same way it was for the apostle Peter at times. I have a relational reflex to be aggressive. When I don't resist that reflex, I yell at people in the store, square off against other men in public, hold eye-contact too long, and push strangers who get too close to me. I also do other things that I don't have the courage to share in this book. And all of that feels so crazy when I claim it in writing. *But it's real, and I have no chance of changing any of it unless I name it and ask for help.*

That's my sticker, or one of them anyway. I "wear it" around my friends who are also trying to resolve hostility. We work together to trace our emotions to their source. At times my friends help me stir empathy in my heart when I really want to choose anger. They nudge me toward humanizing people by seeing them as fathers, brothers, sons, and friends—not adversaries. Sometimes they just ask me, "How would Jesus shop at Costco around people who lack awareness?"

None of this is fun to admit, but it's essential that we see the truth about our lives. The Holy Spirit provides clarity, in safe communities, to reshape our hearts and push back against messages we've rehearsed for years. For me, the more I wear my sticker with safe and helpful people, the more I want to be like Jesus. Because that's how change works when the conditions are right.

It's Hard to See Your Own Sticker

If you wore a sticker right now, what would it say? Do you have clarity about your downside? Can you immediately name some of your growth areas? Come to find out, answering this is one of the bigger challenges for most people.

There are things about us we cannot see on our own because of something like naturally occurring self-blindness. In other words, *we cannot know what is true of ourselves by ourselves*—at least not completely. My buddy Dale Bacon says, "We can't take our own temperature." It's not just that we know and hide our flaws; we certainly do that, but we have a hard time actually seeing them.

Our capacity for self-deception is staggering. This happens when we get squishy on the truth when we look at ourselves in daylight. The reality is, in sober moments, we see things in our words, behavior, and motives (especially our motives), that we don't like—awful things, things we wish were not there.

The problem is we can't make our cringey truth go away altogether, but we can make it "smell better," and that's the problem. Many of us have an automatic—nearly unconscious—habit of relying on excuses and exceptions to explain away our ugly truth and let ourselves off the hook.

We tell ourselves: "This is just a one-time thing." "I'll start on Monday." "If he wasn't so awful, I wouldn't have said those things." "I deserve to be happy." "I'm only a recreational drinker." "I just want to be me." "I'm not going to let this become a habit." "I'm not controlling, I'm intentional." On and on it goes, and on and on we walk further away from the truth about ourselves.

"This Isn't Who I Am"

The core of our self-deception is the twisted belief, "This isn't who I really am." We have the crazy ability to look at data that reveals our sins and imperfections, and somehow tell ourselves, "I'm not really selfish, critical, lustful, gossipy, petty, ungrateful, miserly, angry, controlling, or whatever . . . *those things aren't me.*" The problem is, whatever we can't see and understand—or simply won't look at— we also can't change.

Hue Jackson, former head coach of the Cleveland Browns, in a film session with his team, told his players, "Quit talking about 'This is what we want to be.' *I'm showing you the tape. This is you!*"[2] Somehow, we need to see this too. We need to watch the "tape" on our lives, accept what we see . . . and then look in the mirror and say, "This is you."

Dallas Willard writes, "The initial move toward Christlikeness cannot be toward self-esteem (i.e., confidence in your worth and abilities[3]) . . . because, realistically, I'm not okay and you're not okay. We're all in serious trouble."[4]

We compound that trouble when we allow self-interest to blind us to our true condition. When that happens, Willard goes on to write, "such a situation will only breed self-deception and frustration."[5] Further, he lays all this at the feet of our unwillingness to accept the truth, stating, "Denial . . . is the primary device that humans use to deal with their own wrongness. It was the first thing out of the mouths of Adam and Eve after they sinned, and it continues up to the latest edition of the newspaper."[6]

What's really crazy about all this is that, while we are prone to let ourselves off the hook, we refuse to offer that same blind-kindness to others. We are prone to brutalize people we know over the very truths we work so hard not to see in ourselves. We draw conclusions, mind-read, sum people up and then privately denounce them—all in the name of "truth-telling." Our self-deception is complete when we fail to give others the same benefit of the doubt that we hoard and guard for ourselves.

If you're wondering where this comes from, look to James' letter in the New Testament. In the first chapter, we read there is something in the human heart that allows us to hear the truth of Scripture in light of the truth of our lives, *and then forget what we heard.*[7] Did you get that? There is something in us that makes it hard to stay clear on what is true—about God's Word and about our lives. James explains this through the metaphor of a mirror. We have the inclination to look in a mirror, receive the truth, refuse to act on that truth, turn away, and "forget" it all.

"*I'm showing you the tape. This is you.*" And it's me too!

The Imposter's Phenomenon

John Ortberg writes about the "Imposter's Phenomenon"—what he calls the universal sense that, at some level, we're all faking it.[8] It's built on the idea that "the real me isn't good enough so I'm hiding behind a made-up-me," one I've fabricated to match what's important to the people around me.

The goal is to be accepted by others—to appear worthy and valuable. The price of it, however, is the truth: I must sacrifice the actual truth about myself to live the idealized truth of my community—whatever that community is. The more skillful we get at this, the more distance we create from people and the more disconnected we become from reality.

When our followers give in to this pressure, they surrender any chance of becoming the people God designed them to be. They stop aiming at God's version of their best selves and settle for an alternate version that their community expects. God wants us to live in the truth, but many of our human communities will settle for a made-up, distorted version of that truth.

The greatest danger isn't that loved ones find out they're flawed and sinful. The greatest danger is they never will—that they will look away from the truth about themselves and settle for a fake life. Because our default mode is to minimize, deny, and cover-up our sins and imperfections, it's possible to live our entire lives disconnected from who we really are.

The Truth Really Does Hurt

Let's face it, the truth does actually hurt some of the time—maybe even a lot of the time. It feels dishonest not to admit that, but because we want to avoid that pain, we create elaborate denial schemes and choose not to look deeply at ourselves. It also keeps us on our never-ending quest for the perfect "fig leaf" to hide behind.

But the fact remains, growth and truth are inseparable; you cannot have one without the other. This also means that growth and pain are a package deal.

Dan Allender tells us God meets us in reality. "Reality may be painful," he writes, "but if we want to meet God we have to go there."[9] Henry Cloud and John Townsend take this even further: "It has been said that spiritual and emotional growth is a path further and further into reality. I always try to remind people that as painful as it may be, *truth is always your friend*. No matter how difficult it is to swallow, truth is reality and that is where ultimate safety, growth, and God are. *We need to know the truth . . .* whatever the truth is, it is our friend. And it is where God lives."[10] [Emphasis mine.]

This isn't just for us, to keep our own hearts straight on the cost/benefit ratio of seeing reality. We have to remember, as we nudge loved ones toward the truth, that we're also nudging them toward discomfort.

I was in a leadership seminar years ago led by my friend Rex Minor. As he trained us on essential practices for shepherding, he highlighted the need to help followers metabolize the discomfort that's always a part of growing.

At one point, he invited a young lady from his team on stage and asked her to share how she was dealing with the pain of her own growth journey. She shared her beautiful story of courage and, at one point, credited Rex with helping her through some particularly dark moments.

When she finished, Rex said something I will never forget. He looked her in the eyes and said, "I am absolutely committed to your discomfort." Apparently she had heard those words many times, because her eyes filled with tears as she whispered back, "I know . . . thank you."

His commitment to her discomfort didn't seem hard for Rex, because he knew her pathway to growth ran through truth, and that truth is often painful.

Our loved ones cannot grow without living in the truth—no one can. I'll take it even further: life only works when we live in the truth. You want to talk about pain? Try living your life on the flimsy foundation of truth avoidance. I actually know something about that—I "lived in that neighborhood" for a while—and now I would never exchange the discomfort of living in the truth for the anguish of ignoring it. Life is never more painful than when you collide head-on with the truth you've devoted your whole life to avoiding.

Our World Isn't Kind to the Truth

To make this harder, we all have to live in the world we're in right now. I don't care where you grew up, this world we live in is a rough neighborhood. It's a jungle out there and you can take a beating for being yourself, whether you're careful or not. Someday Jesus is going to change all that, but until then we live in a deeply divided, full-contact, and inherently dishonest world.

It's a mistake not to admit this and say it out loud. We live in a world that is not kind to the truth—for a bunch of reasons—and that makes it dangerous to be yourself out there in the open. I guess you could say our world is not a sticker-friendly environment.

Family Rules for Hiding

For nearly all of us, our struggle to live in the truth started in the families we were born into. Every family has rules to follow—nearly all of them unspoken—and if you pay attention long enough you will discover what those rules are.

They may be simple peacekeeping rules like "Don't hit your sister/brother," or division of labor rules like "Wash your dishes when you're finished." They can also be quite demanding, complicated, and nuanced, rewarding children when they think and value the "right things," yet punishing them when they do their own independent thinking and believing. That said, I actually love family rules when they're flexible, healthy, and inclusive, because they clarify expectations and help us understand how life works at home.

The trouble we get into is when family rules are shame-based and turn toxic. When that happens, it becomes very difficult for children to see who they really are and understand the world as it is.

In shame-based families the rules often teach family members two life-skewing lessons: (1) hide who we are and (2) become a false version of ourselves. Under those guidelines, the family cabal locks their truth away from public view and then lives some alternate version of reality.

We were really good at this in my family growing up. We had three unbreakable, silent rules that made authenticity nearly impossible:

1. **The "No Talk" Rule:** "I know we have dark, terrible secrets and you know we have dark, terrible secrets, but we don't talk about us . . . not with each other, and certainly not with others. So close your mouth and keep your thoughts to yourself."

2. **The "No Limp" Rule:** "Life hurts, so get over it. If you hurt, suck it up and walk it off, but don't ever let me catch you walking with a limp. If you're sick, get up, get out of bed, and get going. If someone hurts you, shake it off and make sure they hurt worse than you. Showing pain in any form is unacceptable."

3. **The "No Help" Rule:** "You're on your own, so don't ask me for help. Don't lean on me and don't count on me. I've got enough in life to worry about on my own. If there's anything you need, figure it out and get it for yourself."

What were the rules in your family growing up? Are you clear on the norms that shaped how you see yourself and the world around you? Were you welcomed and celebrated, and then nurtured to discover your unique self? Or did you live under the heat and pressure of toxic disapproval and expectations, pressing you into an alternate—more publicly acceptable—version of yourself?

Steel will bend quickly under extreme heat, but it also degrades and warps gradually through the constant expansion and contraction of warm days and cold nights. Sometimes our families are like a furnace, other times they're more like the weather, shaping and molding their members over time. Either way, do you know how your family rules shaped your heart?

Every single one of us lives our most vulnerable years in families with rules. Those families may have been kind and nurturing with the truth, or they may have enforced a made-up version of reality. Whichever version our followers lived under, those rules may still be in place and active in their hearts. It's beyond helpful to look hard for those rules and help those who you love and lead understand how those early rules affect their current ability to live in the truth.

And then there's the bigger picture to look at.

Truth-Optional Culture

The gloves are off in our culture these days. Civility is nearly gone, replaced with bare-knuckle brawling. It's as if we've lost our ability to speak to one another, so we resort to lobbing verbal attacks and hiding behind ideology. Social media only adds kerosene to this bonfire.

Don't have an opinion. Don't ask a question. Don't share a thought. *Don't be yourself.* The cultural landmines are everywhere—so much so that it seems impossible not to stumble into some offense or insensitivity in conversation. I won't even trash-talk the Denver Broncos these days, and I'm a card-carrying member of Raider Nation. What is this world coming to?

Seriously though, it doesn't seem to matter which side of any issue you land on, there's always an outraged opposition group ready to carve you up. I've had too many friends tell me they feel so vulnerable to "social attack" that they simply choose to fly under the radar and keep their thoughts to themselves.

Our conversations have become not just bland and impersonal, but strategically cryptic, guarded to the point of confusion, and so qualified with explanations we end up saying nothing. The general consensus I hear is it's simply not okay to be yourself out in the open, which makes me wonder if "tolerance" is failing us.

I think there are bad ideas everywhere. I know for sure I have bad ideas all the time. I also know I can be so entrenched in my ideology that it's hard to see things from another perspective. What bothers me most, though, is that I feel like there are fewer and fewer places for me to talk about my messed-up ideas. I know I have them, I know I don't see things clearly enough, and I know I need help. But where do decent people go these days to talk about their bad ideas in the hope they can discover the better, good ideas with the help of others?

All of this isolates us, locking us into echo chambers where we only hear the stuff we already agree with. The good guys are with us and the bad guys are with them. It's not just their ideas that are bad, they as individuals are bad. They don't simply have misguided, uninformed strategies and plans, they have wicked hearts. We don't disagree with fundamentally good people, those we differ with are evil and their motives are selfish and hurtful. They want power, wealth, and control, and they are willing to abuse and exploit the public to get those things. This is how the lines seem to be drawn today, *and further into hiding we're compelled to go.*

The Bible uses two phrases for a truth-challenged world like ours. In his letter to Timothy, Paul writes we are in "terrible times" and "the last days."[11] He is describing the time we're living in right now—the time between Jesus' ascension to the Father and when he returns.

What makes these last days so terrible? Paul says it's us—the people who live during this time—because of who we are and what we do. He fires off a list of nineteen traits and two core behaviors to describe the way we are right now. He calls us: lovers of self, lovers of money, boastful, proud, abusive, disobedient to parents, ungrateful, unholy, without love, unforgiving, slanderous, without self-control, brutal, not lovers of the good, treacherous, rash, conceited, lovers of pleasure instead of lovers of God, and looking good only on the outside. Wow, that's a lot—this is one of Paul's longer lists.

But then it gets really rough when he pinpoints how these traits show up in our behavior. He says we are prone to deceive and control vulnerable people, and that some of us actually oppose the truth because of our depraved minds. Ultimately, Paul aims all the traits of his list at two dominant behaviors: deception and opposition to the truth.

I've used inclusive "us" and "we" language with Paul's description for a reason. I think it's important that we don't go entirely "us versus them" when we read his words. It doesn't help to point a finger at culture and act like we're untouched by it.

Even as followers of Jesus, we live as a subset of the population Paul describes. That's part of the ugly and painful truth I mentioned above. Maybe we're fooling ourselves if we think our cultural context has no impact on us. Can you claim exemption from all the items on Paul's list? Are you able to read these vices without the familiar knowledge that some of these character traits live in your heart? I cannot do that. If you feel any of this like I do, I think it's because of the constant heat and pressure of the truth-warp we all experience.

Hiding in the Church

This gets very close to home for me, and maybe for you too. It breaks my heart to admit, but those of us in the church are often not kind to living in the truth.

I love the church! With my whole heart, I love it! The church isn't a building, it's a family we belong to. It's the hope of the world, God's only plan for making disciples, and I've devoted my whole life to serving and leading the church. But I'd be lying if I didn't admit how hard we "church people" can be on the truth.

Let me tell you about my friend Elizabeth—she's one of my favorites. A number of years ago I got a call from a mutual friend asking me to reach out to Elizabeth because her life had gotten really hard, really fast. At the time I rarely had enough margin to follow-up on calls like this one, but I felt nudged by God, so I agreed to reach out.

After I called her, we met for coffee and talked about the painful challenges she was facing. Her greatest challenge was the crushing pain of finding her husband lying dead on the living room floor, suddenly making her a single mom to her son Matthew.

I liked Elizabeth immediately. She is far from ordinary. She's extremely smart, articulate, informed, and thoughtfully outspoken about the things that matter to her. When you meet her you also can't help but notice her piercings and tattoos right away. If you ask, she will tell you when she got each of them and what they mean to her. To say she's an open book is like calling the Pope religious. She clearly strolls to the tune of her own kazoo.

In time I discovered the open-book-theme of her life also extended to her car, which will become relevant in a moment. It looked like it was held together by bumper stickers, all of them broadcasting her current big causes—like a clean earth, diversity and acceptance, legal marijuana, and gay marriage. If a cause was left of center—or way left of center—Elizabeth was all about it.

What I loved most about Elizabeth was her brutal honesty and how she approached life with her head up and her eyes open. Conversation with her was easy, efficient, and mostly rooted in reality. She seemed to know, intuitively, that her challenges weren't going to solve themselves. If life was going to work for her again, she had to own her part in the struggle and follow through with positive changes.

So she and I met from time to time to untangle her internal world a bit and focus on the things that kept her moving forward. Most importantly, we talked about Jesus and how he wants to meet her right in the middle of her difficulties. We talked about the truth of the Bible and the way the Holy Spirit leads followers of Jesus.

Eventually, my wife Coleene and I invited her to church, and I helped her find a couple small-group communities to join.

The last big theme Elizabeth and I worked on was being "relentless." We could see the distractions and discouragements that seemed to derail her from time to time, so we decided she would focus on *relentlessly holding onto Jesus*, as a way to stay on track. With each new challenge she faced, we would talk about what it meant to relentlessly follow Jesus through it. It really seemed to be working and she made some nice progress.

One day she called and asked to meet, explaining she had something to show me. When I got to our Starbucks, she had a big smile on her face. When I sat down, she stood up, turned around, and on her back—across her shoulders, in three-inch letters—was a tattoo that read, "Relentless." That's my friend . . . that's Elizabeth! Wow, I was speechless! That's called going all-in on a spiritual practice.

In time, her crisis eased up and life approached something closer to normal for Elizabeth. She became a follower of Jesus and stayed engaged with community, and one day she and I stood in front of our church as she declared her devotion to Jesus, after which I baptized her. She inspired many of us that day.

And then the unthinkable happened. In all honesty, I was always a bit worried about how our conservative, patriotic church would welcome Elizabeth. Our church was khakis and loafers and she was tie-dye. We were red meat, she was vegan. We were NRA, she was Greenpeace. She had big differences with that church and maybe it was denial that made me think everything would be fine.

Deep down inside, I guess I wondered if we would be willing to receive her just the way she was and simply point her to Jesus. Would we love her as-is, speak truth and grace to her, and allow the Holy Spirit to do his work? Would we see past the piercings, tattoos, and bumper stickers, and respond with generous caregiving? Would we elevate safety and acceptance long enough for her to see Jesus clearly and love him deeply? I really hoped we would.

One Saturday night after our evening service, Elizabeth walked to her car in the parking lot—maybe you can imagine how it stood out among the other cars. She backed out of her spot and pulled into line to turn left and head home. A car pulled up behind her, and when Elizabeth looked in her rearview mirror she saw a woman . . . reading her bumper stickers. Elizabeth told me she watched the woman's countenance grow dark and angry the more she read.

Soon the light turned green and Elizabeth and the woman made their turn. At the next stoplight, the woman pulled up next to Elizabeth, rolled down her window and shouted at her, *"I hope you never come back to our church again!"* I have no idea who that woman was, but when Elizabeth related the story, I felt punched in the gut—it was like time stopped a little in that moment.

But I was so proud of how Elizabeth responded to that woman. She did it relentlessly devoted to Jesus. In a split-second decision, she met Jesus in her heart and simply said to the woman, "Well . . . I hope you have a fantastic evening," and drove away.

There is a thread that runs all the way from Adam and Eve, through the church, and into our hearts. When we don't live in the love and acceptance of the gospel, our hearts take on a self-righteousness that cloaks who we are and drives others into hiding. If that false righteousness had a voice it would say to people, "Your flaws and failures make you unredeemable. I disagree with you and that makes you unsavable."

The gospel gives us the safety we need to see how messed up we really are. First, we become sons and daughters of God, and then the Holy Spirit begins to shine his spotlight on growth areas in our lives, ultimately empowering us for life change.

But we create hiding in the church when we make a spotlight of our own to illuminate the flaws and failures of others. This is an illegitimate use of spotlights, and entirely unnecessary. Only the Holy Spirit gets to decide what is illuminated, and when.

Ultimately, each of us decides which side we line up on: the side of shame and hiding, or the side of love, acceptance, and truth. So far we've been looking at the first side of that line, but now we turn to the only side that leads to change and growth.

HELPING PEOPLE SAY "YES" TO THE TRUTH

There is something true about you . . . and you don't know what it is. There is also something true of those you love and lead . . . and they don't know it either. This is the human condition we've been looking at this whole time.

The way Peter Scazzero explains this, each of us is like an iceberg—a small part of our lives is above the waterline and visible to everyone, but most of who we are remains below the surface, out of sight, and not immediately known.[1] He says if we want to live in the truth, we have to figure out how to look beneath the surface.

Jesus Looks Beneath the Surface

Jesus has always known who we are beneath the waterline of our lives; in fact, he knows what's beneath the surface better than we do.

All through the Gospels we read about Jesus seeing deeply into the hearts of people and then talking with them about what he sees. He dispenses the truth to those who desperately need it. He brings reality to those who are unaware of their waterline, and to those who are trying to ignore what's beneath it. By doing that, he offers them the life they've always longed for.

In John's Gospel we read about Jesus sitting at a well around lunchtime. Moments later, a Samaritan woman approaches to draw water. Since she is coming to a well, Jesus initiates a water conversation.[2]

The cultural context of this interaction is stunning—in fact, bordering on forbidden—but Jesus ignores that and plunges right in. It's like he says to the woman, "You're here for water? Great, we all need water, and you seem to think this is the place to get the good water. What you don't know is I have the water that you really need. All these years you've relied on thirsty-again water, but what you really need is never-thirsty-again water. I am the only one who can give you that. It's the best water; it will flow within you and give you life forever."[3]

The woman can't believe what she's hearing—she's been ready for never-thirsty-again solutions her whole life. But just when it seems like she's going to get one, Jesus "looks beneath the surface" of her life with a waterline comment that exposes what she's been relying on for years.

"Go get your husband," Jesus says. There it is. That's the difficult truth she spends her waking hours trying to avoid. "I don't have a husband," she responds. "Yeah I know," Jesus tells her, "You've had five husbands and you're living with a guy right now. You *do* know what the truth is."

This woman, she shows up at the well with water-supply issues and discovers her real problem is what lies beneath her waterline. Her thirsty-again solutions have never resolved her deepest need, and that's where Jesus meets her. He knows all about her—he knows all the details—and he skillfully loves her with the reality of her own truth. Jesus is never okay with our fabricated realities when life-giving truth is within reach.

In case you're wondering, this whole encounter is the best news ever for this woman. She runs back into town, back to the people she has avoided her whole adult life, and tells them, "There is a man who knows everything I ever did." The thing she most wants to hide, she now proclaims to everyone. Being loved by Jesus is the most freeing experience ever for this woman, and she can't keep it to herself.

It's not hard to imagine the words in her heart as she runs back to town. "What you all know about me—the truth that shames me every day of my life—there is a man who knows all of that too, and he gave me never-thirsty-again water. Come and see him, and he will love you too. You no longer have to live like there is nothing beneath the surface of your life."

And they come to Jesus, looking for the same thing the woman received. They too want their never-thirsty-again water . . . and they get it. They receive from Jesus what he first gave to the woman, and little springs of never-thirsty-again water well up in people all over town.

This is simply what Jesus always does—he always points us to the truth. He is the *way* to the truth. He is the *truth* himself. His truth provides the *life* our souls have always thirsted for.[4] He is the light of the world and it's not possible to follow him and remain in the dark, because his words lead to truth and freedom.[5]

The Gospel Makes It Okay to Look Beneath the Surface

Too many of us live an ongoing struggle between looking good and being good. We want to look good because we know, deep down inside, we're not actually good. If you feel that tension, that struggle, you need to know the gospel confirms your suspicion: you are, in fact, not good and you can't be good enough—not on your own.[6] None of us can, me included. It helps to admit that and get it out of the way as early as possible.

But the gospel doesn't stop there. It also tells us we don't have to try to look good because Jesus is good for us, and by "good" I mean he is sinless, without fault, completely perfect.[7]

The most scandalous part of the gospel, though, is "the great exchange":[8] Jesus' righteousness for our sinfulness.[9] When we put our faith in Jesus and follow him, he takes our sin and gives us his righteousness. It's not just that we're forgiven and our debt is cancelled, putting our sin-balance at zero. We're actually credited with all the righteousness that Jesus embodies. And the mind-blowing wonder of it all is that this is Jesus' solution to our depravity problem. If we accept this, receive his forgiveness, and devote ourselves to following him, we leap from massive debt to unthinkable riches.

In his commentary on Galatians, Martin Luther tells us we receive righteousness like the ground receives rain.[10] Righteousness is never something we can acquire on our own. We're made "good" (i.e., perfect, sinless) without any effort on our part, because we have nothing to contribute to our own goodness.

Though we can have confidence, it will never be rooted in our own goodness. Our assurance is in Jesus' righteousness; in his perfect life and in what he did for us on the cross. That means the gospel tells us we are perfectly safe in Jesus.

This is amazing news. Once again we are fully known and fully loved, which means it's okay to look beneath the surface and see who we really are. There is no jeopardy in Jesus. As J.D. Greear tells us, *"there is nothing you can do to make God love you more and nothing that you've done to make him love you less."*[11]

I have come to crave looking beneath the surface of my life with Jesus. I never feel more loved, paid-attention-to, and cared for than when he meets me in the imperfect places of my life. Most of the time when I meet him there, I think I hear some version of the same message: "It's okay . . . it's alright . . . you don't have to worry . . . open your eyes. I won't leave you; I'll help you. It won't be easy, but we can do this together. I know how you can change, and I'll walk with you through it, one step at a time."

Jack Miller, former pastor, professor, and founder of World Harvest Mission, tells us, "It is false thinking that heaven is a free gift to us, but God is distant and angry with me the rest of my life." He goes on to explain, "That's how many of us live: God is angry with me all the time, and only angry, and I don't know what to do with that or how to change it . . . other than behave better."[12]

God's dominant emotion toward us and toward those we shepherd is love, not anger. God loves the same people you love. God isn't indifferent about them. God isn't distracted from them. There is nothing they can do to win or lose his love and favor. And they can come to live in the reality of that truth, which also means they can come to look at the deepest truths of their lives.

Jack Miller tells us, "It is the righteousness of Christ, credited to my account, which frees me to be honest about my struggle and not to be crushed by it—to know that even though I struggle with sin, God is still with me. Even though I struggle and make slow progress, and sometimes no progress, God has not abandoned me. Because that's not the whole story. I have a righteousness that's not my own. Unless we hold onto this truth, honesty is just too hard; it's too frightening."[13]

Truth Is the Foundation for Who We're Becoming

Every one of us is in the process of building the life we're currently living. This life-building happens as we walk through life saying "yes" to some things and "no" to others. Through an ongoing process of consent and rejection, *we are who we are right now, and we're becoming who we will be one day.*

We have built and we are building. We have become and we're becoming. Dallas Willard describes this as "formed" and "transformed," and it's the foundation for the way he explains life-change and growth.[14]

"You have a spirit within you," Willard writes, "and it has been formed." That spirit, he tells us, "takes on whichever character it has from the experiences and the choices that we have lived through or made in our past. This is what it means to be 'formed.'" *We are who we are, right now.*

But transformation is absolutely an option for the future. Dallas explains we never have to settle for who we are at this moment. He says our greatest need is the "renovation" of our hearts. He writes, the "spiritual place within us from which outlook, choices, and actions come has been formed by a world away from God. Now it must be transformed." *We're becoming who we will be one day.*

Saying "Yes" to the Truth

In the Sermon on the Mount, Jesus teaches his disciples how life works in the kingdom of God.[15] He starts out describing who lives the blessed life. Then he highlights the law and clarifies what it means to follow it faithfully, pointing out that true compliance is more about the condition of your heart than the action of your hands. He warns us that it's easy to get preoccupied with looking good on the outside, but we can remedy that temptation with secret generosity, prayer, and fasting. After all, he points out, there is nothing in this world worth treasuring. The only thing worth having, really, is the treasure of our life with God in heaven. So he tells us not to obsess over this life, what we have or want, because God will take care of us. Bottom line, we should seek God first and all the other things we worry about will take care of themselves.

In the end Jesus finishes his message with a couple options for listeners and adds a stunning metaphor. Option one is receiving his message as truth and living our lives guided by that truth. Option two is doing nothing with his message. Then, using that stunning metaphor, he describes the results of those two options.

The one who chooses the first option "is like a person who builds a house on solid rock."[16] That person's house is firm and stands up in stormy weather. The one who chooses option two is "like a person who builds a house on sand."[17] That house—that person's life—is flimsy and it's coming down as soon as the rain falls and the winds blow.

Jesus makes it graphically clear that our lives stand up or fall based on what we do with the truth. We're all building the lives we're currently living. We can build on truth, ultimately settling into a firm life that allows for change and growth. Or we can opt for fiction, believing lies and fallacy and settling for a flimsy life of coping and denial—ultimately struggling under the inevitable stress of phony living.

We shape who we are with truth or lies; reality or fiction. Whichever option we choose, it becomes the source from which we form our values, thoughts, emotions, decisions, commitments, habits, and character. It becomes the foundation for the life we're currently living and for who we will become one day.

Truth Is the Raw Material of Growth

If there is an actual "thing" that growth is made of, I think it's truth. If we want life change, truth is what we search for, consume, and use. It's not something we do. It's not a skill we master. It's not just a thought we think. It's something we take in to become a part of us. It is about us and all around us. We receive it and examine it to understand and use it, as best we can, to shape our lives.

When we want to actively pursue positive growth, we don't just hear truth—we do something with it, like Jesus told us to. We believe something and then behave a certain way because of that belief. Over time our behavior turns into life habits, and out of those habits our character forms. We become someone different because of the truth we believe. Truth is the raw material of growth.

Two Kinds of Truth for Building

There are two essential truths we must focus on for life change: the truth of our lives and the truth of the Bible. This is the great spiritual intersection. It is where we come to understand who we are, how life works, and who we can become. For growth to happen, we must live out the truth of our lives in the context of the truth that God reveals in the Bible. The Holy Spirit meets us at this crossroad and becomes our guide forward.

1. The Truth of Scripture

As followers of Jesus, our essential source of truth is the Bible. We receive it as the direct message given to us from God,[18] and the central figure of that message is Jesus.[19] We look to Jesus, through the Bible, to understand what it means to be his disciple—his student in life—and become more like him.

The Bible isn't relative or subjective. It isn't truth that morphs based on circumstances, nor is it truth based on what we want it to be. The Bible is reality and it tells us what is true.

We believe God speaks to us directly through the Scriptures. For us, the Bible is our primary source on how to become the best version of ourselves. It reveals the truest thing about our lives: we started out far from God, Jesus entered our world to restore us to his family, and now we can follow him as disciples.

Our growth is absolutely dependent on constant guidance from the Bible. We search it, read it, contemplate it, discuss it—all to understand God's influence and direction in our lives. It must be our central resource to guide our thoughts, decisions, and behaviors. Following what the Bible says as a life habit reconciles us to life as it was supposed to be. Most importantly, it helps us know how to love God and love people.

This reliance on Scripture is the lifestyle practice that makes growth a possibility. We cannot grow without a radical core commitment to the truth, and the Bible is the epicenter of that truth. It is what we must settle into and point people toward all the time. It is the place to start and the place to stay.

I have hundreds of books in my library and I love them all; they feel like old friends who help me make sense of life. I've been mentored from a distance, for decades, by the people who wrote those books, and it's hard to imagine life without their wisdom. Books and videos and blogs and podcasts are fantastic; it is mind-blowing how much amazing information is available at the click of a button. *But they are not the Word of God.* As helpful as they are, they weren't written by the Designer and Creator of life itself—though God will use those resources as they align with the truth of Scripture.

Our reflex must be looking to Scripture as a *first response* to the challenges, questions, opportunities, and growth barriers in life. As a disciple, I am always asking, "How would Jesus handle this? What would he say? What would he think? What would he do? How can I become like him in this part of my life?" And then I go to the Bible in search of Jesus and his answers.

This is also the foundation for the way I lead and love followers. We must point people to the truth of the Bible, allowing the power of that truth, along with the guidance of the Holy Spirit, to impact the truth of their lives.

This is a massive topic. Hundreds of books have been written on the authority and centrality of Scripture, and I won't improve on any of them. All I want to do is "hang neon lights" around the power of the Bible for life change.

God created life and he knows how it works best. We do our best work as shepherds when we help people see the truth of their lives in light of the truth of Scripture.

2. The Truth of Your Life

The life you live will tell you what is true of you; all you have to do is pay attention.

My golf instructor used to tell me, "The flight of the ball never lies." Forget the lying part for a moment; the flight of the ball actually tells the truth about your golf swing. The point of impact between the club and the golf ball is the ultimate "rubber meets the road" moment. At that point, pure physics takes over and the flight of the ball is simply the result of a previous event.

In the golf world, the trajectory of the ball is the most honest "cause and effect" moment ever. If I swing my club, strike the golf ball, and get a "wicked slice," a "worm-burner," or a "shank" (all really bad golf shots, by the way), I know exactly what happened at the moment of impact. That's because the flight of the ball tells the absolute truth about my golf swing. The effect—the flight of the ball—points backward and reveals what's true of the cause—my swing. It's actually one of the purest truth-moments in life. But it's still just golf.

Well guess what? There's also a trajectory to your life and it too doesn't lie—it reveals what is true of you. Your life is like the flight of the golf ball; it's the result of a previous cause. That cause may have been a traumatic event, an amazing opportunity, a deep disappointment, a loving community, or a profound moment of clarity. More accurately, it's a combination of all those events along with many others like them. But the ultimate cause of your life is how you've responded to that collection of high-impact events over time.

Another way to say all this is that *results point to reality*. Our lives are perfectly aligned to produce the results we're getting, and those results reveal what is true of us. Who we are comes out behaviorally in the lives we live: the way we love, how we spend money, the way we do conflict, our ability to sacrifice and delay gratification, and even our hopes and dreams.

You can't constantly scream at co-workers and claim gentleness as a virtue. You can't think of yourself as generous, yet never help people in need. Who you are—your ultimate cause—comes out in what you do—your ultimate result. Look at your pattern of behavior over time, and it will tell you what you need to know about yourself.

Jesus talked about this big idea in much the same way, using the metaphor of trees and fruit. In Matthew's Gospel, he says, "You can identify them [false prophets in this case] by their fruit; that is, by the way they act. Can you pick grapes from thornbushes, or figs from thistles? A good tree produces good fruit, and a bad tree produces bad fruit. A good tree can't produce bad fruit, and a bad tree can't produce good fruit."[20] In this passage Jesus is giving us the "law of results" wrapped in divine metaphor and wisdom. *Your life will tell you what is true of you, but only if you're willing to see it.*

It would be so much easier if life was more straightforward, like my golf lessons. Learning to golf, one follows a process of action (or behavior), observation, feedback, and adjustment. And it's all linked to the pure and real-time data of trajectory. What outcome are you going for—what do you want the ball to do? What outcome are you getting—what is the ball actually doing? What changes do you need to make to achieve your desired outcome—how will you change your swing? *Work on those.* There is a ton of nuance to golf and it's a wickedly mental game, but those are the basic mechanics. The flight of the golf ball gives me the information I need to change and get better.

Here's some really good news: the trajectory of our lives also gives us the information we need for change and growth. We can look at our lives, identify the patterns over time, decide on changes, and then get to work on those changes. There is a ton of complexity and nuance to life and it can also be wickedly mental, but we have a framework for change that becomes wildly helpful if we will only pay attention and see what is true of our lives. To be clear, none of this happens quickly—I pray I haven't left you with that impression.

I have an app on my phone called "Flight Radar 24" that allows me to track, on a map, the trajectory of any airplane flight in the U.S. *in real time*. It's actually kind of mind-blowing to me. I can watch my son and daughter-in-law take off at JFK in New York and follow their actual flight path all the way across the country to San Diego.

There is nothing in our lives like Flight Radar 24. We have to use relationships and community to track our "flight path"—to look for and see our life patterns. Come to find out, *that's the only place those patterns actually show up.*

This is what we offer those we love and lead: an opportunity to see the truth of their lives, as we do the same thing with our own lives. When that happens in a safe place, watch out, because courageous growth steps are right around the corner. It just takes some time.

Writing Your Sticker

A keystone is the last piece placed in the top of an arch. It's the wedge that locks the other pieces together and allows the arch to bear massive weight. Without the keystone, everything else falls apart. *Truth is the keystone for everything else; it holds together all the other life-changing conditions.*

When we help others live in the truth, the pieces of their lives come together and they gain the strength they need to bear the weight of life change. If we can't live in the truth, nothing else works the way it's supposed to.

Shepherding people in the truth is all about helping them see, display, and respond to what is real in their lives. It's like helping them write and wear their own stickers.

Trajectory Reveals Truth

Remember from the last chapter, your sticker represents a growth area in your life—it's a part of you the Holy Spirit wants you to recognize and work on. When you "write your sticker," you're claiming a part of your life that needs changing. You're admitting to something you see in yourself that doesn't resemble Jesus. This boils down to identifying a growth area and then talking about what you see with safe people. That's how you write your sticker. *You see it and then you say it.*

But what is it we're actually trying to see when we look at the truth of who we are? The place to start is trajectory—the overall arc of how we live our lives. Trajectory reveals what we value most, because lifestyle always follows affection. In other words, the core motivation of our heart comes out in what we pursue with our lives.

Why think trajectory first? Individual behaviors don't tell us enough about the true state of our hearts; the sample size is too small, so they don't give us the full story. Trajectory—the collection of those behaviors—shows us the bigger picture and reveals the deeper truth about who we are.

Imagine, for a moment, you meet a young lady who became a follower of Jesus a few years ago. Her transformation has been dramatic and now she is devoted to helping young women in Tijuana know Jesus and rise out of poverty through micro-business ownership. But she also smokes cigarettes. She has smoked them since she was thirteen and it's been brutally hard to stop.

The trajectory of her life is locked in and she looks a lot like Jesus, and it would be a huge mistake to shepherd this young lady as though she has fundamental "heart issues" because of her unresolved cigarette habit. Does she need to quit smoking? Of course; it's terrible for her health. But then again, I really need to lay off cake and peanut butter too. Is the Holy Spirit at work in her heart to transform this habit? Absolutely, and her faith community can be helpful too. But it can be easy to miss a trajectory because we get too focused on an individual behavior, especially if that behavior is stigmatized in our faith culture.

There seems to be a "first things first" process to life change with the Holy Spirit. It's almost as if he triages our lives and says, "Oh yeah, let's work on this thing (or these things) first, and we'll get back to those other things later." That "first thing" usually focuses on what we love most and corresponds to Jesus' command to "Love God first and love people like you love yourself." When what we love gets transformed, it's surprising how it fixes so many other things— because what we love is a trajectory issue.

When men love women the way Jesus loves women, they give them the same opportunities and pay that men get, and they choose not to objectify their bodies. When people love the poor, they provide work opportunities and give to organizations that help lift families out of poverty. When we love our families, we create quality time with our children, caring for their hearts and making sure they know they are loved. When the Holy Spirit focuses on the trajectory of our hearts—transforming what we love—it's amazing how the right things become important to us and how we become indifferent to the wrong things. Because, again, behavior follows affection.

Consider this: if you woke up early each day before your family, skipped breakfast to get into the office early, lunched with clients, met with co-workers all afternoon, ate dinner at your desk, and then crunched numbers late into the evening, what would a dispassionate observer say is your core pursuit in life? It wouldn't be work/life balance. It wouldn't be volunteerism. It wouldn't be deepening relationships with family. It wouldn't be physical and emotional health. But it could be workaholism, success and achievement, wealth, performance, and the like.

We could create endless scenarios like this one. What if we plugged your life into the scenario? What if we plugged in the lives of those you love and lead?

Trajectory implies destination, because the way we live our lives indicates what we're hoping for when it's all over. It reveals what we believe is the good life—or the good enough life.

Patterns Reveal Trajectory

The controlling question of trajectory is, "What do I see in my life and what does it mean?" What are the decisions I make? How do I spend my time? How do I spend my resources? What do I study and try to get good at? What do I sacrifice for? Who do I sacrifice for? What is my life really all about? Ultimately, how does my trajectory match up with the trajectory that Jesus lived? How do my values and decisions align with his?

All of this shows up in patterns of behavior. We don't live a collection of isolated, independent, and random actions; we generally live our lives through behavioral patterns. These patterns make up the trajectory of our lives. As leaders, it's really helpful to distinguish between random actions and the patterns we see in followers. What are the patterns we see and what do they tell us?

Gospel-centered churches often talk about the "heart idols" we pursue. Think of an idol as anything we look to for "life" (i.e., significance, purpose, satisfaction) or anything we elevate above God. Pursuing idols is the opposite of what the Holy Spirit is trying to do in our hearts. Caesar Kalinowski lists four of the big idols we tend to elevate above following Jesus.[21] They show up in our behavior patterns like neon at night. Here are those four idols, or four potential patterns:

1. **Control:** I desire to be in charge of my world and call the shots. I insist on certainty about conditions and outcomes. Self-discipline is king for me. Things must be just right, so I tend to over-prepare and obsesses about details. I often feel my preferences as needs.

2. **Comfort:** Privacy, elimination of stress, and freedom to choose are a big deal to me. Feeling good is one of my highest values and my choices get passed through that

filter. There are things in life I deserve. I work hard to eliminate discomfort and inconvenience at all cost.

3. **Approval:** I must have acceptance, affirmation, and peace in relationships. I work hard to prove myself to people. I often defer to others when I need to make a life decision. What others think is a big deal to me. I live with a constant fear that others may not like me.

4. **Power:** Success and influence are essential to me. It's important I'm viewed as competent. I feel the need to be right and in charge. It's my way or the highway. I must prove myself by winning . . . all the time. So I compete, a lot.

Actions Reveal Patterns

Of course, patterns are made up of individual choices and actions. This is truth at the finest, most granular level.

It's important to see the details of our lives, because that's where the Holy Spirit meets us—in the minutiae of everyday living. This is where our individual conversations, decisions, habits, choices, and responses point to the patterns we live. And those patterns reveal trajectory.

Since we live our lives in the details—one piece of life at a time—this is where we collect the data on who we are. Even though I started out focusing on trajectory, the actual order of discovery goes like this:

$$\text{actions} \rightarrow \text{patterns} \rightarrow \text{trajectory}$$

If we are going to understand ourselves and those we lead, we must look for and see the details of our lives—but we have to do that in the context of patterns and trajectory. When we get this wrong, we often end up in the classic "missing the forest for the trees" scenario. We can get so focused on a specific detail (e.g., decision, action, conversation, relationship) that we lose sight of the bigger picture of someone's life. When that happens, it's easy to jump into compliance enforcement and out of heart transformation.

As I lead loved ones, I am constantly asking, "Am I seeing an isolated behavior or is this part of a pattern in their life?" Even though our individual actions make up patterns, we also have one-off experiences all the time. All patterns are made of behaviors, but all behaviors do not make up patterns.

Have you ever noticed how often Jesus encounters people in the details of their lives and then relates to them based on their trajectory? It is inspiring to see him do that all throughout the Gospels. I can't break those scenarios down right now, but it is a fascinating study, worthy of your time.[22]

Wearing Your Sticker

Writing a sticker and then not wearing it is like not writing it at all. When we wear our sticker, we're admitting we don't do our growing on our own. In fact, wearing our stickers is what makes them actually work. They are effective specifically because we're not keeping our truth to ourselves. By wearing them, we're admitting to ourselves and to others that real change and growth happens best in community with safe people.

There is a ton more to say about this, but I'm going to hold off for now. The next two chapters are all about how we wear our stickers the best way. It's an essential component of growing, so be sure you don't miss it.

Responding to Your Sticker

To see the truth and do nothing about it is like not seeing it at all. Seeing must lead to responding, and one way to think about that is simply taking a next step. It's not taking *all* the next steps, just the very next one. *When we continue to do this over time, new life patterns form in us and our trajectory begins to shift, one degree after another.*

Sometimes a next step is *something you do*, and sometimes it's something *you do in you*. There are times when it's best to change a behavior, and other times when it's best to focus on an internal heart change. All this is part of the "weighing out" process of transformation.

So, in a nutshell, responding is doing something with what we've written about on our stickers. What do I see? What does it mean? Now, what is the Holy Spirit leading me to do?

Finally . . . Getting Help with My Sticker

I lived through one of my richest seasons of healing and growth while working for my friend Michael Yearley. He is not only a fantastic teacher and preacher, he's also a world-class leader who created one of the richest growth environments I've ever known.

He created that environment, in part, by asking us to weigh in on how he was leading our staff family. He didn't cloak it in "How are *we* doing?" No, it was a straight-up "How am *I* doing?" moment, and I'm pretty sure that was a first for all of us.

There were two questions he asked in particular that completely dismantled my boss/employee paradigm. He asked: "What am I doing that you'd like me to *keep doing*? And what am I doing that you'd like me to *stop doing*?"

Do you see what those questions imply? By asking them, Michael was telling us, "There are some things I'm doing that are probably right, and they work. And . . . there are some things I'm doing that are probably wrong, and they don't work." Michael was admitting he had both upside and downside, and the beauty of it was he faced it all in the open—and relationally—in our little community. Because of the way Michael led us, we looked for the truth, talked it out, tried to understand each other, and decided together how things would change or stay the same.

Those two questions also changed me. Michael's bold openness, more than anything I remember, made me want to recognize and understand my own downside. I actually wanted to see myself through the clarity one can only get in community. I saw the importance of knowing my growth areas, because Michael lived out that value in front of me.

It wasn't long before I began to ask Michael, "What's my downside?" No sugar-coating, no editing; I just wanted him to give it to me straight. In fact, I asked a version of that question for months—many months—and somehow he always found a way not to answer. I don't know if there is something sacred to Michael about delivering that kind of truth to people, or if he just wanted to be sure I really wanted what I was asking for, or both. But I finally backed him into a corner and insisted on an answer, and he agreed to give me one.

I can still picture the day. We used to meet at a Starbucks each week to talk about ministry and our lives. It was a sunny California afternoon, so we sat outside and I just went straight for it: "Okay, what do you have for me? What's my downside?" I was saying, "Michael . . . please . . . I cannot see my own sticker, will you tell me what it says? Will you tell me the truth about myself?"

And then he told me the truth. It wasn't easy truth to hear, and it hurt more than a little, but I'd had a hunch about it for a long time. When he spoke it, something activated in my heart and I gained clarity I didn't have before our conversation. He told me:

1. **You have low emotional stamina.** There are times when you may not actually be as emotionally tired as you think you are. At those times you may need to push a little harder. If you do that, you may see your capacity expand.

2. **You have a narrow "sweet spot" for ministry.** Your sweet spot isn't about capacity either, it's about comfort (there's that "idol" again). There are things you can and should do, but your discomfort is holding you back.

3. **You have a ton of complexity.** Your heart is complicated and conflicted. If you don't pay attention and allow God to untangle some of this, your emotions may hold you back and keep you from being more like Jesus.

There it was. That's what I asked for. My friend Michael Yearley loved me with the truth. I received his words, weighed them just like he would, and ultimately accepted them as the truth I had longed to know.

Michael was absolutely right about me, by the way. The Holy Spirit met me during that time and told me, over and over again, "This is what's true of you. This is going to hold you back and limit your kingdom impact." God made it clear I had to take some important next steps if I was going to grow through these issues. So I did; with God's help and help from my safe friends, I took some uncomfortable, and risky, next steps and I grew in ways I couldn't imagine . . . but that's a story for another time.

When we know the truth about ourselves in light of the truth of the Bible, we have a chance for real change and growth. This is true for us and, most importantly, it's true for those we love and lead. We can help them see their lives clearly so they can cooperate with the work of the Holy Spirit. All of this is absolutely within your reach.

But there is an essential practice we all have to live out regarding truth, otherwise none of this works. There is a way to welcome people into our lives, and there is a way to be welcomed into the lives of others. That's what we will look at next.

" VULNERABILITY OPENS THE DOOR TO LIFE CHANGE. "

FULLY KNOWN AND FULLY LOVED, ALL OVER AGAIN

07

My wife Coleene (I call her Co) is my own personal computer help-desk professional. She keeps my laptop running smoothly and fixes the stuff I break. During the day, though, she is a Business Intelligence Analyst for a large healthcare system here in San Diego. Trust me, she is clearly the brains of the outfit around our house. (Side note: if the robopocalypse ever goes down, she'll be the one who started it. You've been warned!)

I can't honestly tell you with specificity what she does at work, because it's way beyond me, but I love hearing her talk about the tech projects she's managing. One of the things I do understand is that, generally speaking, software exists in one of two places in the computer world: (1) the test area or (2) the live area. One way to think about this is: *private versus public.*

All new software starts out in the test area. To keep it simple for me, Co explains the test area as a simulated world, of sorts; an area where programmers and analysts test-drive new software to work out the bugs and make sure it's running just right. This is a comprehensive vetting process that happens to prepare all new software to "go live" in the real world.

If the test area is the simulated world, the live area is the real world. When a new piece of software is born, this is what it dreams of. It's kind of like Pinocchio becoming a real boy: software knows it doesn't become "real" until it gets loaded into the live area. Kidding aside, you can do all the testing and debugging you want, but if the software is going to serve its ultimate purpose, it has to exist in the real world.

As it turns out, that's kind of how it works in our lives too.

Every person who has ever lived has both a test area and a live area, a private side and a public side, a side that faces in and a side that faces out.

We take content into our private world—our test area—all the time, from all kinds of sources. Along with receiving that content, this is the place where we collect messages from others, think about our thoughts and then make decisions. Whether intentional or not, we're "mental-modeling" how we think our lives should go. In all of this, we draw conclusions and ultimately form beliefs about ourselves, the people around us, and the world at large.

One highly destructive example of this is the formation of shame in our hearts. Author and shame researcher Brené Brown says that both men and women experience shame, but we feel it differently based on gender messages and expectations in our world. For women, Brown claims their shame centers heavily on appearance and motherhood. The message is: Look perfect and be the perfect mother, but never look like you're trying hard.[1] Men, however, feel shame from two big issues: failure of any sort and weakness in any form.[2] Each of these messages originate in culture at large, but they come to life inside of us.

All of this happens in our own personal test environment—our own private world. We actually simulate life, as we understand it, to debug our beliefs before we "go live" with them in the real world. Sometimes this happens intentionally when we choose the content we consume and then decide on our beliefs and conclusions. Other times it's more like autopilot—our whole internal belief system running outside the realm of conscious thought. But it happens nonetheless.

And then we live our lives. We take what we've "test driven" in our private world—healthy or not—and load it into our public world. We "go live" with the conclusions and beliefs we've been working on (or not working on) in our test area. Those conclusions and beliefs turn into behaviors, decisions, habits, and ultimately a way of life. What starts in our test area ultimately shows up in our live area.

Here's what I'm getting at. How things go in your public world is determined by how they go in your private world. In other words, what happens inside of you determines the life you live. When your worth is settled and you are living from your true identity as you pursue a vision for your life based on calling and strengths—when all of that is online in your heart—you have a great chance at wholeness and lifelong growth. But if you are driven by shame, comparison, and deep messages of disapproval—if those messages go uncontested in your private world—you will suffer your whole life and struggle to stay on your feet.

There's an even deeper issue at play, however. The trouble we get into is trying to manage, on our own, all that happens in our private world. We started on this idea in previous chapters, but let's take another swing at it now. Not only can we not see ourselves clearly, we cannot fully care for ourselves on our own. Survive? Yeah, I guess. Get by for a while? Sure, why not. Thrive? Nope, not at all.

It's really a truism at this point: we were never meant to do life on our own, and this is never more true than when we're trying to make sense of, and direct, the functions of our internal world.

If you take this seriously, it means a couple of things. One, you have to open yourself to the life skill of welcoming healthy and safe people into the private areas of your life. If you've never done this, it will be next to impossible to lead others toward openness—so that's the place to start. Two, you will need to learn how to be invited into the private lives of those you love and lead.

This is where vulnerability comes in.

Dark Places in the Human Heart

Let's do some of the hard work first.

There are all kinds of seemingly good reasons *not* to let others see who we are in our private world. I think it's one of the bigger mistakes to not admit that up front. We all feel it after all—that cringey emotion when we think unfiltered thoughts about the dark places in our hearts. What would people think if they knew my awful unedited thoughts or the lusty desires I accommodate? How about the humiliating blunders I've made or the sins I've willfully pursued? The capacity for evil in the human heart is crushing to look at, let alone admit. Why in the world would we ever let people in on that stuff?

Dallas Willard writes about "the ruined soul." He comes in hard on this, explaining that "soul corruption" has touched everyone due to the Fall.[3] His point is that radical evil isn't just a part of the world at large, but that there is evil in the human heart as well. He writes, "In the ruined soul, the mind becomes a fearful wilderness and a wild intermixture of thought and feeling, manifested in willful stupidities, blatant inconsistencies, and confusions, often to the point of obsession, madness, or possession. This condition of mind is what characterizes our world apart from God. Satan, 'the prince of this world' . . . holds sway over it."[4]

The Bible isn't subtle about the condition of the human heart when it remains untouched by Jesus. The prophet Jeremiah gives us quite a stark picture when he writes, "The human heart is the most deceitful of all things, and desperately wicked. Who really knows how bad it is?"[5] That's lovely: even the prophet admits we can't see the bottom of this poisoned well.

Jesus, too, cut straight to the point with his disciples about the condition of our hearts. Get this, though: before he delivers his reveal of the human heart, Jesus scolds the disciples for not seeing the obvious. "What, are you stupid?" (Okay, that's not precisely what he said; it was softer, but not much.) He asks, "Are you so dull?" And then Jesus goes on to say, "It is what comes from inside that defiles you. For from within, out of a person's heart, come evil thoughts, sexual immorality, theft, murder, adultery, greed, wickedness, deceit, lustful desires, envy, slander, pride, and foolishness. All these vile things come from within; they are what defile you."[6] See? It's like I said, all that stuff starts out in the human heart—these traits aren't add-ons we pick up later.[7]

R. C. Sproul famously said, "We are not sinners because we sin. We sin because we are sinners." In other words, what we do comes from who we are—and who we are can be tough to look at.

When we consider all this, many of us feel the flinch to look away and make sure the darkness of our heart never sees the light of day. We want advanced encryption for our hearts so that when others query our internal world—when they try to get to know us— all they get back is confusing data, or an "access denied" message. But is that really what we want? Really?

The Culture of Cruelty and Shame

Now add to that a little cultural context. Our world is brutally mean right now, and it doesn't look like it's going to turn toward civility any time soon—you might as well forget about kindness. And I'm not talking "playground mean;" it's way beyond that—more like "prison-rules mean."

Take social media, for example. It's always an easy target these days. I don't think I know a single person who has posted some opinion online and not taken a beating for it—you probably know exactly what I mean. As a rule, we seem to jump right past the idea in a written statement and judge the heart of the writer, and this is never more obvious than in the online universe.

Something has changed in culture. Cruelty and shaming are so common, and our reach is so wide because social media has given us not just a voice, but also a means to speak directly to the people—celebrities and politicians—we never had access to in the past. The net effect is public pillory on a scale we couldn't imagine even fifteen years ago (Facebook launched in February of 2004).

John Oliver, host of the wildly popular *Last Week Tonight with John Oliver* on HBO, recently devoted an entire show to the theme of public shaming.[8] It was ironic watching someone as crass and belligerent (and crazy funny) as John Oliver champion a move toward civility. (And for the record, I feel like I need to post a "shame disclaimer" right here to disavow myself from any beefs you may have, or not have, with John Oliver. I'm just telling you what happened.)

He started the show saying, "Public shaming! Or as we call it in England, parenting." Okay, I thought, here we go—it's game-on!

He continued, "Thanks to the internet, it's never been easier to pile on to a public shaming. In fact, it is now one of America's favorite pastimes." Anyone want to try and dispute that? I certainly can't. Oliver called this "The golden age of internet shaming," and claimed that "Some people, online, are just looking for a reason to be angry."[9]

The surreal part of the show was watching John Oliver shame shamers and create criteria and ground rules for "acceptable public shaming." "You may be expecting me to say that all public shaming is bad," he said, "but I don't actually think that. When it's well directed, a lot of good can come out of it . . . It can increase accountability."

I'm not sure about that. Maybe it does more than keep the public accountable. Maybe even "appropriate shaming" simply pumps more toxic emotion into a culture overflowing with it.

Maybe there are other consequences for bad behavior that don't add to our over-saturated culture of contempt and cruelty.

Arthur Brooks, author of *Love Your Enemies*, a book about disagreeing and our culture of contempt, says that a key feature of public discourse today is "motive attribution asymmetry."[10] It's the idea that I am good and honorable, but you're a jerk. If we disagree, I attribute wicked motives to you, but virtuous motives to myself. It's not just that you are misguided or uninformed, you're actually a bad person with hate in your heart; while I, on the other hand, am wise, upright, and loving.

All of this, Brooks says, leads to contempt for others which he defines as, "The unsullied conviction of the worthlessness of another."[11] You are misguided. "Shame!" You are wrong. "Shame!" You are evil. "Shame!" You are worthless—the ultimate shame.

Shaming is simply what we do now, everywhere, and if you really want to hurt someone, shame is absolutely the right weapon to use. It fires an emotional missile right past our bad behavior and plunges deeply into our identity. That's where shame does its greatest damage. It is an attack on who we are.

The general rule these days is that guilt is about what you do, but *shame is about who you are*. The message of shame says, "You didn't just do a bad thing, *you are bad!*" This is the stew that our culture soaks in, and I fear it might be here for a while—until Jesus changes it all.

Shame Stands in the Way of Vulnerability

I'm making such a big deal about what we all seem to know because ambient shame, along with the focused and personal version of it, does massive damage to our relational default settings. The conclusion many of us draw is: Keep yourself to yourself! Don't let anyone into your private world. Reveal your true self to no one. Lock it down and melt the key.

When I talk to leaders and groups about vulnerability, I often speak of it as a drawbridge. It's a vivid picture and a helpful tool for gauging how open we feel toward the people in our lives. I will often ask, "Where's your drawbridge these days? All the way up? All the way down? In the middle somewhere? Would you show us how open you're feeling right now?" And then group members simulate the position of their emotional drawbridge using their arm, revealing how open they are to being vulnerable. It's a fantastic visual.

That said, I think I see a massive trend toward living with our drawbridges all the way up, closing us off from deep relationship. It simply feels like the safe option these days. Everywhere we look, publicly (with internet shaming) or privately (in the darkness of our hearts), it feels like bad news. *But I will not settle for that, and I hope you won't either.* We don't have to leave our loved ones locked inside the prison of their own internal world. Pulling up the drawbridge might feel safe to them for now, but it's not what they desire most.

Shame is the great enemy of vulnerability, which also makes it the enemy of relationship, community, and transformation— and ultimately the enemy of joy. We cannot enter life-changing environments without also allowing others into our lives. Toxic shame makes that nearly impossible, triggering a cascade effect in our private world: I feel shame. I am bad. I hide myself from others. I live outside of community. I lose hope and joy. I feel shame . . . *and on and on the cycle goes.*

The Human Heart Is (Still) Made to Be Seen and Loved

We don't have to give in to any of that bad news—the cruelty and the shaming and the dark places in our hearts. If our loved ones are going to push back against the pressures that shut down their private world, they must return to their deepest original longing.

Even in the darker places of shame, if we pay attention we can detect the essence of Eden. That essence is the scent that comes from our very first taste of being fully known and fully loved: *"The man and the wife were both naked, and they felt no shame."* Two people in perfect relationship; nothing hidden and fully accepted—that is the scent that draws us.

Nearly every child I've ever known wants to be seen. Before we know risk or actual danger, we want to be looked at by those who love and care for us. Just think about that for a second. Children believe that being seen is a really good thing. What they seem to love most is being seen doing a "great thing," and then celebrated for who they are.

So the motto of safe children everywhere is their universal request, "Look at me!" The two-word version is, "Watch me!" That request is one of the purest desires born of a secure environment, and it remains our yearning until we find out it's no longer the safe thing to ask for.

All of this starts out in the human heart. We long to matter to important people in our lives, to be noticed and celebrated with genuine interest and care. That innocent childhood desire—"look at me"—is more than a request, it's a flashback to the ancient remnant of joy in the human heart to be seen and loved.

"I See You. I Am Here."

In the *Fifth Discipline Fieldbook*, the authors write about tribespeople of northern Natal in South Africa. These men and women have a common greeting that they speak to one another, *"Sawu bona,"* which literally means "I see you." The common reply to that greeting is, *"Sikhona,"* literally translated, "I am here."[12]

The authors write, "The order of the exchange is important; until you see me, I do not exist. It's as if, when you see me, you bring me into existence." These tribespeople have a deep connection to community, but also a high regard for each individual in the community. They live out a value that says, "I'm looking for you and I long to be seen by you."

In this Ubuntu ethic it is right and normal to both look for and be seen by others. In fact, these tribespeople have a Zulu saying, "*Umuntu ngumuntu nagabantu*," which means, "A person is a person because of other people." To them, a fundamental part of identity "is based on the fact that you are seen—that the people around you respect and acknowledge you as a person."[13] To these people, life outside of eye contact is such a foreign concept, it's essentially like ceasing to exist.

I think these wise people may have it just about right. We aren't valuable because we are seen, but being seen and loved in community is a full expression of life as it's supposed to be. If you have even a trickle of that desire in your heart, that may be a win these days, but it's worthy of your best effort to turn that trickle into a full-flowing part of how you do life with others.

Brené Brown says that, "Connection is why we're here. We are hardwired to connect with others, and without it there is suffering."[14] Deep down inside, don't you already know that? Don't you? Being both known and loved aren't preferences. We're not talking about vacation options or picking food off a menu. Being known and loved are like sleep and vitamin C. The human heart withers under the severe neglect of indifference and isolation because we're made to be seen, known, and loved.

Getting Naked and the Gospel

In his book *Getting Naked*, Patrick Lencioni contrasts vulnerability with the world's obsession for projecting only competence and strength. Though it feels counterintuitive, he claims that vulnerability is how we get what we really long for.

"Without the willingness to be vulnerable," he writes, "we will not build deep and lasting relationships in life. That's because there is no better way to earn a person's trust than by putting ourselves in a position of unprotected weakness and demonstrating that we believe they will support us."[15]

Did you catch his language? He says that "unprotected weakness" is the key to deep, lasting relationships. If this is true, who would sign up for it? The fear of "getting naked"—of unprotected weakness—may be the very thing that keeps our loved ones from real change and growth.

Ironically, most of us are for vulnerability in others, but against it when it's our turn. I can't count how many times I've seen people, myself included, encourage a friend to "just open up and let it out." But when we're the ones who need the emotional reveal, we lock down the mechanism.

We must never forget that when everything went sideways in Eden, the first thing we did was cover ourselves, and the second thing was hide. The opposite of what we need now is covering and hiding. The bullseye of what we need is getting naked again—that is, learning to practice vulnerability in a safe place with helpful and loving people. And if you don't know it already, this is one of the essential features of the gospel.

The Gospel Loves Vulnerability

Like I said, vulnerability doesn't feel like good news to a lot of us. No one signs up for the vulnerability club at school. It's not recreational, like bowling night or fishing on Saturdays. People write shocking "tell all" books about others, but they write "memoirs" about their own lives.

This is the paradox of vulnerability, and it's what makes this such a tricky issue. We admire vulnerability in others but hate it when we are the ones opening up. It feels good and honorable in you, but bad and awful in me. Brené Brown writes that, "We love seeing raw truth and openness in other people, but we're afraid to let them see it in us."[16] It may be the same behavior from both of us, but we experience those behaviors completely differently. "I want to experience your vulnerability," Brown says, "but I don't want to be vulnerable. Vulnerability is courage in you and inadequacy in me."

So our hearts are divided over vulnerability. We haven't closed the rational gap yet between the behavior of vulnerability and its benefit. We fail to receive it as the essential and amazing growth tool that it is. In our hearts, it simply feels uncomfortable: it feels like risk, exposure, potential threat, and even doom. Bottom line, vulnerability in us feels like bad news—maybe really bad news. But we have that entirely wrong.

If the gospel is good news, then so is vulnerability. In fact, vulnerability is at the very heart of the gospel—I'm not sure you can have one without the other. Through the gospel we see brokenness in our world, but also brokenness in our hearts. We admit to our sinfulness and acknowledge that we are not our own solution. When we welcome Jesus into the reality of our lives, there is no more room for hiding and covering. We ask him for help, for a complete and total renovation of our lives. Through the gospel, Jesus makes vulnerability one of our essential solutions. "Good" isn't even close to the right description for news like that!

To be vulnerable is to come out of hiding and uncover yourself. The good news of the gospel is that you can finally do that without suffering judgement, guilt, or shame. In that respect, vulnerability is good for everybody, not just *everybody other than you*. To become vulnerable with the right people is one of the best things ever, and that is the heart shift we need to help followers embrace and normalize. When they do that, transformation and growth become possibilities.

Fully Known and Fully Loved . . . All Over Again

Our reflex with guilt and shame has always been to *cover and hide*. We do this in a bunch of different ways, but it never really works for us. Thankfully, our hiding never works for Jesus either.

In Romans chapter five, the apostle Paul pulls the cover off the human condition. The backstory of his big reveal—the four previous chapters—starts with the mess we've made of the world, our own lives, and our relationship with God himself. Our mess is so bad, in fact, and our corruption is so complete, that we need to be saved from ourselves. Paul tells us the good news is that Jesus is the answer to our depravity. Jesus offers a righteousness, through faith, that we can only get through him.[17] That's when we get to chapter five.

> *"You see, at just the right time, when we were still powerless,*
> *Christ died for the ungodly."* (Romans 5:6)

In the nick of time, we read in this verse, Jesus became the solution for the "ungodly." You know, the people who messed everything up in our world—the ones Paul mentions in earlier chapters? Yeah, those guys. Jesus takes care of the mess they made.

If that's how we understand Paul here, we're absolutely wrong.

Without a careful reading, it might be easy to think that here Paul is pinning the world's depravity problem on someone else—like he's pointing back to the troublemakers he was talking about in earlier chapters. After all, doesn't he explicitly label us here as "helpless," or "powerless," or "weak," or "*utterly* helpless" depending on the translation we read?

But then—*record scratch*—we realize he's actually talking about *us* in this verse. This is the first time in Paul's letter he puts the blame specifically on our shoulders: it's you and me; we're the problem and our problem is our willful, sinful behavior.[18] We are the "ungodly" he's referring to, and our ungodliness is what makes us utterly helpless.

Because of our sinfulness, we are powerless to do good—we can neither save nor fix ourselves. Like a magician dropping a veil, Paul pulls off the curtain . . . Flash! Bang! Smoke! . . . and there we stand, center stage, as the ungodly.

"Very rarely will anyone die for a righteous person, though for a good person someone might possibly dare to die." (Romans 5:7)

At this point, in verse seven, it seems like Paul eases the tension with a hypothetical, but he is actually building to his big point—the biggest point ever.

He mentions two guys: let's call them the "letter-of-the-law guy" and the "law-of-love guy." The letter-of-the-law guy does everything right; he satisfies the rules and always does what is required—nothing more, nothing less. Paul says it's feasible someone might die for this kind of rule-keeping guy. We could imagine that, if we try really hard.

But the law-of-love guy . . . oh we love this guy, because he loves us too. He's just a good guy who isn't preoccupied with satisfying rules. He wants to do the right thing, because that's who he is. Now this guy, he's the kind of guy people might jump on a hand grenade for.

Forget these two guys, though, just for a moment. Let's go back to the people Paul mentions in the beginning of his letter. Remember, the really awful people? We haven't considered them yet. In Paul's world, they are just about the worst of the worst; nobody would die for those guys—that's just unthinkable!

Not true though. Paul says that not only would someone die for people like this, *he reveals we are just like those people.* It is a stunning connection! The word "ungodly" he uses to describe us in verse six, that's the word he uses earlier in his letter to describe the "really terrible people." Again, we are them, and they are us; without Jesus we're all the same. At the very moment we understand this, Paul brings God into the picture.

> *"But God demonstrates his own love for us in this: While we were still sinners, Christ died for us."* (Romans 5:8)

You see, our sin simply isn't big enough when you compare it to God's love, and that's what Paul does. He rolls out the mother of all magnifying glasses and places it right in front of God's love, contrasting it with our depravity. It's feasible someone might die for a rule-keeper or for a really good guy, but for goodness' sake, who would ever die for deplorable people? Someone with love as vast and pure as God's, that's who. Jesus died for deeply flawed people, and that's shocking news because every one of us qualifies for membership in that club.

I love vulnerability in you, but I hate it in me. Paul doesn't give us the option to pick who gets to be vulnerable here; he pulls back the curtain on all of us. We are all exposed. We are all uncovered. We are all vulnerable because of our sin. When Paul refers to us as sinners, he uses real-time language—he's referring to our sinful behavior happening now in the present tense.

And then all of us are loved at that very moment! Jesus knows all about you; he knows all the details. He knows your hateful, murderous thoughts. He sees how easily you become the epicenter of your life and require that the world revolve around you. He sees your petty jealousy and your insecurity. He watches you cling to comfort and control above loyal love. Oh, wait a minute, actually all of those traits are mine! That's what he sees in me. But he sees things just like these in you too. He sees everything in all of us.

And then he lets us see his love. In fact, he *"demonstrates"* his love for us in real time, right now, in the present tense.

In response to our sinfulness, God puts his love on display. You think your flaws and sins are bad? Watch how well he loves you in response, as he calls you to himself. His love goes up on a billboard; he pulls it on a banner behind a plane; he writes it in smoke in the sky—whatever big metaphor you like for making the biggest point ever. The dark and ungodly places in your heart are nothing compared to the love that God has for you. *That is the big reveal that Paul makes here in this passage.*

The cry of our childlike heart is, "Look at me! Watch me! See me!" And Jesus does—he actually looks, watches, and sees us all, and then says to each of us, "You are worth my life. I will set aside my rights and privileges to come into your messed-up world. I will pay for your offenses. Let me help you with your messy life. Allow me to renovate your heart. *Follow me.*"

The return to Eden—to perfect love in the perfect relationship—begins in our hearts, if we will allow it. Finally, once again, we can be fully known and fully loved.

Because vulnerability is at the heart of the gospel.

THE ACTIVE INGREDIENT IN VULNERABILITY

08

"I am so sad right now and I feel so alone. The pressure in my life is overwhelming and I'm no longer coping. School is a disaster. My family are strangers. Ministry is at a standstill. I've drained my tanks dry—I have nothing left to give. I am not well.

"I am barely holding on. My life is a crescendo of self-hate. My desire for an end has never been so strong. I am exhausted by this constant obsession. Quite literally, I am reaching the end of my supply of courage and hope.

"My life ended twenty-seven years ago, when I was born; that was the beginning of it anyway. Everything has been a funnel to this very moment. And I'm here now. I hate my life, and I hate living. I am anxious, distressed, and tense all the time. I tremble when I'm awake and I grind my teeth at night.

"Worst of all, I am locked inside myself, behind a fake smile. I am unhelpable by the people around me. I need their help; I crave their friendship, but the chain around my neck is my shame and it keeps me just beyond reach of their caregiving. I don't deserve their friendship and love.

"This is me. Focus. You're a bottomless hole, never to be filled. You're an abscess. It just doesn't matter."

On Tuesday, November 28, 1989, I sat in my office in Simi Valley, California, and typed those words into my journal.

What a terrible day that was. It was like most of my days back then. Two days later, I was admitted to the Behavioral Medical Unit at Memorial Hospital in Gardena, California, where I lived for the next ten weeks or so.

I've debated for a long time about whether or not I would let you dear readers in on this part of my life: this journal entry, my hospitalization, and the truth about my emotional crash.

I'm simply afraid to let you read those words. That's how I often feel when I talk about that episode in my life. I feel the tug of shame pulling me back into darkness and hiding. I'm pretty sure this confession gets me voted off the island and thrown out of the club. Which island and which club? I'm not sure, that's just how it feels. And that's how shame wants me to feel: "If you speak up and let others know the truth, it's over for you; you're done."

The moral of the story from that time in my life is about hiddenness. I was in a lot of trouble mentally and emotionally, *and I couldn't tell anyone about it*. It wasn't just that I was struggling; everyone struggles from time to time—some of us more than others. I had stopped coping. Life was no longer working because some essential function in my heart was busted.

But that wasn't my biggest problem or my deepest illness. I had come to believe that hiding my flaws and broken parts was the right thing to do. The flavor of indifference I believed at the time was, "Keep yourself to yourself. *They don't care anyway*." So I did just that. I lived in silent contempt for as long as I could, and then simply flew that plane into the ground. The "crash" was spectacular to see.

The Enemy of Vulnerability is Shame

The enemy of vulnerability is shame.[1] It's the core emotion that keeps us in hiding when we know we should open up and allow others to help us with our messy, flawed, and unchanged lives. The message of shame is that you're so unlovable in your current state that you must keep yourself hidden. Nobody else must discover what Lewis Smedes calls "the actual you."[2] If they do, you're out. You will be rejected, exiled, ignored, abandoned, forsaken, or dismissed. You will be voted off the island and thrown out of the club. Which Island and which club? I still don't know and it doesn't matter to your heart, because the fear of authenticity isn't rooted in reason.

If shame and vulnerability were actual people in our lives, they would speak very different messages to us.

Shame Harasses Us With . . .

"You are not enough."[3]

You're not good enough, thin enough, smart enough, articulate enough, successful enough, tall enough, witty enough, bold enough, strong enough, sexy enough, clever enough, unique enough, fun enough, perfect enough, etc. I've even been in churches where I felt like I'm not "gospel-y" enough. How 'bout that?

"You are flawed, 'less than,' unacceptable, and unworthy."

Lewis Smedes writes that, "The feeling of shame is about our very *selves*—not about some bad thing we *did* or *said,* but about what we *are*. It tells us that we *are* unworthy. Totally. It is not as if a few seams in the garment of ourselves need stitching; the whole fabric is frayed."[4]

"You are alone."

You are the only person as flawed as you. You are unique in your messed-up-ness. You're the president of the club . . . and . . . the only member.

"You can never change, so you'll always be unlovable."

You've heard the phrase, "You can't fix stupid"? That's how many of us feel about our toxic shame. Shame pokes us in the chest and says, "You can't fix you, stupid."

"You are doomed to your fake life."

Your only option is to project a fake version of yourself to become acceptable to others. But never forget you're still *actually* unacceptable and unlovable, because it's just your fake self that people like.

"You deserve the shame you feel."

Lewis Smedes writes about the time he internalized his own shame:

> "When I was a boy, and I was hanging around, sluggish, dreaming about nothing in particular, my tongue had a tendency to droop out of the side of my mouth. The sight of my languid tongue annoyed my mother considerably, drove her, in fact, into a moment of madness. One early August evening, close to my seventh birthday, I was sprawled out on a porch swing, taking in some grown-up gossip going on between my mother and some neighbors who had stopped out front to pass the time. I yielded my torpid mind to the toneless murmur. My jaw sagged, and my tongue slid outside of my mouth without any thought of going anywhere, just dangling there like the soft end of a limp belt. My mother caught the tongue in the corner of her eye, and it was too much for her. She raised her arm, unleashed the back of her hand, and caught me where my tongue and I hung in front of the world."
>
>   "I did not move an inch. Didn't bawl. Didn't complain. I felt only a deep deserving; I must have had it

coming. Anyone with a hopeless tongue like mine must deserve to be smacked in public. *I swallowed my mother's shame of me and digested it inside of myself until it was all mine.*"[5] [Emphasis mine.]

Vulnerability, on the Other Hand, Whispers in Our Ears . . .

"I'll love you forever, I'll like you for always."[6]

I actually cried in front of everyone the day John Ortberg read the words of this dear children's story in one of our Sunday services. I still remember thinking, "Is that possible? Could someone actually feel that way about me?" What you won't find in that story are qualifiers for love, like "if" or "because" or "when."

"I am for you."

I'm for you before I'm for myself. Like Jesus, I will set aside my rights and privileges to love you in a way that serves you first. You are worth my best effort.

"I am with you."

I'm not going anywhere, so you can eliminate this from your list of things to fear. We may not run together for the rest of our lives, but I will not reject you or cast you out. We're together, you and me.

"I want to know the real you."

You are a masterpiece, crafted by Jesus himself. When I look at you, I see what Jesus loves about you. I want to see and know who you are. You fascinate me.

"I believe in you."

You have what it takes. You may not see it right now, but I do. You're going to get through this and thrive.

"I will help you."

Another way to say this is, "You can change; I can help." Consider me a resource in your life when you need me. I won't leave you the same; I will help you become your "true self": the "self" Jesus created you to be. I will pay attention—along with you—to the work of the Holy Spirit in your life.

The Pre-Gospel Resting State of the Heart

Shame is the pre-gospel resting state of the human heart. It is who we are, deep down, without the ultimate acceptance and love Jesus offers. I think of it as the starting line of the human condition. Without the gospel we're left to hustle and prove ourselves to get accepted, all the while covering our unworthy parts.

Brené Brown talks about this as the "Shame 1-2-3s": (1) We all have shame; it's our common human condition. In fact, she says only sociopaths live free from shame, and no one's signing up for that. (2) No one wants to talk about their shame. (3) The more we ignore it, the more it pushes us around.[7]

Toxic shame twists and binds the human heart, one half turn of the vise at a time. It's subtle at first, just a bit of pressure, just a touch of discomfort. Eventually it builds like steel bands tightening around our chest, depriving us a full breath of air. Very slowly—one neglect or ridicule or abuse at a time—shame constricts our hearts, leaving us to sip and suck for the acceptance we were born to gulp and guzzle. Like a body robbed of oxygen, something in the human heart fails to thrive in a low-grace, high-shame environment.

That's difficult news to accept. The double-whammy with shame, however, is that it also diminishes our ability to course-correct our lives. Shame locks us out of our own growth process by spiking our compulsion to cover ourselves and hide from others.

When we feel guilty, we try to *hide what we've done.*

In a moment of temporary insanity, I once took apart my father's radio. I grabbed one of his screwdrivers out of the garage, pried the back off the radio and started the disassembly. Huh, who would've thought it would be so hard to put a radio back together? Not my nine-year-old self, I'll tell you that. Long story short, I didn't get it put back together right, and I left the screwdriver at the scene of the crime. My father came after me right away and I used every skill I had to deflect, deny, and cover my guilt. But the DNA came back on the screwdriver and I was a 100% match. I was caught red-handed.

Shame is different; when we feel shame, *we hide ourselves.* We are the offense. We are the crime scene. We're not waiting for DNA to come back against us, because the offense is in our genetic code—it's us! It's who we are, not what we've done.

Countless times as a frightened boy, I stood crying uncontrollably in front of my raging father as he ridiculed the emotions I was unable to keep to myself. My crime was my heart; it felt feelings too deeply for a raging alcoholic like my father, who only really wanted to look away from his own pain.

I don't actually remember many details of life with my dad, but I've never been able to purge from my memory the disgust he felt for me on his face. I can actually picture him right now, and I can hear his names for me: "Cry baby;" "Fat head;" "Tit baby;" "Dumb head;" "Sissy." My father looked me in the eyes and sentenced me with those messages for years, and I simply accepted them as a terrified young boy. Over time, his disapproval cinched up tight around my heart and I learned to live on less: less attention, less approval, less love, less help. Eventually, I lived on nothing from him.

Shame puts us in perpetual fear of being discovered and seen. I learned from my father that being my true self was a punishable offense, so I came to live in fear that people would see me and find out who I was. Come to find out, that wasn't a burden I could bear my whole life.

When we are in the grip of fear, the only thing we reach for is survival and safety. We simply don't think outside those options. In that state, we cannot innovate, create, change, and grow without first becoming ourselves. If we're not our authentic selves, our hearts will hang-up on that reality and forward progress will slow dramatically or stop altogether.

Controlled by shame, our lives become all about satisfying the requirements for acceptance. We're trying to earn our way back onto the island or into the club. Which island and which club? Any of them that will take us.

This is just another way shame derails what God wants to do in the lives of those we love. Shame says, "Here's your to-do list. Get busy. When you're done with that one, I've got a bunch more." Jesus says, "Don't worry about lists. I will help you become who I designed you to be—who you really want to be. We will work on it together."

As a lifelong shepherd, I've seen that it's nearly impossible to yield to the Holy Spirit under the severe pressure of shame. But there is actual hope: I know, I've experienced it myself. Through the mercy of my own "emotional crash" Jesus led me to what I had always needed. Since then, I've seen thousands of others jailbreak their way out of shame, and our solution was around us the whole time.

Vulnerability Repels Shame

Lewis Smedes says, "The good news is that shame can be healed." Only one thing really heals our shame; it's a return to what we are created for: being both known and loved. Our garden rebellion got the shame ball rolling, but it's the cross that stops it with grace and acceptance, and one day Jesus will exile shame from the human heart forever. It all starts now, though, with vulnerability.

Life Isn't a One-Person Job

When I have work to do and others are around, they often ask, "Do you need help with that?" If I can't figure out how to break the job into parts I usually say, "I think it's a one-man job." Making sense of the human heart isn't like that—it's never a one-person job. We need help with the messages that live in our hearts, and *vulnerability is how we get that help.*

So when it's safe—with the right people, at the right time, and in the right place—we may open up to others. Vulnerability is our response to safety. In fact, there is so much overlap between safety and vulnerability, it's hard to talk about one without the other. Everything I wrote earlier about safety points to everything I write here about vulnerability. We only get one after we've first gotten the other.

Vulnerability, in its simplest form, is sharing our lives—it is letting the right people in on what we experience and feel. So easy to say, yet so hard to do for most of us.

Vulnerability is coming out of hiding. It's understanding what our fig leaves are—what we're hiding behind—and then figuring out how to take them off. It is the human response to God's call to Adam and Eve after the fall: "Where are you?"[8] Calling back, "Here I am!" is the first act of vulnerability.

Fig leaves lead to fake lives. When we live behind fig leaves, we prop up false versions of ourselves to keep our true selves hidden and our fake selves accepted. This is the front line of our shame battle, and the tip of our spear is vulnerability.

John Bradshaw writes, "To heal our shame . . . [we] have to be willing to expose our essential selves." "To find one's life," he continues, "one must lose one's life. This is a literal truism for shame-based people. We must give up our delusional false selves . . . to find the vital and precious core of ourselves. Hidden in the dark reservoirs of our toxic shame lives our true self."[9]

Brené Brown helps us with the balance of vulnerability. "Vulnerability is based on mutuality," she writes, "and requires boundaries and trust. It's not oversharing, it's not purging, it's not indiscriminate disclosure, and it's not celebrity-style social media information dumps. *Vulnerability is about sharing our feelings and our experiences with people who have earned the right to hear them.* Being vulnerable and open is mutual and an integral part of the trust-building process.[10] [Emphasis mir.e.]

I wish I could ask you how you feel about vulnerability. I wonder what you'd say. You may not like it—not at all; most people don't at first, but no one gets to ignore it forever. Vulnerability is not a part of life we get to opt out of; there are no vulnerability-free zones. No one is afraid of nothing. No one feels strong all the time. Life brings everyone to their knees eventually, because to be alive is to be vulnerable.

Vulnerability and Shame Can't Live Together

Vulnerability and shame can't live together in the same life for long. These two entities are going for entirely different outcomes because they have different aspirations for our lives. If shame wins, we go into hiding. If vulnerability is up and running, we allow good people deeper into our lives. However this goes, one or the other gets tossed out eventually.

Vulnerability is a courageous act of truth and honesty—it's a gentle reveal of our true selves. Shame is a hostile takeover, a bullying cover-up, and an emotional hijacking by our fake self.

Vulnerability thrives with words; shame festers in silence. When we attach words to feelings and then speak those words to safe people, we give our true selves a voice. When shame wins, our hearts are muted and we opt for cover-up as a relational habit. If we allow shame to determine our word count, it controls not just the conversation, but our thoughts as well—and that's where the battle is won or lost.

Brené Brown tells us, "Shame derives its power from being unspeakable." So the remedy is exposing shame with our words. "If we cultivate enough awareness about shame to name it and speak to it," she explains, "we've basically cut it off at the knees. Shame hates having words wrapped around it. If we speak (the message of) shame, it begins to wither."[11]

Vulnerability flourishes in "story;" shame metastasizes in secrecy. Shame wants us to believe that our story is what makes us so unworthy and unacceptable. It holds our story against our head and threatens to pull the trigger. As long as our stories remain unspoken, shame holds power over us. But when we come out of hiding and trust the people who care about us, we disarm shame.

I remember sitting in the hospital, all those years ago, wondering how I would recover—not from my broken emotions, but from the fact that I had become so broken I required hospitalization. How would I ever reenter my life with that on my record? I was still thinking secrecy, not story. How could I craft the right cover-up to sneak back into my life without anyone knowing I'd been gone? That question alone derailed the beginning of my healing for a long time, because I was allowing shame to hold my story against me.

Then I read these words from John Bradshaw:

> "The best way to come out of hiding is to find a nonshaming intimate social network. The operative word here is *intimate*. We have to get on a core gut level because shame is core gut level. Toxic shame masks our deepest secrets about ourselves; it embodies our belief that we are essentially defective. We feel so awful, we dare not look at it ourselves, much less tell anyone. The only

way to find out that we were wrong about ourselves is to risk exposing ourselves to someone else's scrutiny. When we trust someone else and experience their love and acceptance, we begin to change our beliefs about ourselves. We learn that we are not bad; we learn that we are lovable and acceptable."[12]

I had to decide what it was going to be: people and healing or shame and hiding? Because one of them had to go.

No One Grows Alone—Vulnerability, Change, and Growth

Vulnerability is literally the way we become a part of life-changing relationships and communities. When I say literally, I mean it: vulnerability is what we do to enter a relationship or community. Until we allow others into our lives, we remain on the outside with them. We become insiders by coming out of hiding with other insiders.

Without vulnerability, we're not participants and members of the community; we're observers, still on the outside looking in. We may be in the room, sitting in the circle, speaking to other people, but if we don't let them into our lives it's as though we are not there at all, at least from a growth standpoint. I tell leaders all the time, "You have their bodies, but their hearts may be far, far away." Vulnerability is the way we get into the community, and then the community gets into us.

Safe community is where we come to know who we really are. Shame wants you to settle for an alternate, distorted version of yourself, but it doesn't work that way in life-changing communities. When we feel safe with caring people, it becomes natural to talk about ourselves and feel our feelings in their presence. It's this very process of talking and feeling that helps us understand our truest self. By helping others know and understand us, we're providing ourselves the very same clarity.

You cannot know something until you give it words. Have you ever thought about that? I've heard people say, "I know what I'm thinking (or feeling), I just can't say it." Nope. No you do not. Not yet. Meaning and understanding require language. Legendary broadcaster Harry Reasoner once said, "No thought has any meaning until it is spoken or written." Another way to say this is that you don't know something until you can put it into words.

That applies to our lives too: we don't know what is true of ourselves until we attach language to our reality. This is what we do through the act of vulnerability. By talking and sharing, we actually discover and come to understand ourselves in ways we never would without allowing others in.

This is an amazing gift we give to followers. "Walk me through that." "Help me understand what you're thinking and feeling." "Talk about what was going on for you when you said or did that." "What words describe what you're experiencing right now?" When we ask questions like these and then sit with someone as they reach for the right language, we help them with self-discovery. When they answer, they are uncovering, coming out of hiding, and coming to know who they really are.

And that's when their hearts become accountable to their own intentions. By reaching for the right language and sharing it with someone else, our loved ones not only gain clarity, they solidify their intentions to live and be a certain way. They gain strength and resolve when they go public with who they are and what they intend to do next. In this way, vulnerability is an essential part of their growth process.

Living Out Vulnerability—Going "Real Time" with the Right People

I've used "turbo groups" ten times or so over the last twenty years to create a group of leaders who then kick-start some big initiative in a church. I describe a turbo group as an *accelerated and intense leader development process.* Think Navy Seal training for church leaders. I'm kind of serious about that.

One of the things I ask for from people considering one of my turbo groups is "crediting us—the group—with safety we haven't earned yet." In other words, I'm admitting up front we're not going to take the appropriate amount of time to build trust and safety. We're going to act like it's already there from the beginning, and then we're going to do some really risky and vulnerable things together. I describe this to potential turbo-groupies as, "locking arms and stepping off the edge together into community." It's actually quite thrilling . . . and scary . . . and wildly productive in that setting.

About ten years ago in one of my turbo groups, one of the guys kept talking about "coming real." He would say things like: "I need to *come real* with you guys on that." "Thank you for *coming real* with us." "Are you going to *come real* about that?" I had never heard that exact language before, but I liked it a lot. In fact, his phrase become a motto for that turbo group, and then somewhere along the way we malapropped it into *"going real time."* Since then, I've watched hundreds of people utter those words before making a risky personal reveal: "I need to *go real time* with you guys about something . . ."

Going real time with safe people is a consummate act of vulnerability. There is a difference between talking about sins and flaws in the past tense and letting people in on our struggles right now. I will talk for days about how I used to fail—that's in the past; it's who I used to be. But letting friends see my pain, struggle, or temptation in real time is another thing entirely. I can tell you about being a disappointment to my father, or I can cry with you and feel my emotions in your presence. One of those is reporting, the other is going real time.

For the record, reporting is a great start with vulnerability. It gets us talking about ourselves with other people. It also helps us connect with feelings from past hurts. It's almost like practicing for going real time. But going real time is always what I'm hoping for with loved ones.

The Mechanics of Going Real Time

I help people understand what it means to go real time with three words: *look, feel, and share.*

1. **Look inward:** I wrote at length in previous chapters about seeing what is true of ourselves. What I want to highlight here is the ability to recognize our emotions. In my experience, people are often in the dark about what they're feeling at any given moment. They're feeling their emotions, for sure, but they find it difficult, at best, to actually name what they're feeling. Vulnerability is a huge solution for this, but it takes a little time.

   Emotions have great potential to push us around and make us do really unhealthy and unhelpful things. That's true of feelings we recognize and name, but it's more true of the feelings we're unaware of. Just because we can't name our emotions doesn't mean they stop influencing us.

   Vulnerability is a tutor that helps loved ones build an emotional vocabulary over time, allowing them to become emotionally fluent with their own hearts. All of this starts with looking in order to see what we're feeling.

2. **Feel what you see:** We identify emotions by feeling them in the moment. When we allow an emotion to surface and live with it for a while, we have the chance to attach language to what we're feeling.

   Almost daily, I become aware of some particular emotion bubbling up within me. I've gotten in the habit of stopping at those moments and asking, "Okay, what's happening right now? What am I feeling?" Those questions are a simple device for clearing away distractions so I can actually feel what I'm feeling. I can't emphasize enough how easy it is to skip this step and miss a chance to know who we are.

3. **Share what you see and feel with safe people:** If I am going to help someone understand me, I must understand myself first—or at least at the same time. When I talk about what I see and feel, both of those things happen. Through vulnerability we don't just connect with other souls, we also gain clarity and understanding of our own soul. That's the double benefit of opening up to safe people. But make no mistake, without this third step of sharing there is no vulnerability.

    I don't want to imply that vulnerability is without complexity—trust me, I know it's complex and I feel it. In fact, I think I'm the king of complexity. But having a simplified mechanism—*like look, feel, and share*—is extremely helpful for leaders, and invaluable for people trying to locate themselves in their growth process.

Empathy Is the Active Ingredient in Vulnerability

If you want to know what makes vulnerability so toxic to shame, look no further than empathy. *Empathy is the active ingredient in vulnerability.* It is the antibiotic of the heart, the antigen to shame.

Brené Brown writes, "If you put shame in a petri dish and cover it with judgment, silence and secrecy, it grows out of control until it consumes everything in sight—you have basically provided shame with the environment it needs to thrive. On the other hand, if you put shame in a petri dish and douse it with empathy, shame loses its power and starts to fade. Empathy creates a hostile environment for shame—it can't survive."[13]

I feel like I've seen this a million times. Vulnerability goes well when it's met with active empathy, but openness without empathy seems to confirm shame's accusations. Without empathy, shame takes our exposure and tells us, "Ha! I told you—I was right all along. You are garbage and they don't care."

I think of empathy as connecting my heart with someone else's heart. I'm not connecting to their experience, because I can't live their life; and I'm not connecting to their thoughts, because I can't get inside their head. But what we do have in common is human emotion. I don't have to go through the same events to connect emotionally with someone else, I just need access to the full range of feelings in my own heart.

The essential function of empathy is an emotional response: it's allowing your heart to feel along with someone else. I don't know what it's like to endure the crushing pain of infertility, but I do know what it feels like to have a lifelong dream snatched away forever. Those two situations aren't the same—not at all—and I don't want to imply that they are, but the emotions they evoke come from the same family of feelings. Empathy is about identifying with what someone is feeling, not necessarily the details of what they're living through. It is climbing into their emotional world to feel along with them.

Empathy is face to face, not shoulder to shoulder. It happens best when we square-up on loved ones, close the distance and meet them eye to eye. When a loved one goes real time with me, I often imagine turning my heart loose, allowing it to go wherever the conversation leads. This means I have to focus, remove distraction, and squint with my heart. As it turns out, all of this comes quite naturally when I love them deeply and their worth is settled in my heart.

One last note: Shame has a secret weapon against empathy you may not know about. *Apathy kills empathy on contact.* There may be nothing more toxic to vulnerability, and a response of empathy, than apathy. Every single one of us has the power to kill empathy if we react to openness in others with a drowsy, distracted, or indifferent response.

Apathy is a resounding confirmation of shame's message of contempt and worthlessness. It is lovelessness in one of its cruelest forms. It communicates the message, "You have such low value to me, I don't even care to consider you."

In most cases, if you give off the scent indifference—intentionally or not—your empathy is finished and the powerful impact of vulnerability becomes off-limits for you as a leader. Most of us will not open ourselves to people who appear not to care. Why would we endure the risk of exposure with someone unwilling to look up from their phone and give us eye contact?

Vulnerability Is Hard; Shame Is Much Harder

As an expert in the law, the apostle Paul had firsthand experience with the shame and condemnation of failed rule-keeping. He knew what it was like to be "not enough." The beauty of his leadership is he never kept that to himself:

> *You know how I lived* the whole time I was with you, from the first day I came into the province of Asia. (Acts 20:18, emphasis mine.)

> I came to you *in weakness with great fear and trembling.* (1 Corinthians 2:3)

> For I wrote you out of *great distress and anguish of heart and with many tears*, not to grieve you but to let you know the depth of my love for you. (2 Corinthians 2:4)

Oh, dear Corinthian friends! We have spoken honestly with you, and *our hearts are open to you.* (2 Corinthians 6:11, NLT)

I am asking you to respond as if you were my own children. *Open your hearts to us!* (2 Corinthians 6:13, NLT)

You know we never used flattery, *nor did we put on a mask* to cover up greed—God is our witness . . . Because we loved you so much, we were delighted to share with you not only the gospel of God *but our lives as well.* (1 Thessalonians 2:5, 8)

Paul never implies that any of his vulnerability is easy. On the contrary, a number of times he talks about the suffering he endures as a leader in God's Kingdom.[14]

In *Journey to Ixtlan*, a wise native guide tells his apprentice, "We either make ourselves miserable or we make ourselves strong. The amount of work is the same."[15] I get his point completely, but I think it's actually worse than this when you're talking about vulnerability.

Vulnerability is hard; shame is way harder. Growth is a challenge, but staying the same will turn your soul to dust. It's up to each of us to decide which we will choose. We will either endure the soul-sucking work of hiding and cover-up, or flourish under the life-giving work of vulnerability—*looking, feeling, and sharing.*

Those we love and lead may or may not understand the crushing effect of shame on the human heart—the shame that robs us of freedom and clarity. But we get a say in how that goes when we introduce them to their truest selves through vulnerability. It is the door held open that every shepherd offers to the ones he or she leads.

Like Paul, we can open our hearts and show followers the way to opening their own hearts. We can come out of hiding in their presence and gently invite them out of their own hiding. By taking our own risks first, we show loved ones that taking this courageous step is infinitely worthwhile.

"AFFIRMING THE RIGHT MESSAGES AND REFUTING THE WRONG MESSAGES. "

MESSAGES SHAPE
THE HUMAN HEART

If you could "say the word" and speak something into existence, what would you say right now?

This is one of those hypotheticals we like to sit with for a while. It's like the genie-and-three-wishes scenario. When we're having fun with this idea, most of us try to create a loophole, like "I'd wish for a million more wishes." But forget loopholes for a moment and stick with the question: What would you speak into existence, if you could? World peace? Vast wealth? Clean oceans? Breathtaking good looks? Raiders win the Superbowl?

In some Jewish mystical traditions, they believe they can actually do something like this. They believe words create reality; that the words they speak go out from their mouths and change the tangible world in real ways.[1]

Based on the creation story in Genesis, they claim that words are the raw material of creation. In Genesis one we read six times, "God said," and then a part of our world is spoken into existence. The crescendo of this is God creating man "in His own image" on day six. So their syllogism goes like this: God spoke the world into existence. We are made in God's image. We speak things into existence.

As I understand it, those who believe this take it very seriously. They claim that, as divine image bearers, we carry a partnership with God in the ongoing creation of reality. In other words, we can continue to speak our world into existence. One author writes, "The words you use actually bring things to life—and when you stop using those words, or change them, you will inevitably create something completely new."[2]

All that said, I'm not sure how they explain some of the atrocities they've lived through over the last four thousand years. If they can speak parts of the world into existence, how do they understand four hundred years of slavery in Egypt? What do they do with the Roman occupation of Israel in the first century? And for goodness' sake, what sense do they make of the holocaust? At some point, this idea seems to crumble under the weight of their own history. Either they're not speaking the right words, or their words are not literally "creating" in the material world.

I first heard about this "words create reality" idea studying Hebrew in seminary. Our professor mentioned it as one explanation for the social weight of blessings and cursings we read about in the Old Testament. For example, why was Esau so distraught when he heard his brother Jacob stole his blessing from their father Isaac?[3] *It was stolen!* How does a stolen blessing stand up in real life? Why doesn't Isaac throw a fit, renounce his blessing over Jacob and give it back to its rightful owner?

I've got dozens of twenty-first century solutions for their blessing problem, but they did not see the problem then the way we see it today. Isaac's words were spoken over Jacob, not Esau, and they would impact Jacob's life in the real world in a way that Esau would never know—period, end of story.[4] Most likely, they believed this was true because the words they spoke created reality in the real world.

Susannah Heschel writes of a midrash (i.e., a commentary or parable on Scripture) that asks how Moses was able to get an audience with Pharaoh to demand the release of the Jewish slaves. Pharaoh was the greatest leader of the day; Moses was a fugitive murderer. She asks, "How could just anyone march into the palace of a ruler . . . and gain the ear of Pharaoh?" She answers, "The midrash explains that when we speak truly from the heart, our words go *directly to the heart of our listener*."[5] My translation? Big words have a big impact on the people around us. Words spoken from a place of deep conviction have a way of getting around our defenses and reaching deeply into our hearts and minds.

In this way, I think the Jewish mystics are on to something. I've never seen a single person change the physical world with well-spoken words, but I've known many hundreds of people who either soar or struggle from the messages that live in their hearts. In that way, we do create real things in the real world with our words. And we do it all the time.

Call a boy "Dumb head" long enough and that boy will settle into a stupidity of his own making. Tell a girl she can't keep up with the boys and before long she will accept life this side of that fiction. Poke a man in the chest with the notion that "soft feelings" are weak and he will forsake a part of his heart that makes him feel most alive. Allow a woman to believe that perfect motherhood and perfect children are life requirements, and she will hide quietly behind a veil, covering her flaws and feelings of inadequacy.

As it turns out, words do, in fact, create reality inside the human heart. There is something you believe because someone spoke a message to you, and then that message came to life in your heart. And it's not just you; that's the way this works for all of us. We come to believe messages of good and bad, life and death, blessings and cursings. They are messages about our own lives and about life in general. Something lives in your heart and in mine that wasn't there before because of words spoken and received.

The Receiver Is Always On

The one thing none of us can do is shut off the flow of messages, unless we decide to move to a cave in the desert. The other thing we can't do is shut off the "receiver" in our minds. We are always "on" and scanning for information, because we were made to send and receive messages.

In college I studied communications, and really loved it. For a minute there I thought I wanted to jump into the world of news media, and that path led through the world of rhetoric and critical thinking.

One of the things we spent a ton of time talking about was the primary "communication model," or how communication happens between people. It included ideas like filters, encoding and decoding, channels, interference, zones, feedback, modes and mediums, and much more. On and on it went, from surprisingly simple to nearly incomprehensible.

What all these theories had in common, though, were three core ingredients: senders, receivers and messages. Those three things are the irreducible minimum for communicating between people. However we structure it, the model tells us that everyone is both sending and receiving messages all the time.

Even when we're trying to mind our own business, people barge into our lives with their messages. When I was in seminary, a nearby church allowed me to study in a tiny unused room in the back of their sanctuary—they're called empty storage closets. I would drive over early in the morning, park under a tree behind the buildings and enter through a back door. For months I did that, never seeing another person. One afternoon, after I finished studying, I walked out the back of the building and noticed a note under the windshield wiper of my truck. Written on the back of a church offering envelope was a nasty message from someone about my rude selfishness for taking too much of the shade from that one tree in a vast empty parking lot. There's the model: sender, message, and receiver.

Entirely by chance, I recently discovered a website wholly devoted to this "windshield communication model." Maybe I'm new to the game on this, but the creativity I found on that site inspired me . . .

- "Thanks for always parking across the path. It gives me the chance to be a movie star and slide across your hood now and then. Try it, it's awesome!"

- "Many three-year-olds have trouble staying within the lines. Maybe if you practice coloring this turtle, it will help with your parking." (They drew an awesome picture of a turtle on the note.)

- "When you park like a fool you make people mad. When you make people mad, they write notes. When they write notes, they're wasting their time. When they waste their time, they get more mad. Or is it madder? Now they're doubting their grammar. Don't make people doubt their grammar. Don't park like a fool."

- "Learn to park, Helen Keller." (Love the sarcastic simplicity of this one.)

- One person even left a message on his own windshield for the traffic cop who kept leaving tickets: "Please stop giving me tickets. I already have three this week. I am obviously broke already. I have ordered my new sticker. It's in the mail. I can't make it get here faster. Have some mercy, you are ruining my life."

Sometimes I wish the mean messages only showed up on our windshields. We could have friends triage our wiper blades each morning to weed out the really hurtful things people say. Sadly, that's not the way it works. People pin messages to our lives all the time, every day. So let me say it again, you're never not receiving messages—that's the one part of this big topic none of us get to control.

The Analysis of Critical Messages

One of my favorite classes in college was "Critical Analysis of Messages." It was fascinating to learn what goes into the "sending" part of a message to get people to believe certain truths on the "receiving" end. We have massive industries compelling us to eat their pizza, buy their tires, wear their clothes, and brush our teeth with their toothpaste—along with a million other behaviors. The strategies may look different and unique, but ultimately they all want to shape the way we think, feel, and—most importantly—behave.

All of that, and much more, makes up the macro side of messaging, but it's the micro side I'm most concerned with. The micro version happens in our personal lives every day with the people we know and encounter. Sometimes these personal messages are big and obvious; other times they're small, subtle, and nearly imperceptible.

Our Big Messages

I had a birthday last weekend, and my son and daughter-in-law hosted a party for me at their house. It was just about perfect: a few close friends, simple conversation around the table, and ribeye steaks. Some people like splashy parties with lots of people; I like them small with people who aren't stingy with their big messages.

I got a few big messages at that party, some in the form of "e-s-t messages." Ever heard of those? They're superlative, literally, because they're made of "e-s-t words": b*est* . . . kind*est* . . . great*est* . . . strong*est* . . . bigg*est* . . . happi*est*– you get the idea. When I'm given words like these from credible people who know me, and the words seem to fit my life, they fill me up. They make it hard for my skeptical heart to slough off the sender's message and look for self-disqualifying loopholes or exceptions.

Big messages are indisputable in most settings, at least as far as clarity is concerned. They don't sneak up on you or leave you wondering what someone is getting at. You don't have to replay them in your head looking for clues or debrief them with a friend to mine for subtle meaning.

Sending big messages is irresistible to me at this point in my life. I crave the clarity and documentation they provide. When it comes to my really important people, I can't live with the thought of them being unclear about my love, acceptance, and joy for them. I don't want them to question that for a single moment of their lives. So I look into their eyes and say the big words and create the big moments. I also write the words in notes and letters so that they have hard evidence they can look back on later. I go "on the record" with big messages. I go public with my favor and blessings. I'm pretty sure this makes me awkward at times too; maybe a little over the top, but never unclear or confusing.

Then I reinforce all that big stuff with the small stuff.

Our Small Messages

Our small messages happen where we live our lives, day in and day out. If we save our big messages mostly for special moments, it's our small messages we send every day. This is where our truest sentiments, intentions, and interests show up, because we can't hide for long any incongruence between what we say and what we believe. Who we are shows up in the details of our lives—especially in our everyday words and gestures. So when I use the phrase "small messages" I don't mean insignificant; I mean routine, authentic, subtle, daily, or habitual. Here are a few of those messages you might recognize.

1. Word count. *Word count* may be the most common small message we send. This isn't about the content of our words, it's about the actual number of words we speak to someone. If you want to punish someone with low access to your life, and do it in a hard-to-confront way, low word count is your ticket. You can send a "speak to the hand" message by pruning your responses to the fewest words possible, and people will get the point. Low word count shuts people out of your life in a way that also maintains plausible deniability—it's nearly impossible to prove intent with unspoken words.

   The flipside happens when someone floods us with their words—in a really good way. A friend calls and says, "I couldn't wait to tell you what happened." And then they do; they bestow trust and value by telling us everything, holding back none of the details. A husband returns home and says to his wife, "You wouldn't believe what happened today." Then he unpacks the details in a way that makes her feel like a fully participating member of his life. A young daughter protests, "Sally was so mean to me today at lunch!" And then she lets her daddy in on the playground politics that make fourth grade so hard on a nine-year-old girl. He may never understand the nuance of her playground life, he's just happy she's telling him about it.

   Word count is more significant than many of us understand. High word count is an honor, an invitation. Low word count can feel like a vote of "no confidence" or low interest. When it's just right, it seems to say, "We belong together, you and me, and I want us to be current with our lives."

2. Eye contact. *Eye contact* is another potent small message. Each week, it's my job in our family to shop at our local big-box store. A few weeks ago I had one of those bigger shopping sessions, the kind you have when you're out of everything. So I wound my way through the store, getting what we needed, finally arriving in the checkout line with an insanely stuffed cart.

   When it was my turn at the check stand, the young clerk processed me through her line without ever acknowledging me. She and I had a five-minute financial transaction, exchanging payment cards and goods, and she performed the whole thing without ever looking at or speaking to me. We've all had uninspired customer service, but this was a whole new level of indifference. I couldn't look away.

   The last thing she did was hold out my receipt toward the exit, so I took the hint and kept moving. I could have robbed the place and she wouldn't have been able to tell the police a single detail about me: not hair color, age, height, ethnicity—nothing. In all fairness, it's not hard to imagine she was simply having a really bad day—so no harm, no foul.

   It's one thing to be ignored by a store clerk, but another thing entirely when it happens between spouses, parents and children, or with friends. Eye contact is both subtle and significant. With it we bestow honor and value, but without it we're left feeling insignificant and overlooked—even invisible.

   Eye contact is the first gesture of worth attribution. It's a micro-vote that says I want to see you more than

I want to read my newspaper, watch that television, read this post, or snap that chat. I pick you before I pick all those other things. Eye contact is one of those nonverbal gestures that communicates more than "I see you." Through eye contact we tell each other, "It's good, to me, that you're here."

3. Attention. *Attention* bears a family resemblance to eye contact, the big difference between the two is sustained focus. Like eye contact, attention honors the presence of a person, but it adds interest and pursuit.

    I think we communicate attention best with the front of ourselves, and I mean that literally. When I think about paying attention, I picture in my mind something like relational geometry. If there's a straight line that runs between my shoulders, I want it to be perpendicular to the straight line that runs between you and me. I want to square up my body, eliminate distractions, close the distance and be fully present with people I love. That's what happens with the gift of full attention.

    This is a literal reorientation of your life in the moment. It is a physical act with a subtle and irrefutable message that says, "I'm turning toward 'us' right now, and that starts with focusing on you." Like eye contact, when I turn my attention and my body toward a person, I'm also turning away from everything else.

    This kind of attention starts out in our hearts—that's where all our behavior comes from. When my heart turns toward a loved one, my body simply follows. I think we understand this intuitively, and when someone turns their attention toward us, we often feel significant—maybe even special.

It's no mistake, then, that when God wants his people to know his blessing, he instructs Aaron to tell them they have his full attention:

"The Lord bless you and keep you; the Lord make his face shine upon you and be gracious to you; the Lord *turn his face toward you* and give you peace."[6] [Emphasis mine.]

4. Everyday words. *Everyday spoken words* are the most tangible small messages we send. We might wiggle our way out of the other small messages, but we can't deny what we say—it's in the public record. I'll explain more about this later, but it's critical that we see *the collective impact of everyday conversation.*

Our "everyday words" reveal more about us than most of us know. It's not hard to manage what we say in short bursts, but over time who we are comes out through our mouths. You might say that our true self eventually leaks out in our language. And it's not just who we are; through our words we also reveal what we believe, value, and long for.

What most of us don't know—and the hidden danger in all this—is that everyday language has a nearly imperceptible, incremental impact on us over time. Years of endless wave action will empty a beach of its sand. The constant freeze and thaw of water shears massive sheets of granite from a rock face. Thick Cyprus trees lean permanently away from the sea under the endless pressure of ocean winds. *And everyday words shape and shear and change the human heart.*

This is especially true of families. Author Peggy O'Mara says that, "The way we talk to our children becomes their inner voice." The collective glossary of a family becomes a child's narrator, defining the way she thinks and feels about herself, along with what she believes she can pursue in life.

If this isn't landing for you, if you're not feeling the full weight of this, I hope you'll slow down, reread the last few paragraphs and contemplate how everyday words have shaped your own heart. Think about the different communities you've been a part of (e.g., staff teams, your family growing up, sports teams, classes, platoons, clubs, churches, etc.) and ask yourself how each of them made you feel. Think about the way people spoke in those settings: what they would and would not discuss, how they talked to each other, the slang they relied on, what was funny and offensive, the nicknames they handed out, and how they spoke of their aspirations or defined success. The sum of our everyday conversations has a cumulative effect on how we think and feel, and because that effect is slow, we rarely see our heart changes until they're etched into us. But when you slow down and take a careful look, can't you actually see those inscriptions?

It's possible that all these small messages might seem too subtle to accept as actual communication, and if you believe that, my friend, you'd be wrong. Small messages create the ambient environment of our relationships. In reality, they often mean more to us than the big messages, because it's our small messages that either validate or refute the big ones. When someone speaks big words of blessing and favor, but treats us like trash every day, their big messages mean nothing to us. But when a person's small messages and big messages match up, our hearts tell us, "Yep, those big messages are legit—you are free to believe them."

A relationship is a living entity, enriched or undermined cumulatively over time, the result of a thousand small messages.[7] Our minds gather all this big and small relational data effortlessly, along with dozens of other cues we will never detect with the naked eye. That is the power of messages between people, and it is fundamental for shepherding followers.

Good Buckets and Bad Buckets

Every one of us carries two buckets through life: a *good bucket* and a *bad bucket*. In our good bucket we collect positive and affirming messages, and in our bad bucket we collect negative and critical messages.

In our *good bucket* we collect messages like:

"I love who you are."
"I have plenty of time for you, what do you need?"
"I'm so sorry that hurts, can I help?"
"You are worth a big effort to me."
"I believe in you. You have what it takes to get this done."
"You are a gift to me."
"I won't abandon you."
"It's good that you are here."
"Here's what delights me about you . . ."
"I'm with you—let's figure this out together."

In our *bad bucket* we might collect messages like:
"You are a disappointment."
"I knew you'd fail; you always do."
"You're not—*fill in the blank*—enough." (e.g., smart, thin, good, tough, ladylike, funny, handsome, etc.)
"I've had enough of you, I'm leaving."

"You'll never change."

"You're just like your father/mother."

"You're important when you get things done."

"I'll give you something to cry about." (*My personal favorite.*)

"Why can't you be more like . . . *fill in the blank*?"

"Don't lean on me. Don't count on me. You're on your own."

The bad news is many of us have tiny thimble-sized good buckets, and great big dump-truck-sized bad buckets. Some people I've known seem to have no good bucket at all—they have no way to retain the good messages people long to leave in their hearts. It's like they're armor-plated against good messages, but lined with Velcro for the bad ones. Because of that, the good messages have little to no shelf-life in their heart while the bad messages pile up and fester.

Our Messages Shape Us

Every one of us is impacted by the messages we've received—none of us get a pass on this. Dallas Willard writes that, "Nothing enters the mind without having an effect for good or evil."[8] Whether or not we're aware of the messages in our buckets, they either push us around or propel us forward.

In my sophomore year of high school I lost a very important wrestling match to the reigning world champion in my weight class. In hindsight, it was actually glorious. I knew I had virtually no chance of winning, but I thought about my opponent for weeks and created a game plan that put winning into the realm of feasibility . . . if you bent the laws of physics and believed really hard in unicorns.

The match started out great. I surprised everyone, my opponent included, by quickly getting the opening takedown. From there the match went back and forth and after two rounds we were tied at five points apiece. In the end, though, I just didn't have enough to win.

I failed to score in the final round and he shifted into overdrive and easily ran away with the match. It was a blowout.

In the moments immediately following the match, I was so happy with how I went into that competition. It may have been my greatest strategic effort as a wrestler, and in the end I earned a bit of respect from a world champion and a tiny ration of praise from a tough wrestling coach.

But that's not how my father saw it. To him, competing well without winning was nothing more than losing. As I stood in our kitchen later that night he badgered me with his disappointment and humiliation. With drunken sensibility and slurred speech he summed up my loss, "I don't care how hard you tried, and I don't want to hear your excuses. I just need to figure out how to live with the disgrace of being your father." That message was my second loss of the evening—the one that did the real damage. I simply didn't have the maturity or the courage to fight back, and by that point in my life, I'm not sure I even disagreed with his condemnation.

Lewis Smedes writes that, "To be disgraceful to people who care for us means that our own people have no grace in their hearts for us. To be disgraceful is to be . . . found unacceptable to those who we need most to accept us. It is, in short, *to be despised and rejected by our own.*"[9]

The actual message I collected that night in my bad bucket was, "The only thing that matters is results." Preparation and effort are irrelevant if you don't win or produce. More than that, your strategy and effort are all bad if you don't meet the expectations, reach your numbers, hit the target, or exceed the results of your last win. I've been bullied by that message most of my life. By withholding a blessing, my father condemned me to a life of running on a treadmill that only got steeper and faster. I pushed harder, I ran faster, and I never got anywhere. Somehow, I had to figure out how to step off that machine.

Mandy Smith says we learn untrue stories about ourselves. That's her language for what we do with the messages we collect in life.[10] She says that over a lifetime, we accumulate these stories at an emotional level, and then they become the way we see ourselves. I think she's right, but if we can learn untrue stories, we can learn the true ones as well.

Actually . . . It's Our Response That Shapes Us

A number of years ago, I spent a day in Donovan State Prison, a high-security correctional facility here in San Diego County. I had a friend who got into some trouble and was serving a short sentence there, so I used my "pastor card" to visit him by tagging along for a day with the chaplain of our church's prison ministry.

After the long process to enter the prison, I met my buddy on one of the prison yards. It's hard to describe the feeling I had when I saw him—maybe a mixture of fear, vigilance, or concern, and a touch of hope. Right away he began to tell me about prison life, starting with the population, broken down along the typical ethnic and social lines. He also pointed out different areas of the yard, describing where he could and could not go, and who he could and could not speak to. It seemed like a steep learning curve, with painful consequences for getting it wrong.

One detail that caught my attention was the fact that each group in prison has a "shot-caller." Just like it sounds, he's the guy with the most power in each of the groups; he calls the shots for everybody else. Ironically, as we stood outside catching up, one of the shot-callers walked right by us, heading into the chapel service we were about to attend.

Technically, I was inside the prison that day as a chaplain. I guess I didn't think through what that would mean once I got inside the facility. What do chaplains do? Well, for one, they lead chapels.

So it was a huge surprise to find out I was the guest speaker that morning for a couple hundred prisoners. I remember thinking, "Wait a minute! I haven't written my prison sermon. I'm just here to visit my buddy." That surprise assignment was not good news to me—not to mention the fact that my new shot-caller-friend was sitting in the front row. I was kind of freaking out—no exaggeration.

I'm not quick on my feet in impromptu speaking scenarios. I've said a million times that I have a slow-twitch brain, and that means it takes me a while to put a message together. Under pressure, and with people watching, my mind would lose a sprint race to a glacier. That said, I sat in the room with all those prisoners and prayed to Jesus for an idea or a theme or a Bible verse—anything I could use to get through the next thirty-five minutes.

And then I got an absolutely ridiculous idea—I mean actually dangerous if things got out of control in that setting. I'm in a cement-block room with hundreds of men, each of whom has been convicted of some crime. There are no fences, no catwalks, no sally ports . . . and no guards—just me and all of them. The doors are in the back of the room and I'm standing on a small elevated stage up front. All right . . . let's do this thing!

After walking onstage, I looked out into the crowd, found a scary looking guy about fifteen feet away, pointed at him and told him to stand up. Surprisingly, he did what I said, so I kept going. I poked my finger at him and asked, "What are you going to do if I come over there and put my hands on you?" I wish you could have seen the looks on these guys' faces when I asked that question. A short white guy on stage with his suit and "little boy" haircut, trying to get all "hard" with an *actual* tough guy. He didn't know what to say, so I went on to the next guy.

I found another scary guy, a little closer, and repeated my routine, this time stepping off the stage toward the front row. That second guy didn't have much to say either, and I think everyone saw what was coming next. I walked a few steps to my shot-caller-buddy, looked him in the eyes and asked, "Now what are you going to do? What if I put my hands on you right now? What if I push you around?" That was the craziest question I've ever asked in my life—think Sheldon Cooper picking a fight with Khal Drogo. What was I thinking?

Neither of those three men answered me; they just looked like they were ready to deliver the beatdown of my life. So after that last question, I backed up slowly—no sudden moves—and spoke to every man in the room. I said, "None of you would let me push you around, right?" They actually laughed, shook their heads and answered together, "No way!" (They actually used a different two-word response, but let's stick with "no way.")

"If that's true," I replied, "if you won't let me put my hands on you, then why in the world do you let other things in your life push you around? Why would you say 'no' to me but 'yes' to them?"

Then I asked them to think about their lives and create a mental list of the hurtful people they've known. I asked them to identify how those people and the destructive events of their lives have shaped their identity. I asked, "Who in your life has told you what to do and who to be? What were the hurts and abuses that shaped you? What happened in your life to make you who you are right now?" Those are hard questions to consider seriously with a shot-caller in the room.

As I looked at those men, I could see the message was landing in their hearts. I told them all of us have something—a message, a person, an abuse, or a hurt—that has the potential to derail our lives . . . permanently, if we allow it. Then I made a final request, "Would you tell us about some of the people and circumstances that have pushed you around? Would you find the courage to let us in on that for you?" I can't even begin to imagine the high risk of a question like that for a group of men in prison, but one after another, they shared about the conditions that have brutalized them: drugs, violence, institutional foster care, abusive or absent fathers, actual hunger, gang recruitment, cultural stereotypes, poverty, disadvantage, and the like. I can't say for sure, but I wondered if that was the first time any of them had pushed back on their hurts in a productive way. It was a beautiful moment.

While I sat in that prison chapel before the service, scrambling for teaching ideas, I had a high-clarity moment with God. In that moment I felt a wave of calm come over me as I heard God say, "Don't be afraid. They look scary, but every one of these tough guys has been pushed around by life. *And so have you.*"

And so have you. And so have all your loved ones. If you're like the rest of us, you haven't gotten through life unscathed. You've taken damage. You've been hurt by important people in your life. Even if you had the best parents, they parented you imperfectly. Even if you went to the best schools and lived in the best neighborhoods, you still lived through the cruelty of puberty and adolescence. And if you had none of those advantages, you probably know what it's like to live on less than enough.

Life touches every single person with a kind of brutality that is hard to explain at times. All of these difficulties, hurts, abuses, and injustices become data for our interpretation of life, and ultimately they land as messages in our hearts. We collect both the interpreted and actual messages of our lives, all along the way.

But it's what we do with those messages that makes all the difference—it's how we understand and respond to what we've received that either holds us back or propels us further in our growth journey. *That's what we will look at next.*

HELPING PEOPLE PUSH BACK 10

Back before they wrote all their books, I was in a therapy group led by Henry Cloud and John Townsend. Those of us in the group came to love their uncluttered approach to health and wholeness. I remember one time when Henry called a timeout with our group because we were behaving like powerless martyrs—*my words, not his.* He told us, "You've been run over by a drunk driver and now you're lying in the street expecting him to come back and heal you." His metaphor cut right through my emotional fog—I immediately knew he was right. In fact, that one sentence has been an essential guide for me ever since.

The fact that we've been hurt and that life is hard isn't the most important truth in the room. Rather, our ability to do something about those hurts is the big difference maker. Ultimately, it's not the messages we receive or the hurts we experience that shape us; it's how we respond to them. It's up to us. We actually get to choose what we do next—whether we know it or not. We can continue to "lay in the street," beaten and bruised by the hurtful messages we've collected, or we can take ownership and push back.

Before we do any pushing, though, let's unpack the mechanics of message collection. The internal progression goes something like this:

messages → beliefs → agreements → vows

Messages Become Our Beliefs

The messages we carry in our good and bad buckets become our beliefs. Imagine, for a moment, you had a parent who repeatedly told you, "You are worth my best effort, so count on my help when you need it." Lifted by the abundance of that message, it would be reasonable to believe the world is filled with helpful people. Based on that belief, you'd "just know" there are resources all around you, and that it's absolutely okay—normal even—to ask for help. And that's what you would do. When things got too difficult or you backed yourself into a corner, you'd reach out to helpful people. Not everyone would say "yes" of course, but some would, and chances are you'd make your way through life energized by a belief in abundance, free from the burden of perceived scarcity.

Flip that coin now. What if you didn't receive "count on me" messages from parents or mentors? What if their core message was, "You're on your own. Figure it out for yourself. If you need something, it's on you to get it." That is a crushing message to grow up believing. In that scenario, scarcity would almost certainly become a controlling fear, and you might come to view people as adversaries to defeat as you struggled and hustled to "get yours" in a zero-sum world. Being self-made might become a life value for you—but believing in generosity, a mistake made only by chumps.

We come to believe the messages we've collected. I don't want to overlook the complexity in all this or imply there isn't a process in the message-to-belief migration. But this is generally how our messages work—which is really great news when we're talking about positive messages, but a nightmare when our messages are destructive.

The beliefs that form from the messages in our bad buckets often become barriers to growing up in Jesus. They keep us from the gospel of truth and grace. They stand between us and a loving heavenly Father who desires only the best for us.

When our dark messages dominate, they don't simply coexist with the healthy messages. Our bad-bucket messages have a way of canceling out the healthy ones. For a bunch of reasons, life on the dark side of messages is usually extreme, lopsided toward self-accusation and condemnation, and hostile to grace and acceptance. Dark messages also tend to create a momentum of their own, slowly increasing in speed and size until we're caught up in a distorted cycle, sometimes leading to hopeless gloom. At some point objectivity may become out of reach, making it nearly impossible to recognize healthier and more productive choices in life.

Life centered on good-bucket messages, however, usually has a kind of balance to it. From that place we live with enough security to accept both our strengths and weaknesses, our upside and downside. Our bad-bucket messages aren't cancelled out; they simply no longer dominate the internal conversation. We factor in those accusing messages and weigh them in our search for the truth, but they no longer define who we are by default, or discolor the entire landscape. We simply no longer allow them to push us around as we live from the center of a hope-filled future.

Beliefs Turn Into Agreements

Again, the messages we collect turn into our beliefs—about ourselves, God, others, and the world in general—and from those beliefs we draw conclusions.

A conclusion is the end of a matter, a process, or an event. Through a conclusion we reach a judgement about how things are based on the "facts" we believe. Often with conclusions we close our minds off to considering new and different information and messages. Either intentionally or not, at some point in our hearts the gavel drops and the decision is made: This is who I am. This is how life is. And this is how my life will go.

We get on the healthy side of this when we hold our conclusions loosely—open for modification as new information comes in—allowing them to focus our attention on our strengths, gifts, and passions in order to carve out our unique path in life. But this turns quite dark when our conclusions come from warped beliefs that are built from a stockpile of toxic messages. When that happens, our conclusions chain us to a harsh and desperate life, mastered by self-disregard and bullied by fake living.

The hardest life you'll ever live in the free world is the one that doesn't belong to you. The good news is that such a thing can only happen with your consent. The bad news is that too many of us surrender to that kind of life all the time.

Conclusions imply agreement; in fact, they require it. When we collect a message, believe it and draw conclusions based on that belief, we are implicitly agreeing with that set of ideas, ultimately giving our approval to live inside their perimeter. *We make agreements with our beliefs*, either by default or by decree.

In seminary I took a class called "Ministry Life Evaluation." It was fascinating because, in that class, our individual lives were the field of study. Over the course of the semester, our professor walked us through a battery of roughly thirty assessments to help us discover and understand who God made us to be. It felt like looking into a mirror reflecting near absolute truth, and it was the gift I had needed all my life. Through those assessments, I dug deeply into my heart and mind, guided by my desire to finally know myself.

At the end of the semester I wrote a fifty-page summary of what the assessments revealed—much like painting a self-portrait. In the end, I decreed, "This is me." From that honest look, I finally landed close to the bullseye of God's design for my life. I had nothing to do with the formation of that design, but I finally saw who I was for the first time. I gathered up the messages, examined my beliefs, drew fresh conclusions, and agreed with God to live out his design for my life.

Since that time, all those years ago, it's been my job to stay clear on who I am and stick to that agreement. Kierkegaard famously said, "Now with God's help, I shall become myself." That's the agreement I signed on to.

Making Bad Agreements

Jesus wants your loved ones to become precisely who he designed them to be, and Satan wants to destroy them. There is zero nuance to this. If we miss this, if we fail to understand this existential struggle, we're missing a fundamental reality of the world we live in. We were born into a world at war and we have a spiritual enemy who has been assaulting us from the beginning.

Lewis Smedes writes, "The devil struggles with God, and the field of battle is the human heart."[1] That means the front line of the war is within us, and the weapons of warfare are messages, beliefs, and agreements. Satan wants all of us—our loved ones included—to believe destructive messages and then live our lives based on agreements with those messages. But Jesus wants us to believe the gospel and live from the foundation of his grace and acceptance.

The very first picture we see of Satan describes him as a serpent "more crafty" than any of the other animals in creation.[2] When you read "crafty," maybe you think shrewd, cunning, sly, or tricky, and those would be accurate descriptions. You'd also be right to think of characters like Keyser Söze (*The Usual Suspects*), Petyr Baelish (*Game of Thrones*), or Frank Underwood (*House of Cards*).

When the Hebrew Torah was translated into Greek, the word the Hebrew scholars chose for "crafty" (Greek, *panourgia*) means tricky and cunning, but it also carries the additional sense of, "ready to do anything."[3] That's a great way to understand our enemy: slippery, underhanded, and ruthlessly *willing to do whatever it takes* to accomplish his purposes. It doesn't matter what he has to do to control the hearts of people; he will do it.

So what does he do? The Bible indicates his weapons are drawn from who he is. In this way, Satan is like anyone else—what he does stems from who he is. Here's a quick survey of how the Bible describes our enemy:

- **Tempter:** His temptation of Adam and Eve ushered in the fall of humanity. He also tempted Jesus—unsuccessfully—in the wilderness. The point of his temptation is to get us to question the goodness of God and then substitute death for life.[4]

- **Murderer:** Jesus says Satan has been a murderer from the beginning.[5] In other words, his intention has always been our actual death—physically and spiritually. What he did, then, in the garden was an attempt to murder the entire human race: the crown jewel of God's creation.

- **Liar:** As the old saying goes, "If his lips are moving, he's lying." How much truth is in Satan? Jesus says there is absolutely none! That means he has no capacity for non-deceptive language. Lying is his native tongue; it's what he speaks best, and as the father of lies, all lying originates from him. This is the explicit and direct language Jesus uses to describe our enemy.[6] By definition then, when we believe his messages, we internalize false information and turn away from the truth.

- **Schemer:** At least two times we read in the Bible that Satan is scheming against us.[7] If you really want to grasp how dangerous this is, imagine some of the really heinous schemers from recent history. Think of a combination personality—maybe someone with the calculated ruthlessness of Bernie Madoff and the "charming" brutality (and violence) of Ted Bundy. When I reach for context like this, the true danger of Satan's ruthless scheming becomes real to me; he becomes less abstract and more literal.

What terrifies me most though is that Satan has been scheming for thousands of years with billions of people. This has to change the way we think about him. We will never comprehend his strategic competence and his proficiency with distortion and deception. Bottom line, we have no chance against him on our own—without Jesus, his Word, and the guidance of the Holy Spirit.

- **Predator:** It's a dreadful mistake to believe Satan is indifferent or forgetful about humanity. In fact, his greatest deception may be allowing us to forget he's even there. We must live knowing that, as followers of Jesus, we are always in his crosshairs.

  My wife, Co, and I went camping last week near Lake Tahoe. The weather was perfect and the setting was breathtaking. One afternoon we hiked along the swift-moving Big Silver Creek, swollen by recent spring rains, up to the crashing and tumbling, hundred-foot-high Bassi Falls. It was truly stunning . . . but I was a bit distracted our entire hike.

  Maybe I've seen too many "When Animals Attack" videos, but throughout our hike I couldn't help scanning the trees, wondering about potential predators. The area is actually known for bears, and where I come from we see mountain lions from time to time. So watching closely seemed like the right thing to do, because predators never warn before they strike. They hunt, conceal, ambush, and pounce. Their strategy is secrecy and then a sudden, overwhelming attack.

The greatest danger is not being stalked; the greatest danger is being stalked and not knowing it. *You are being stalked, along with everyone you know and love.* The apostle Peter uses this language specifically: "Your enemy the devil prowls around like a roaring lion looking for someone to devour."[8] This metaphor tells us Satan's intentions are vicious—he's on the prowl to tear his prey limb from limb.

Peter's remedy is to be self-controlled and alert. He's saying, "Look up! Scan the tree line! Stop strolling through your life as though nothing is out there." The Greek word he uses actually means, "Wake up!" It's as if Peter shakes us to our senses, waking us to the looming threat of our enemy.

- **Accuser:** Satan opposes everything God does. In fact, the word "Satan" literally means "adversary." The focal point of his opposition is the place where Jesus does his most important work. That place is your heart.

  In the book of Romans we read that God works for the good of those who love him, and that he helps us become more like Jesus. All this is possible through Jesus' justifying work on the cross.[9] That's the gospel.

  But then Paul asks what seem like curious questions:

  "If God is for us, who can be against us?" "Who will bring any charge against those whom God has chosen?" "Who then is the one who condemns?"[10]

  Wait a minute, what is all this opposition language? Paul starts out with goodness and "likeness" and now we're talking opposition, allegations, and condemnation. There must be an implied question, doubt, or charge Paul is responding to with these questions. We don't raise hypotheticals for no reason, so there's something going on here for Paul.

To be precise, Paul isn't asking "what" questions; he's asking "who" questions, and this is where Satan—*the Accuser*—comes in. This is what Satan does, what he has always done.[11] He is against us, he accuses us, and he condemns us—all because of the acceptance and grace Jesus offers to everyone. If Satan opposes everything about God, tops on that list is the gospel message Jesus wants all of us to believe.

But wait, there is another "who" in the Romans passage—it is Jesus himself. The Bible tells us Satan stands in God's presence accusing us, but Paul tells us Jesus is there too: "Christ Jesus who died—more than that, who was raised to life—is at the right hand of God and is also interceding for us."[12]

Jesus is our advocate; Satan is our accuser. *For every truth Jesus wants to birth in our hearts, Satan has a corresponding lie to bludgeon us with.* Jesus wins when we believe his gospel of free grace and acceptance. Satan wins when we make agreements with the condemning messages he leaves in our bad bucket.

By the way, in the Romans passage, Paul never mentions the actual charges against us. He simply reveals Jesus as our advocate and then answers the unnamed allegations. The defense Paul makes is the love of Jesus.[13] In spite of anything we may have done or any messages we've collected in life, the acceptance, grace, and love of Jesus are our ultimate defense.

Like it or not, this is the actual struggle we are locked in. We have an enemy who contemplates us, assaulting us with all of his cunning and resources. He has a game plan for each of us and he wins when we make agreements with the beliefs that come from his lies and accusations. Dwight Pentecost describes it like this, "Satan is more concerned with what you think and what you believe than with what you do. Satan's desire is to control your mind so that he can control your actions. Satan does not spend his time in peripheral things; he concentrates his efforts on his goal, to control what you believe."[14]

Agreements Turn Into Vows

Finally, we vow to live our lives based on the agreements we've made—whether good or bad. There is no ceremony involved or documents to sign; we simply give consent to our agreements and sign on to the life they define. We allow and invite certain beliefs to thrive in our hearts, and they begin to call the shots for us. We begin to live a life based on a worldview that starts from the messages we collect in our good and bad buckets. All of this is true . . . for better or for worse.

Becoming Your True Self or False Self

Messages shape our identity. We are always moving toward our true self or our false self. These two selves stand in opposite corners of the room, and Lewis Smedes says that the one who stands between them is our actual self—the person we are from day to day.

He writes that the true self is "like the design for a building still under construction or the original design for a building that needs restoring. It is stamped in the depths of us like a template for the selves we are meant to be and yet are failing to be."[15] I like to think of this as the ideal version or the "Jesus version" of ourselves: the version the Holy Spirit is helping us become.

Our false self is a fake, made-up version of who we are. It is twisted and pressed into shape from the destructive messages collected in our hearts. We receive those messages, believe them and agree to live under their tyranny, ultimately taking on an imposter identity. Smedes writes that, "Our false self is an image of what we ought to be that is concocted out of false ideals. The false ideals are imposed on us by other people. They do not come from our true self, from the self we are meant to be. They are planted in us by sources that try to create us in their image."[16]

Speaker and blogger Morgan Snyder likens the false self to the gyro of a bicycle wheel. It has a gravitational center in itself, so it has to keep spinning and perpetuating the false self to stay upright.[17] Our true self, however, places the gravitational center in Jesus. And in that case, we remain firmly on our feet when we follow him as best we can, in order to become who he designed us to be.

Ultimately it's all about the messages we choose to believe— they lead us either toward the "Jesus version" of ourselves or toward our fake selves. How we respond to the messages we take in determines our identity, and we never live beyond who we believe we are.

You cannot grow a false self; only your actual self can become more like Jesus. What you can do, however, is fabricate a fictional you, usually from the parts and pieces of people you know. You also cannot relate to people from a false self. If you live a fabricated life—intentionally or not—your relationships will always be aimed away from who you actually are. Sometimes the discomfort from that deviation is slight; at other times it's excruciating—like you've been alone in this world your whole life.

All of this leads us to a given destination. If messages shape our identity and relationships, there's no way they don't also shape our future. What happens for us downstream in life may be most affected by how we view ourselves and the way we relate to others.

Very early in life I abandoned my true self. Why wouldn't I? I didn't know a single important person who celebrated, affirmed, or loved that early version of me. At some point, I believed they were right, and I implicitly agreed to forsake myself and build a new identity from their values and aspirations. As a teenage boy I used to tell myself, "I will become anyone I choose to be." That was an actual mantra I spoke over myself all the time, whenever I needed to push back against the pain of my fake life. My agreements and vows became ironclad, but the pressure on my heart from fake living would become more than I could take.

None of the people in my life at the time are responsible for the decisions I made—truly! It was me who chose my fake life. I decided to leave my real self and self-transform into some chopped-together fabrication of a made-up person. I believed the destructive messages I collected and agreed to a life that God never intended for me.

Helping Loved Ones Push Back

I see this same self-abandonment in people everywhere I go. As it turns out, it's quite a challenge to become one's actual self: the person Jesus designed you to be. The longer I live, the more I recognize that sources outside our lives—whether family and friends or culture norms—push us around and press us into molds of their making. And all that pushing and pressing comes at us in the form of messages.

I don't know when this changed for me; I can't pinpoint the exact time, but I can't take this anymore, and I don't mean for myself, necessarily. I cannot bear the thought of my loved ones living under the pressure to accept disfigured lives, battered and pushed around by evil and destructive messages. It makes my blood boil!

Jesus doesn't pressure anyone, and he isn't trying to crush us into a mold that looks nothing like us. He simply points us to what's real and calls us to the truest version of ourselves. Isn't that what you really want—what we all want?

John Ortberg, in his fabulous book, *The Me I Want to Be*, writes, "As God helps you grow, you will change, but you will always be you." He goes on to say, "Some people think that if they seek to grow spiritually they will have to become someone else. But God won't discard your raw material."[18] What a comforting idea. I spent much of my early life trying to become a version of myself that I wasn't, and it was exhausting.

"Here's the good news," Ortberg writes, "When you flourish, you become more you. You become more that person God had in mind when he thought you up. You don't just become holier. You become you-ier."[19]

You can help with all this! You can absolutely be the difference in the lives of your loved ones. We see all over Scripture that Jesus uses his people to shape and grow his people. It's a beautiful picture of mutuality and reciprocity that is hard to find anywhere else.

Pushing Back Against a Fake Life

Pushing back doesn't come naturally to everyone, because it's just not nice. The civilized crowd neither pushes nor pushes back. In fact, what do we tell our children from the moment they understand us? "Kids! Stop pushing! Keep your hands to yourself! I don't care if she pushed you, do not push her back!" For most of us, pushing back was not an option growing up, and in some families it could cost you thirty minutes in the time-out chair.

We have a funny (funny to us, at least) experience forever captured in our family lore. It's about a father we saw scolding his son, Shawn, at Disneyland. Shaking Shawn's arm, as Shawn's little brother stood by smirking, Shawn's dad screeched, "Shhwaann, da shecond kid alwaysh getsh it!" And then Shawn "got it" from his dad. The moral of the story? It's a bummer when your dad shouts your name in public over and over. And you may get pushed, but if you push back you'll be the one who "gets it."

I'm telling you to forget all that. When it comes to some of the messages we've collected over the years, I'm advocating for the opposite of what you've always heard. Many of us need to figure out how to act more like five-year-olds and *not keep our hands to ourselves.* I'm telling you we need to learn to push back.

I coached wrestling for ten years. One of the hardest things to help young wrestlers with is *effectively* matching the aggression of an opponent. Your opponent is trying to force your body into positions you don't choose. He puts his hands on you, pushes and pulls, trips and throws, all to exert his will over you. He wants to push you around. At some point, *you have to figure out how to push back productively.*

The apostle Peter writes about pushing back, using the word "Resist."[20] Pushing back is about resistance—the right kind of resistance. It's about deciding not to give in to the hurtful influences that damage our hearts. In Peter's case, he's referring to the lies and accusations of our enemy, but it could apply to any message that causes us to abandon our true self.

We need to take charge of the messages that land in our hearts. We have options. We get to decide which messages live or die, stay or go. We don't have to remain victims, and we aren't passive spectators observing our hearts from the outside. When it comes to messages we can affirm, challenge, dispute, confirm, receive, refute and replace, restrict, shut off, accept, weigh-out, or believe.

All of these options are available to us if we become discerning and a bit militant about what we allow to live in our hearts. That's easier said than done, trust me. The last few pages might make it seem like I have a handle on this, but when it comes to the messages in my own heart I'm a push-over . . . and I know it. In fact, that's where my family and our community of friends come in. Because I can't handle my messages on my own—because I'm too easily pushed around by them—I constantly include my wife and close friends in my internal conversations. I do this to help identify the messages I need to welcome and the ones I need to send packing. And I don't think I'm out of the ordinary on this. *We push back best when we push back together.*

As shepherds, this is what we offer our loved ones. Since we're always trying to help followers look to Jesus, anytime we see a destructive message gain traction in their hearts, we simply point them back to him. When we do that, the question we're trying to answer is, "What does Jesus have to say about the message you are tempted to believe?" Most often, in my experience, this simply leads back to the gospel. *What does your message mean in light of the gospel? How does the gospel deny, change, challenge, or refute it? How does it confirm, enhance, or support it?*

Ultimately, we're always trying to make Jesus the leader of the resistance in the hearts of our followers. We think Jesus knows best how to overthrow the influence of the enemy in the lives of those we love. So turning to him for clarity and understanding becomes a relational habit of the communities we lead.

Pushing Back Starts by Paying Attention

Paying attention is essential in the growth process—I've said this all along. It's never more essential than when we're trying to make sense of our messages and beliefs. This is where the shepherding metaphor really serves us well. A good shepherd pays attention and knows when his or her sheep are in good shape and when something's wrong.

Paying attention is all about looking and listening. What patterns do you see in those you lead and love? Do their decisions make sense? Are they rooted in reality and truth? How about the way they use their time? What does that tell you? What do you hear in their words? How do they speak of themselves and others? What are the dominant moods and emotions that come out in their language? What doesn't sound like joy and peace? What sounds like struggle and dissonance? What sounds like Jesus and the gospel, and what doesn't? What am I seeing and hearing? What are they seeing and hearing? It all boils down to questions just like these.

Keep in mind, all your looking and listening must be built on the foundation of safety and permission; if you don't have those, it doesn't matter what you see and hear. But when followers feel safe with you and grant you permission to lead, you've got the green light to respond to the messages that come to the surface.

The Serendipity of God's Message

God has a message for everyone, and each message is as unique as the one receiving it. If you don't follow Jesus, his message is, "Come to me. Follow me and I will give you the life you long for most deeply; the life you've been looking for this whole time." It's as simple as that.

If you already follow Jesus, his message often focuses on how you can become more like him, and this is where personalized growth and specificity come in. It's an amazing adventure to see how God shows up in our lives, places his message before us, and calls us to take next steps. We don't always see that coming, so it's a wonderful experience when it happens. It's the serendipity of God.

Finally . . .

Messages have both wreaked havoc and birthed blessing in my life. If I had to estimate the ratio on these, I'd say it has been about seventy-thirty, havoc over blessing. That's a challenging ratio, so I've had to work pretty hard to fight back against hurtful messages.

Because of the power of bad-bucket messages, I believe it's essential to "hang neon lights" around our good-bucket messages when we receive them. Sometimes we hang our own lights; at other times friends and family hang them for us.

On Father's Day 2012, my son Timmy and I were having one of our typical father-son scrums. It was rough! I don't know how else to explain it. We bickered constantly, always trying to find ways to out-jab each other. I'm not proud of the way I showed up as his dad that day; it's just the way I allowed it to be. Not period. Not end of sentence. Not full stop.

Little did I know, he had a Father's Day gift for me. At the time, he used to "cover" popular songs at local music venues, so it was normal for him to play his keyboard too loud and belt out The Fray, One Republic, or Coldplay. That's what I thought he was going to do for me that day. I assumed Coleene reminded him it was Father's Day and since he hadn't given it a moment's thought, he could just play a quick song and be done with it.

My wife called me into our living room and Timmy sat down and started to play his song. At first I was trying to recognize the song he was covering, so I focused on the melody and lyrics. When he got to the chorus and I still didn't recognize the song, I finally understood what was going on. *"Wait a minute,"* I thought, *"he wrote this song for me."* He spent hours on his own, crafting an actual song to give to me on Father's Day. And it just broke me wide open.

My hard shell cracked. I began to cry uncontrollably because of what felt like radical generosity and thoughtfulness. My boy contemplated me with love and truth, and then put his thoughts to music.

In hindsight I can see how badly I needed my son's message. I was in a difficult job that was a daily, soul-sucking challenge for me. I wanted out, but it was good for Timmy that I stay put in that job. His song was almost like God saying, "I see you. I know what you're doing. Let me remind you why you're choosing your hard life. And know that I'm pleased with your effort. Don't stop."

God has used that message over and over to nourish my heart and re-center my relationship with him. That's how words of affirmation work in our hearts. It's also how God uses you in the lives of those you love and lead.

So go to war! Affirm the right messages in the hearts of loved ones—and refute the messages that hurt and harm them.

"CAREGIVING VALIDATES THE LIFE-CHANGING CONDITIONS. **"**

CAREGIVING EQUALS TRUSTWORTHY

11

Every once in a while I get all worked up because I think my computer has been hacked. But it hasn't; not yet anyway. I guess I find it hard not to be a little tech-cautious these days—maybe even a little paranoid.

We hear about hackers refining their strategies and improving their "skills" all the time. A recent *60 Minutes* episode told the story of hackers seizing control of big computer systems, then demanding ransoms to release control back to the rightful owners. They hit major cities like Newark, Atlanta, and Sarasota, along with Cleveland's airport and the San Francisco transit authority.

Sadly, we know this happens on an individual level too. My son Zach used to make his living helping people remove ransomware from their PCs. What a nightmare—a faceless stranger seizes your computer and locks you out of your own personal information, holding it hostage until you pay up.

Okay, actually one time my debit card did get hacked. I still have no idea how it happened though. Out of the blue, while on vacation, walking on the National Mall in D.C., I got a call from my bank's fraud department asking if I was withdrawing a bunch of money back in San Diego.

Apparently somewhere there's an ATM video of someone taking out wads of cash from my account using a cloned card and my stolen pin number. What a creepy and violating feeling.

After I hung up, still standing in front of the Smithsonian, I had a mini Liam Neeson moment in my head. I wanted to call those hackers and say, "I have a particular set of skills that make me a nightmare for people like you." (I don't.) "I will look for you." (I won't.) "I will find you." (Nope, not that either.) I got over my moment pretty quickly.

The threat of hacking became real to me that day, because it is real—it happens every day, all day long. Someone who doesn't belong anywhere near it barges into our virtual life. They kick in the door or secretly pick the lock, gaining access to our personal information in our social media accounts, financial information, emails, cloud accounts, pictures, texts . . . you name it. Once they're in, they control it.

I'm not a digital native so this threat seems particularly outrageous to me. How has all this happened, and why can't we stop it? Apparently I'm a digital immigrant,[1] which means I remember life before computers when we used paper, pencils, Wite-Out® and typewriters (by the way, you can see all those on display at the Smithsonian), and when our threats were local and tangible. Nowadays, nearly every person has a global online reach along with their own unique electronic footprint, so our threat is global too. This makes trust more precarious than ever before.

Just about everybody knows how dangerous hackers can be. *The trick is figuring out how to allow the right people in while keeping the wrong people out.* This is one of the great challenges of our digital age.

Living a Hacked Life

I've heard stories about how hard it can be to come back from a hacked computer. Apparently, it can take many months to recover data, restore accounts, and in some cases reacquire your own identity. Sometimes you never recover everything. No doubt that's a brutal reality, and so far we're only talking about online hacking.

Just to be clear, hacking isn't just a virtual threat. Way more destructive, the relational version of hacking has led to wounded hearts and ruined lives for a hundred generations. Malicious people also find ways into our actual lives, without permission, and then do real damage.

Hackers You May Know

One of the things that makes middle school such a nightmare is the fully formed, yet brutally unrestrained, ability to bully one another. Thirteen-year-olds have enough creativity and sophistication to inflict real damage, but none of the maturity to hold it back. We adults have taken that creativity to the next level, yet many have failed to grow their maturity at the same pace. So the bullying continues into adulthood, refined and focused by years of experience.

You'd think we'd grow out of this, but social media is again the mirror that tells us who we are. Spend ten minutes on the Nextdoor App—a social network for helping neighbors connect and collaborate—and you will see some truly next-level bullying. It shocked me at first to see neighbors treating each other so badly, and now I'm surprised when people have an opening and don't pile on "the guy down the street" for his naïve or preachy post.

Nearly everyone knows what it feels like when a bully is in the room. Preston Ni writes that a "bully can be an intimidating boss or colleague, a controlling romantic partner, an unruly neighbor, a high-pressure sales/business representative, a condescending family member, [or] a shaming social acquaintance."[2] These people, they're everywhere, trying to hack into our lives and make us submit to their pressure.

That's bullying, and nearly everyone feels it from time to time. But I could have mentioned any number of other malicious players in our lives:

- You may have a "strategic" friend who values your relationship—not for the gift of friendship with you, but for what they can get from you.

- Maybe you know a toxic person who feels socially boosted by spreading shame, gossip and condemnation to friends and family . . . about friends and family.

- Then again, maybe you have a leader—a boss, teacher, parent, or coach—who disregards your needs and aspirations, and instead uses you to serve their agenda or add to their net profit.

Relational hackers come in all shapes and sizes, but their bottom line is getting a payoff that you end up paying for. They want to benefit at your expense. They want something from you and they're willing to barge in and take it without asking.

Going Offline Relationally

When we get enough of this, it's natural to want to go offline relationally. When it feels too risky, we step "off the grid" and build massive firewalls between our hearts and everyone else. We've had it—*enough already*—and we've decided that life behind a protective barrier is the way to go.

For the record, I'm not talking about having healthy boundaries. Those are appropriate, and they usually keep most of the hackers away. I've heard Henry Cloud speak of personal boundaries as a fence line. He says fences help you know what belongs to you—what's inside your fence line, and what belongs to others—what's outside your fence line. He also says fences are great for keeping the safe people in and the dangerous people out.

So a healthy fence line is great, but the Great Wall of China isn't, when it comes to relating to people. I fear that healthy caution is tipping toward fearful isolation as more people worry about their own personal "invaders from the North."

If we miss this fear, as shepherds we can end up on the wrong side of that wall, locked out of the lives of those we love.

Two-Factor Authentication (The Relationship Version)

Some people should be allowed into our lives; others should be kept out. That's entirely reasonable and healthy, but too many of us are unclear on the criteria for allowing access.

Recently I got a new laptop, which meant (surprise to me!) I had to re-verify my virtual identity in order to get access to my online accounts. I guess there is something like a "device identifier" on each computer that gets associated with you and your password credentials. When you switch computers or attempt to log-in on a different computer, many websites want added proof that you are who you say you are. At that point, they require "two-factor authentication;" by sending a one-time code to your phone or email, which you have to enter along with your password to be allowed access to your accounts. (Wow, you just experienced the far edge of my tech capacity right there. You're welcome.)

If you got lost in my tech explanation, I apologize. All I'm trying to say is there are times when you have to use two pieces of identification, online, to prove you are who you say you are. In fact, that's becoming the norm.

The much bigger point is that *our relationships have always required two-factor authentication.* Brené Brown explains this with the words "professing" and "practicing." "As we think about shame and love," she writes, "the most pressing question is this: Are we *practicing* love? Yes, most of us are really good at *professing* it— sometimes ten times a day. But are we walking the talk? Are we being our most vulnerable selves? Are we showing trust, kindness, affection, and respect to our partners (or our followers)? It's not the lack of *professing* that gets us in trouble in our relationships; it's failing to *practice* love that leads to hurt."[3] [Emphasis mine.]

What we say isn't enough; it must be verified by what we do. We can tell people we love them and that we live with their best interests in mind, but that may not mean much in our hacker-filled world until it gets verified by our lifestyle. Why? Because followers don't trust who we are until they see what we do.

Caregiving Confirms Who You Are

Caregiving confirms that you are who you say you are. It's the second authenticating factor that identifies you as one of the healthy people to allow inside the fence line.

To this point, we've spent a bunch of time looking at the other four conditions that lead people to life change: safety, truth, vulnerability, and affirmation. Caregiving is unique, however. It is the life-changing condition hackers won't try to fake for long, because a caregiving life is hard and it requires sacrifice. It's a uniquely generous and unselfish way of living that confirms the other life-changing conditions are authentic and can be trusted.

Caregiving sends a bona fide message that loved ones come to believe. "I'm not just your project," they conclude, "and no one is forcing you to love me. You take the time and effort to get out of your own world and love me in mine. *My heart is now free to trust you*, because you show up in my life and love me in tangible ways." If you don't know it yet, it's nearly impossible to deny real love like this for long.

Ultimately, *caregiving is an invitation to vulnerability*. It empowers the other four life-changing conditions. It validates your love for followers, providing hard evidence that it's reasonable to trust the safety you offer. It assures loved ones that "opening the gate" and welcoming you inside the fence line is absolutely the right thing to do.

There isn't a ton of technique to talk about with caregiving. When it's right, it's simply a function of the love that already exists in your heart. When we love people in a fashion that in no way serves our selfish interests, our pure and sincere intentions become obvious and undeniable. At that moment we become trustworthy in the hearts of followers. This is precisely what I witnessed, firsthand, with our friend Ivana.

I met Ivana in one of the small groups Co and I led in our home years ago. We loved her immediately; she was naturally thoughtful, kind, and funny in a slightly self-deprecating way. The only real challenge I had with Ivana early on was understanding her thick, eastern-European accent.

During our first "get to know you" session in the group, we found out she had fled communist Czechoslovakia as a young girl. As she explained it, her entire family attempted to flee the country, but only Ivana was able to make it out. Just imagine that for a moment; try to wrap your head around that one. She flees with her entire family from the brutality of an autocratic government, only to end up on her own—exposed and vulnerable, a young girl alone in the world. They write movies about stories like this.

Fast forward a number of decades and Ivana lands in our small group as a member of our brand new "family." She faithfully shows up to our group, week after week, for many months. She is delightful to be around, engaging and chatty, even a bit assertive with her opinions—and we come to love her . . . a lot. I remember thinking we were becoming something like a new family for Ivana.

But it seemed like she was keeping something from us. As time went on, our group became a safe place and we began to let each other in on our hurts and struggles. We started to lean on each other and talk about parts of our lives we wanted to change and grow. We were clearly headed in the right direction as a group, but I noticed a divergent trend with Ivana. She had plenty to offer when we "came real" about our lives, but virtually nothing to say about her own life. So I began to gently probe and turn the conversation toward her any time it looked like she was willing to "lower her drawbridge" and let us in. But nothing worked; she continued to keep us at arm's length, because that's how her life had always been. She grew up on her own, solving her own problems, leaning only on herself, and it was going to take something big to change that. Little did we know, that big thing was just around the corner.

One evening Ivana showed up at our group and we noticed right away something was wrong. It was dramatic: her body language was closed down; she engaged no one, and her face was etched stone. I couldn't help wonder what had happened, so as the evening went on I continued to gently "knock on the door," hoping she would crack it open a bit.

Finally it happened; the weight of her private burden became too heavy to bear, and her drawbridge came crashing down. In the seven days since we had last seen Ivana, her job was eliminated, her landlord sold the house she was renting and—this is where it really turns dark—she found her roommate lifeless in bed, having died in her sleep in the night.

There are details I've left out, but that's not really the point. What is the point is how our small community responded to her—it was extraordinary. In that moment, she leaned into our little family for the first time, allowing us to ask details and walking us through all that had happened. And then the best thing happened: we stepped into her life with caregiving and helped her with the burden she couldn't carry on her own. We loved her actively and on purpose. It was one of the most undeniably loving moments I've ever seen.

We walked with Ivana through that season of her life, and we did it as a family. We helped her find another place to live, including giving her money for a deposit and rent. We helped with funeral arrangements for her roommate, who we discovered also lived without the care and comfort of a family. Bottom line, we heaped generous amounts of care into Ivana's life.

The best outcome, however, was the change in how Ivana showed up in our group. She no longer sat outside our circle, watching us do life together; she became a fully participating, transparent member of our family. That, my friends, is the life-changing power of caregiving.

Caregiving and Care-keeping

We have options when it comes to the supply of care in our control, and most people know it. We can give our care to anyone or anything we choose. You should see my fishing gear: it's beautiful. Dozens of rods and reels, all in nearly new condition, because I choose to take some of my care and apply it to the upkeep of that gear. *Most of my care, however, I give to the ones I love.*

That's how this works. I can take my care and hand it out anywhere I choose, to whomever I choose. But I can't give care that I don't have. In other words, there's a limited amount of care I have to offer, so I have to be intentional about how I give it out. In that way, care is a lot like time or money—it's a limited resource that we choose how to spend. I think most people understand this, so it's a big deal to them when they are on the receiving end of our caregiving.

I am an active love kind of guy, mostly because I've experienced firsthand how active love has changed my own heart. I'm simply grateful for it, and now I can't resist offering that same active love to others. When I do, it's not uncommon for people to respond effusively, with big gratitude—almost as if they're surprised to be receiving active care and kindness. Or maybe it's because actual caregiving is rare these days. It's like they think, "Wait a minute!

You're taking some of your valuable care—care you could spend on yourself—*and you're giving it to me*?" Yep, that's exactly what I'm doing!

I don't know what heightens their gratitude, I'm just trying to make a point—and that's what I tell them. I say, "You're welcome to my care! You matter to me and I want you to know you are worth a big effort." By giving them care I not only want to help with their needs; equally important, I also want them to know they are worth my best effort. I want to convince their hearts of my love.

Keeping our care is an option too, of course. In fact, I think care-keeping is way more common these days than caregiving—maybe it always has been. My hunch is that a lot of us today take our care and apply it to our own lives. Don't get me wrong, I'm all about healthy self-care, because we can't do any caregiving if we're always running on empty. I just think that care-keeping goes beyond self-care to something else. It feels inflated and a bit grandiose to me, like we're fulfilling some ethereal obligation to ourselves because the "universe" says it's our personal right and we deserve it. If that's true, why would any of us give any of our care away?

I recently read that the self-help industry generated nearly ten billion dollars in 2016. Experts say that number will rise to thirteen billion by 2022.[4] That is real money for an industry that exploded onto the scene in the 1950s with books like *The Power of Positive Thinking* by Norman Vincent Peale and Dale Carnegie's *How to Win Friends and Influence People.*

Well, not exactly. Come to find out, self-help has been around for thousands of years. Author and social observer Jessica Lamb-Shapiro traces the roots of our current self-help craze to the "Ancient Egyptian genre called 'Sebayt,' an instructional literature on life."[5] Much later, in the eighteenth century, Lamb-Shapiro tells us, "Conduct books told men how to behave in polite society." She writes that these books covered topics like, "'Loathsome and Filthy

Things,' 'Blowing the Nose,' 'Hair Cut Round Like a Bowl-Dish,' and 'Beards of a Frightful Length.'"[6] You can't make this stuff up.

Nearly everyone who writes about the history of self-help points to Samuel Smiles as the father of our current version of this genre. Robin Ince tells us that Smiling Sammy Smiles (That's not actually what they called him, but wouldn't it be great marketing for a self-help author?) was a Scottish parliamentary reformer who, in 1845, wrote a series of lectures for the working class on the power of persistence.[7] He went on to coin the phrase "Self Help" by publishing those lectures in a book of that title, which became the international bestseller of the day, outpaced only by the Bible.[8]

We seem to have a love/hate relationship with self-help. In culture, we can't get enough of it. We buy millions of books and downloads. Podcasts, blogs and TED-type talks appear on every medium. Oprah's built an empire on self-determination. Tony Robbins made the "Law of Attraction" ubiquitous. Brené Brown has a Netflix special. And the whole time in our heads we hear Doctor Phil asking, "How's that workin' out for ya?"[9] I think I'm with the comedian George Carlin: *"If you're looking for self-help, why would you read a book written by somebody else? That's not self-help. That's help! There's no such thing as self-help. If you did it yourself, you didn't need help."*[10]

For the record, I do believe that self-help is actually helpful— you can't look at my bookshelf and draw another conclusion. I just think it has a mythical quality to it. It feels like an oversold fantasy that we can generate within our imperfect selves the kind of help that fixes humans and humanity. History simply does not sign-off on that notion—not at all.

My biggest knock on the genre, though, is that I think it creates a culture obsessed with aiming all, or most, of its care at itself. One core theme of self-help comes directly from Samuel Smiles, who wrote the famous line, "Heaven helps those who help themselves."[11]

My mother used to preach that as Scripture. Problem is, it's just not in the Bible—not the actual words, nor the concept itself.

Mutual Caregiving in Community

What *is* in the Bible is something like what Dallas Willard calls "reciprocal rootedness."[12] He writes about having love for one another that grows out of Jesus' love for us, resulting in "circles of sufficiency."[13] I think the opposite of Willard's idea is inflated self-importance and self-absorbed love, leading to *islands of insufficiency*. Ultimately this comes from the credo that life is up to us—our ideas, our motivation, and our solutions—and we provide our own answers to what needs changing, fixing, and optimizing in our lives. When this settles into our hearts, we're often left with vigilant self-interest and self-dependence that keeps us outside the fence line of the collective care and love of community.

The Bible is filled with radical expressions of caregiving and receiving. In the Old Testament, God tells his people how to care for marginalized individuals in the world and how to uphold justice for the weak.[14] In the New Testament, the early church lives out extreme generosity and mutual caregiving that has its roots in the love and care we first receive from Jesus.[15] Both of these expressions of caregiving originate from the care we receive from God: in the Old Testament, from the relational covenants of loyal love between God and his people; and in the New Testament, from the grace and mercy of the cross. Jesus sums all this up with, *"Love each other. Just as I have loved you, you should love each other."*[16]

In this way, Samuel Smiles had it all wrong: God doesn't help the already helped, he helps the helpless. The prophet Isaiah writes, "For You have been a defense for the helpless, a defense for the needy in his distress, a refuge from the storm, a shade from the heat . . ."[17] In Romans, Paul gives us the foundation for the help that none of us can live without: "When we were utterly helpless," Paul writes,

"Christ came at just the right time and died for us sinners . . . God showed his great love for us by sending Christ to die for us while we were still sinners.[18]

As shepherds—as lovers of loved ones—we can live this value by giving out of the care we've already received from the One who loved us first. When we do that, we're choosing not to cling to our care, but rather to give it away—knowing that mutual caregiving is normal when God's love defines a community. Even though our personal supply of care is limited, the collective community overflows with it, because Jesus couples his divine resources to the church. By following Jesus, a new source of life flows within us: a pure source offered only through Jesus, guided and directed by the Holy Spirit.[19]

What if we created communities filled with mutual caregiving? What if, instead of keeping our care for rainy days, we kept each other and then leaned into community by offering mutual care when life gets stormy? What if, instead of resting our weight on our ability to help ourselves, we actually lived our lives in "circles of sufficiency" as we learned the rhythm of caregiving and receiving? That kind of trust can become the new normal. I know it; I've seen it myself.

Caregiving Generates Trust

One Hebrew word for "trust" means to be careless. I first heard this from Henry Cloud in his book *Integrity*, but I didn't understand it right away.[20] How in the world do "trust" and "careless" fit together?

The Hebrew word I'm referring to is *batah* (The first "a" is long, followed by a real hard "t," ending with an "h" like you're clearing your throat). It's often used to express ideas like reliance, safety, confidence, *or carelessness*.[21]

We don't have a word like this in English, but one way to think about this is to picture a sense of well-being and security because you're loved by the right person. David uses *batah* of God in Psalm 22, writing, "In you our ancestors put their trust; they trusted and you delivered them. To you they cried out and were saved; in you they trusted and were not put to shame." Back and forth David goes, in this psalm, between distress and trust; admitting the fear and difficulty of his life, and then trusting God because of the way he rescues and cares for his people. David is free to "care less" about what worries him, because of God's "care-fullness" for Israel.

Caregiving builds trust like this because it reveals the giver's devotion, love, and favor for others. When we give care, it becomes evidence that we're looking out for the needs and interests of followers *first*. We aren't about our own bottom line, goals, agenda, or personal success. We don't start with our own aspirations; we start with Jesus' aspirations for those we love and lead.

Leaders who do this well believe that caregiving is about loving people—not because they've earned it, or because some day they will return the favor, but simply because we have it to give. We have been loved perfectly by Jesus, and out of his grace and mercy we're passing that love on to others.

When people receive this kind of care from you, they naturally open their hearts and welcome you into their lives. They no longer feel the need to scrutinize you as a leader because they don't have to worry about your intentions. *They can care less.* They are free to be *care-less* about you because you are *care-full* about them. They no longer need to watch their back with you, because they come to believe that's what you're doing for them.

All of this happens through caregiving. Jesus makes it clear that followers don't exist for leaders; rather, it's the other way around—we exist for them.[22] Caregiving keeps that order clear in our heads and alive in their hearts. When we believe in care like this, it's easier to show up authentically in the lives of loved ones. When they believe it, it's easier to open the gate and invite us in. However we view it, this is one of the things Jesus did best and one of the ways we are most like him—when we're wildly generous with our care, people see Jesus' love in us.

Caregiving in the Real World

So the big answer with all of this is being generous with our care and, equally important, generating caregiving in the community. Again, this isn't a technique to master; it's an honest expression of our love for others. It usually requires some wise living on our part, and a touch of good planning. That means you'll need to allow margin to grow and remain in your life so you have the space to give to others.

All that said, *how would you define caregiving?* What do you think of when you hear that word? Allow me to do a little exercise right now. I'm going to take a five-minute break from writing and list as many examples of caregiving as I can. In fact, you could take a quick break too and do the same thing—it's up to you. Here I go, back in five . . .

Okay, here's my list: mow a friend's lawn, set up a meal train,[23] watch a friend's child, write an encouraging note, buy some groceries, lend a car, provide a guest room for a friend, host a party, fix a faucet, send a thoughtful text, appear in court, meaningful touch, check-in with a friend, write a reference, clean a house, sit in a waiting room, call around for estimates, pay for a repair, assemble IKEA furniture (Uugghh!), organize a moving party, throw a birthday party, remember details, foster-parenting, rides to the airport, gift certificates, ask thoughtful questions, stay current with a friend, call first, rally help from others, pay an overdue bill, provide an evening out for a single mom, invite a single friend over for a holiday, listen . . . just listen.

When I talk about this with leaders, I tell them that caregiving is all about actively meeting someone's need. It's as simple as that.

I have this silly quote I read to leaders about caregiving, "This is a lawn-mowing, wall-painting, food-fixing, car-repairing, rug-vacuuming, money-giving, baby-sitting kind of need meeting." Find out what's needed and then give that need some of your care.

Maybe you notice the wide range of caregiving in my "five-minute list." The range is so wide because the scope of human need is vast and specific. Honestly, it's often less about what you actually do, and more about how you show up. *That's the big idea, in fact, with caregiving:* it is showing up in someone's life *in a way that helps them with their real needs*. It starts with them, not with us, and we do this best when we pay attention, recognize a need and *simply show up* to rally help.

A Theology of "Showing Up"

Showing up is rooted in the gospel. I once heard Tim Keller summarize the gospel with these three words: manger, cross, and crown.[24]

Through the *manger* Jesus showed up in our world in human form. He didn't stay away, keep his distance or send someone else. He became one of us to begin the process of meeting our greatest need.

Then Jesus showed up on the *cross*. That's where we belonged—where we were destined to show up ourselves—but he stepped in and took our place. In the greatest act of showing up, Jesus substituted his life for ours. Tim Keller says the essence of the cross is substitution.[25] John Stott, in his classic book *The Cross of Christ*, writes that, "the essence of sin is man substituting himself for God, while the essence of salvation is God substituting himself for man. Man asserts himself against God and puts himself where only God deserves to be; God sacrifices himself for man and puts himself where only man deserves to be. Man claims prerogatives that belong to God alone; God accepts penalties that belong to man alone."[26]

Finally, Jesus rose from the dead and now wears a *crown* as the champion over death and Hell.[27] One day he will return with the armies of heaven to judge humankind and renew the world for his followers.[28] Until then he continues to show up at the right hand of God, representing us to the Father as our advocate of grace and acceptance.[29]

Jesus meets us right in the middle of the mess we've made of this world and our lives. He comes to us—he shows up—because we have an essential need that we can never handle on our own. It's like he tells us, "It's my life for yours. You owe, I'll pay." In that way, the manger-cross-crown gospel is the greatest act of caregiving the world will ever know. When we understand the gospel in this way and finally yield to his caregiving, something happens in us and we're forever changed.

In the next chapter we look at how our heart-change generates the kind of caregiving that helps loved ones transform and grow.

CAREGIVING BY "SHOWING UP"   12

Being rescued—I mean legitimately rescued, like you might not have made it without being saved—does something to you.

2019 marked the ten-year anniversary of the "Miracle on the Hudson" when captain Chelsea B. "Sully" Sullenberger successfully crash-landed an Airbus A320 on the icy Hudson River. It's an iconic rescue story because in that terrifying incident, one hundred and fifty-five people were utterly saved from certain death. Jet airliners don't simply fall out of the sky . . . and everyone survives. It's almost always the other way around, but not on that January afternoon in 2009. That day the plane still fell from the sky, but not a single soul was lost.

Have you ever considered what that flight was like for those on board? The entire flight lasted roughly four and a half minutes from takeoff at LaGuardia Airport to touchdown on the Hudson river. *Four and a half minutes!* I can't fill the gas tank in my truck in four and a half minutes. Pretty sure I can't even decide which show to watch on Netflix in four and a half minutes. But that's all the time those people had—four and a half minutes: 270 seconds.

One minute into that four-and-a-half-minute flight, the A320 flew into a flock of Canadian geese, causing the airliner to lose power in both engines. Passengers described it as a loud "bang" followed by a sound like tennis shoes in a dryer. At that point, nearly all the passengers knew they were in serious trouble, and within sixty seconds most were certain they were living the last minutes of their lives. One passenger quickly grabbed one of his business cards, scribbled a love note to his wife and children and then jammed the card deep into his pocket, hoping that rescuers would find it on his lifeless body and somehow get it to his family so they would know he was thinking of them in the last seconds of his life.

I don't mean to be morbid, and certainly not insensitive, but the last time I flew out of LaGuardia I couldn't help thinking about that doomed flight. In fact, I looked at my watch the moment the wheels of our plane left the runway. At sixty seconds I thought, "bird strike." Three and a half minutes later, after banking away from the airport and with Manhattan and the Hudson river still in view, I thought to myself, "touch down on the Hudson."

How significant is four and a half minutes in a lifetime of living? Assuming those passengers survive to a reasonable age of 75 years old, they will live over 39 million minutes. Over a lifetime, then, that four-and-a-half-minute flight amounts to roughly one ten-millionth of their lives. It's almost like a blink of the eye.

Have you heard what many of the passengers call that "miracle" day they survived on the Hudson? They refer to it as their second birthday—like they were born a second time into a completely different life. One passenger, Barry Leonard, claims, "It was a one-in-a-billion chance . . . that we're here today. So we feel like we're on our second life and we're 10 years old."[1] In fact, he calls the ten years since the crash landing a "ten-year bonus life."

All in all, most of the survivors on that plane talk about an overwhelming feeling of gratitude for being saved. They were spared that day through heroic action and allowed to live more of the minutes of their lives. But their gratitude goes beyond feeling; many have chosen to live their "second lives" guided by a new set of priorities.

Barry Leonard says that, "Without these people (i.e., the pilots, flight crew, and first responders), my children would not have had a father. My mom would not have had a son . . . Giving back became a mantra for my life. There is much I have done, with the help of others, and much more I plan to do."[2] Some survivors reevaluated their work/life balance and chose to take different jobs to have more time with family. Others sold houses and moved to be nearer loved ones. A few of the passengers have written books; others travel around the world speaking to thousands about reordering one's priorities in life. Bottom line? Not a single person on that plane claims that life is the same after landing on the Hudson that frigid winter day. Why? *Because being rescued from certain death changes you.*

When people understand the gospel—I mean when they truly grasp what Jesus wants to save them from and save them for—it changes their hearts. It's like realizing your plane is falling out of the sky, and you're living the last moments of your life. That's what life in this world is like against the backdrop of life in the next world. It's not just four and a half minutes out of a lifetime; it's all the days of your life on earth compared with all the days of life forever in the new heaven and new earth. Jesus says all those days of the second life are ours, if we want them.

As it turns out, the language the survivors of that flight use for their rescue is surprisingly close to the way Jesus describes the new life he offers to everyone. In the Gospel of John, Jesus tells Nicodemus he must be born again,[3] that he has to have a second birthday in order to start not a "bonus life," but his best life—the life his heart has always wanted.

It took a near-tragedy for the Hudson River survivors to realize the lives they were living weren't enough. Jesus takes it further: he tells us our lives apart from him simply aren't what we really want; that we need entirely new lives—the kind we only get through him.

Through the gospel, we discover we're offered life that never ends; a kind of life we've always longed for. If ten years of "bonus living" can radically change the lives of one hundred and fifty-five fortunate people, what happens in the human heart when we realize Jesus offers us a forever-life filled with the joy, adventure and meaning we were always meant to enjoy?

J.D. Greer writes, "The gospel is that Christ has suffered the full wrath of God for my sin. Jesus Christ traded places with me, living the perfect life I should have lived, and dying the death I had been condemned to die. Second Corinthians 5:21 says that he actually *became* my sin so that I could literally *become* His righteousness. Saint Athanasius called this 'the great exchange.' He took my record, died for it, and offers me His perfect record in return. He took my shameful nakedness to clothe me with His righteousness."[4]

The Propulsion of Grace[5]

This *great exchange* births a grace narrative in our hearts when we choose to follow Jesus. When we accept Jesus' offer of new life, we're actually receiving what only he deserves. This is a wildly outlandish offer that makes no sense in our transactional world. We're not only rescued from certain death, but we also trade places with our rescuer who then dies in our place. Once again, it's his life for ours.

Understanding this grace narrative changes the way we see ourselves, others around us, and God himself. We begin to live a different story—the grace story of the gospel. In living out this story, our identity begins to change from what the apostle Paul describes in Galatians as a status-shift from slavery to family.[6] In time we begin to see ourselves as daughters and sons of God himself, enjoying the full status and privilege of family. We start to accurately believe this is what God has always wanted for us. We come to see we belong to God in a way that can only happen through the gospel . . . and that changes everything for us.

In gospel terms, this the "propulsion of grace." The gospel creates new desires in the human heart. The reality of the gospel makes us want to do better and be better—we want to love like we've been loved. Jesus becomes not only the focus of our gratitude, but also the object of our affection. We simply want to become more like the One who loved us and rescued us with his own life. When we come to understand the scale of his rescuing and saving, we're propelled forward into change and growth. We not only become someone new, we start behaving like that new person.

At Serge—formerly World Harvest Mission—they say the gospel nudges us forward, changing the way we live. They write, "The [gospel] renewal that God is bringing into your life leads somewhere. There's a push behind it. There's propulsion in it."[7]

Following Jesus is an inward heart-movement of grace and acceptance that results in an outward life-movement of love for God and others. J.D. Greer, in his book *Gospel*, shares a "Gospel Prayer" he prays every day. I pray it too, because it helps me stay clear on Jesus' love, and how his grace heals and satisfies my heart. Here are the four parts of his prayer. Take your time with these:

1. "In Christ, there is nothing I can do that would make You love me more, and nothing I have done that makes You love me less."

2. "Your presence and approval are all I need for everlasting joy."

3. "As You have been to me, so I will be to others."

4. "As I pray, I will measure Your compassion by the cross and Your power by the resurrection."[8]

The *first two parts* of J.D.'s prayer focus us inward, helping us connect to the reality of God's unconditional grace and acceptance.

When we live in Jesus' love, we experience joy and contentment we can't find anywhere else. Jesus calls this the abundant life,[9] and it becomes our normal life as our dependence on him grows.

The *third part* of the prayer reveals what happens in a heart that has been changed by the gospel. When we finally know we are loved and accepted by Jesus, we want to love and accept others. This is the natural pivot in the heart of Jesus followers. Because of the contentment and joy we find in Jesus, our hearts naturally turn away from "me-first" living to "you-first" living. We no longer need to scrape and scratch to get ours, because what Jesus gives us is infinitely better than anything we might gather on our own.

These are the mechanics of caregiving in the hearts of Jesus followers. This is how the transformation goes from care-keeping to generous caregiving.

Finally, the *fourth part* of the prayer, I believe, moves us to audacious acts of faith and generosity—all because of the realities of parts one and two and the heart-change of part three. The compassion of the cross and the power of the resurrection together act as a launch pad for great and risky acts of kingdom living.

Caregiving as "Showing Up"

When we're changed by the gospel, it gets hard to keep our distance from people. This makes sense, when you think about it. In the gospel we're not believing a "what" necessarily, we're believing a "who." The gospel is that Jesus, the Son of God, closed the distance and came near to us. Since Jesus didn't keep his distance, neither do we.

Caregiving happens best when you show up in someone's life and help them with their needs. That's it: simply show up and do the right thing—the thing Jesus would do in your place. If you didn't catch anything else, this would be enough.

Showing up Is Burden-Bearing

At the end of Paul's letter to the Galatians, he tells them to "Carry each other's burdens, and in this way you will fulfill the law of Christ."[10] However, a few verses later, he also tells them, "each one should carry their own load."[11] Wait! What!? Carry burdens, but not loads? Just hold onto that second thought for a bit and we will get back to it. For now, let's stay focused on Paul's burden-bearing idea.

The common meaning for the word "burden" in the original language is *one's body weight*. If Paul was being literal here, he would be saying, "When things are so hard that someone collapses under the weight of their own body, climb under their arms and carry them along."

Years ago, I trained as a rescue diver. Part of our training was to stabilize an injured diver on the surface of the water and then bring them out onto dry land. That meant carrying fellow students, as dead weight, out of the surf and on to the beach. That's what Paul's word means literally—to bear the body weight of another. But Paul isn't being literal.

The word "burden" in this verse is a metaphor. Paul is referring to things in our lives that are heavy, like an unconscious body is heavy. My father died when I was twenty-five, taking with him all the chances I would ever have to finally win his approval. We have friends who had a fire in their building, ruining their furniture and making their home suddenly unlivable. A single mom in our church who has two young daughters was diagnosed with an aggressive and debilitating cancer. I know a man whose son went missing. A young couple on our staff team lost their infant son to a senseless congenital disease. Like an unconscious body, these are heavy burdens that are virtually impossible to carry on our own, and Paul says we're not meant to.

Now think about that "burden" metaphor a bit—what it means and what it asks of us. Someone has a pain, fear, crisis, obligation, or need that has become too heavy for them to carry on their own. Helping with that burden means we move in close and give some full-contact care. It means we have to go "hands on" with some of the heavy things in that person's life.

If I were to actually carry you, I would have to grab hold, get my hips underneath me, and push hard with my legs to lift you off the ground. As a former wrestler, I've done that about a million times and I can tell you, there's nothing dainty about it. I can also tell you, I can't do any of that lifting from a distance—I must step in close and make contact.

Paul tells us there's a law we satisfy when we step into someone's life and help with heavy burdens. He says, "in this way you will fulfill the law of Christ." That's such an interesting phrase: "the law of Christ." It only appears twice in the Bible, both times in Paul's writing.[12] Paul is pointing back to Jesus' own words when he was confronted by a religious leader who asked which commandment was the greatest. Jesus answered, saying we are to love God and love our neighbors.[13]

It's significant that Paul would link Jesus' command to love with active burden-bearing like this. Paul seems to think we're very much like Jesus when we show up with others and help them with what's too heavy in their lives.

A life-changing community looks needy because it's safe enough to reveal needs, and because the people in it are generous with their care. What emerges from that neediness is burden-bearing and generosity. Let me hit this one more time: caregiving isn't a technique or system to soft-hack someone's heart. It is active kindness from a heart that's been shaped and changed by the care and grace of an outrageously loving God. Caregiving people, in life-changing communities, view their resources—their time, money, possessions, skills, and gifts—as kingdom resources, and they leverage those resources for kingdom purposes. In those communities, when life gets really heavy, the people get really close.

Showing up Starts with Them, Not with Us

My wife, Co, once told me, "Please, don't ever buy me a big diamond." "Okay!" I said, "You got it. No diamonds." Whew, that was a close one—it could've gone the other way.

Here's the thing, Co doesn't have much jewelry because it's just not a big deal to her. She has virtually no jewelry from me, because I know that receiving gifts is not one of the ways she feels loved.

So, no big diamonds for Co, but I cook her dinner most nights and clean up the dishes when we're done. I also take her car and scooter to the gas station when they're low on fuel, because I know she hates pumping gas. I keep the house clean and make our bed most days too. When something needs fixing, I try very hard to get on it quickly. When she has a "honey do" item on her list, I try to knock it out right away. *I do all these things, and others, because I know my wife feels loved when I do things for her.* Understand that I'm not special because I do these things; she is special to me, so I do these things. She believes she matters to me when I take care of our needs, which is great news to me because I'm trying to make a point—I intend for her to know that I love her more than anyone on the planet.

This is how caregiving works too, especially because it's an act of love. It doesn't start with my preferences, agenda, or even my resources. I like to think it starts best with their needs, their timing, their solution, and in their way. That's the place to start with our care, though it doesn't always remain there. Sometimes our caregiving changes after we jump in to help out, but starting with their needs bestows respect and dignity to loved ones, and shows that we take them seriously. They may or may not know what they really need, but starting with their assessment gets the caregiving process off on the right foot.

There is a saying, "Unsolicited advice is criticism." Well, if that's true—and I think it is—then unsolicited caregiving may be intrusion. Getting permission for caregiving may seem like an unnecessary step, but it's not. It creates buy-in for the help you're offering and cooperation from the one you're helping. Sometimes people are not ready to receive care, and at those times it's a huge gift when we simply remain close, available and ready to go.

If you don't know it yet, it's possible to give care in ways that aren't helpful. That usually happens when we don't step in close to find out what effective caregiving looks like for a unique person in a specific scenario.

I recently saw a report on catastrophic aid that pours in after natural disasters. Apparently, agencies know that a part of the aid process often involves dealing with truckloads of donations that don't actually help anyone. Take clothing for example. People instinctively want to send tons of clothes when a hurricane decimates a region. The big problem, I understand, is that there's no infrastructure in place for the massive job of processing the clothing and then distributing it to people. So it piles up, gets in the way and rots—and then the already troubled community has yet another problem to deal with.

We deliver some of our best care when we decide ahead of time not to allow our own context or our personal history to determine our caregiving with people in need. Showing up happens best when we start with them, not with us.

Showing up by Following Through

Years ago, I was a handyman for about a minute. I've always been handy around the house so one time between careers I decided to be handy for a living. It didn't really turn out well, because apparently I'm a horrible businessman. I was fine with the work, but every customer seemed to need a deal, so they got one. Good for them, bad for me. But I digress.

One thing I didn't struggle with was getting customers. I found out all I needed to do was: (1) show up and (2) finish the job. Seems pretty straightforward, right? Well I guess it's not, because I was shocked to find out how many of my handymen competitors didn't do those two things. Many agreed to take on a job and then never showed up, or they agreed to do a job, bought materials, started the job and then never came back to finish the job . . . or get paid. That's when I often stepped in and followed through on a job someone else had started.

Failing to follow through is one of those things that make a hard situation harder. Follow-through is the completion of a declared promise, the fulfillment of a pledge to help someone struggling with their heavy things. Since burdened people live under the weight of their difficult lives, they get their hopes up when promises are spoken and plans are made. That hope is a lift; their lives actually feel lighter because the difficulty is coming to an end. And then it doesn't! All the struggle and pain they carried before the promised care comes crashing back, along with the added weight of disappointment from failed follow-through.

Lack of follow-through diminishes a leader's influence faster than maybe anything else. When we don't come through on promises to help, people rightly believe they can't rely on us. When we become known for that, it's like turning down the volume on our influence. We can still lead and show the way, and people may still listen to us, but they're likely to keep their distance emotionally to protect against disappointment. People may still follow, but our leadership is muted and diminished.

I haven't met anyone yet who trusts a handyman who doesn't follow through on their word. So my handyman pro-tip is simply this: follow through. That's it; that's the secret I discovered to having plenty of customers.

That's my caregiving pro-tip too. Saying you want to help someone with their heavy things, and then never showing up to help, is worse than not saying anything at all. I'm not saying don't offer help. I'm saying offer help . . . and then help.

What Caregiving Isn't . . .

Let me do this quickly. Here are some of the things that will cause a breakdown in your caregiving, or turn it into something entirely different.

- *Caregiving is not helping outside your span of care.* If you've forgotten what "span of care" is, go back and check out chapter two real quick. There is an appropriate size and scope when it comes to the number of people you give your care to, because your personal resources aren't limitless. You cannot help all the people you know who have needs, even if they have really big needs. You aren't automatically required to deliver care outside the scope of your leadership unless you're clear that God is asking for that. I know what unlimited caregiving looks like, because it almost took me out completely. When we give in to unreasonable pressure like that, we not only experience burnout, we also take our care from those who deserve it most.

- *Caregiving is not "doing it all" on your own.* I saved this until now so you didn't minimize all that I've written about so far, but this is a really big deal. Remember Ivana, the young lady I wrote about earlier, who received help from our small group? It was our small group that did the helping, not just me. I helped out, for sure, but we held the weight of her burden together. Sometimes I find myself "directing traffic" by connecting resources to the people who need them. At other times I'm the one delivering the care. But very rarely, almost never, am I doing all the caregiving on my own.

- *Caregiving is not carrying someone else's load.* Remember that in Galatians chapter six, Paul tells us to carry each other's "burdens" and then three verses later he says to carry our own "load." You can think of this as the difference between a truckload and a backpack. "Burdens" are heavy like a truckload, but "loads" are light like a backpack. In fact, "load" is used in ancient literature to describe the pack a soldier carried. In that way, one's "load" is the weight of what you need for living your normal life, day to day. That means, under normal conditions, we need to pull our own weight. It's a mistake—and not caregiving—when we pull the weight of someone else's daily responsibilities, when they can do that for themselves.

- *Caregiving is not owning someone else's problem.* Even though we are to carry burdens for each other, Paul never tells us to make someone else's burdens our own. Giving care is a decision and a gift, not an acquisition. When we give care we are contributors to the solution, not the new owners of the problem. Someday we may have a burden too heavy to carry. When that happens, we may receive help from others, but we don't quitclaim those burdens to our helpers. The burden still belongs to us, and we remain the ultimate owners of the solution.

- *Caregiving is not enabling bad or irresponsible behavior.* Irresponsible living is "dropping the ball" and expecting someone else to catch it. Caregiving gone wrong is when we keep catching the balls that someone else keeps dropping. When we do that, our caregiving goes from helping to hurting, because the "ball dropper" never feels the consequences of their bad choices. We all make mistakes and sometimes it's right to come to the rescue when that happens. But when it becomes a pattern, the most loving thing we can do is to allow someone to know what it feels like when their ball hits the ground.

This isn't a complete list, for sure, but it's important that we balance the caregiving equation with some reality. If we met as a group, I'm sure we could come up with a more comprehensive list, but allow this to get you started.

Finally: Heaven or Hell?

Ultimately, this is all about mutual caregiving. It's hard to give my care to you when I'm worried about having enough of it for myself and my family. Must it be that way, though? What if there wasn't a shortage of care in the family of God? What if we watched each other's backs before we watched our own? What if our reflex was mutual and reciprocal caregiving, before self-caregiving?

Years ago I was thinking about how to punctuate this idea and a story came to me.[14] It goes like this: One day, an angel appeared to a man walking along the road. Realizing he was in the presence of an angel, the man asked what heaven and hell are like. The angel responded, "Let me show you."

The angel takes the man to hell first. He is surprised to see that hell is a huge banquet hall filled with tables extending as far as the eye can see. The people in hell gather around the tables, each of which is piled high with all manner of decadent and delicious foods. Whatever the people desire, whenever they desire it, that food appears in front of them at their table.

As the man looks closer, however, he sees the people are in anguish. They're emaciated and weak, many weeping uncontrollably as they struggle, yet fail, to eat the delicacies in front of them. The problem is their hands. As extensions of their arms, they have three-foot-long spoons where their hands used to be. They reach the food with their spoons and lift the food from the platters, but because the spoons are too long, they're never able to place the food in their mouths. The angel explains to the man this is their plight for all eternity.

Then the angel takes the man to heaven. When he arrives, he is shocked at what he sees. It's the exact same scene he saw moments ago in hell: a massive banquet hall with countless tables piled high with the best food imaginable, all surrounded by people with three-foot long spoons where they once had hands.

But the people—this is where the story turns—oh the people, they bubble with joy and contentment. They live a celebration of friendship and fun as they feast on the food piled in front of them. The people are filled, healthy and thriving. Then the angel says to the man, "This is their blessed great fortune, forever and ever." *End of story.*

When I share this story with leaders, I always pause at this point and ask, "What is the difference between heaven and hell?" And every single time, nearly everyone in the room answers, "In heaven they feed each other."

Yep, that's it, that's the right answer. We all seem to understand this right away. I've got a real knack for the obvious, I guess.

After all these years, I admit this story is a bit corny (maybe a lot corny), but I love how, in it, our hearts are the difference between heaven and hell. This is just a story, and you won't find it anywhere in the Bible, but I think it says something that's true about the human heart. I think we get to decide how caregiving is going to work in our communities and in our relationships. It's not too much to say that every day we get to choose: heaven or hell, us-first or me-first, mutual or exclusive, care-giving or care-keeping.

We do some of our very best shepherding when we cause caregiving to be released in our communities. Jesus prayed to our

Father, "Your kingdom come, your will be done, on earth as it is in heaven." What starts in the God-community of heaven can continue here on earth. Jesus showed us that. *When our loved ones begin to see caregiving as a normal part of life, they open their lives to healthy people.* They also become more like the One who made them. And the fear of being hacked by predators gets replaced with reasonable hope and trust, all because of the active love they receive from you and me.

PART THREE

*Creating the Life-Changing
Conditions—a Primer*

WEAR IT, ASK FOR IT, AND SEE & SAY IT

13

"*Sooo . . . what are we doing again?*"

This is one of my least favorite questions ever, because when I get it I know it means one of two things: I haven't been as clear as I need to be, or the instructions I've given are incomplete, or both . . . usually both. Bottom line, when this question comes up, I haven't given people enough information to take next steps.

Here's the ironic part. For nearly ten years I taught thousands of leaders the five conditions in this book and stopped right there, expecting them to create those conditions on their own. It's kind of like a football coach who draws up a couple dozen plays on the white board just before kickoff and then sends his team onto the field to run those plays in a game. That was me all those years, describing the life-changing conditions and then sending leaders into the real world to figure out how to create them.

Many of those leaders came back to me puzzled about how to bring these conditions to life in their relationships. In their own way, they were simply asking, "What is it, again, I'm supposed to do now?"

I'm embarrassed to admit, at first I was a little baffled. I thought, "What do you mean 'What are we doing now?'" We're doing what we've been talking about this whole time. You know, those five things? Safety, truth, vulnerability, affirmation, and caregiving? Create those in the world you live in, with the people you love and lead.

Pretty simple, huh? Not exactly.

Essentially, they were telling me they understood the five conditions, and recognized those conditions when they saw them in the real world. But they were not clear about how to create them on their own. I had to help leaders not just understand the conditions, but also explain how to bring them to life in the communities they led.

It's Not Rocket Science

Creating the five conditions isn't rocket science; just about anyone can do it, but that doesn't make it easy. In fact, the simplicity of the structure can be deceiving. This kind of culture doesn't make itself; you will have to put in the work to create it. That said, even though it requires effort, don't forget that creating this culture is absolutely worth doing. Remember, these conditions are what we all want— they are what our hearts are made for.

Explaining the conditions to leaders was the right place to start all those years ago. You can't do a thing unless you understand what that thing is. I simply needed to take the next step and walk them through the install process. That might be what you need too.

By now, you know all about these conditions that foster change and growth in others, but how do you create those conditions? I have a short and long answer to that question, or better said, a "getting started guide" and a bigger "full manual" version of the instructions.

What I provide in this chapter and the next is the getting started guide you need to begin creating life-changing conditions. And by the way, I've already finished my companion book to this one—so the full installation manual is on the way. But there's no need to wait on creating conditions for growth, because what you read here is plenty to get you going.

I've broken down the next steps into five parts, using five action statements you can begin practicing right away. Keep in mind, however, there's a chronological order to the steps, so be sure to start at the beginning and work your way through. Another way to think about this is that there's an order for *starting the steps*, not completing them—because we never stop doing any of these if we want to sustain the right conditions for life change. I think you'll understand completely after you read through them.

Okay, let's jump in and start creating!

1. Wear It: Be the Person You're Helping Others Become

The big idea behind "wearing it" is that we generally add things to our lives that we see working well for others. The thought goes something like this, "That looks good on you, that really works for you, that is a great solution for you. *I wonder if it works for me too?*" And then we try it out. We "put on" what is working for someone else to see how it "fits" on us.

We all seem to be looking for options, upgrades, solutions, or recommendations that make life work better. Where are we looking? To each other, of course. Just think about online reviews, for example—Yelp in particular. I love reading about "five-star" experiences—in fact, I rarely go to restaurants with average reviews lower than four stars. It's hard to choose a three-star business when there are so many four- and five-star options.

About six months ago my wife realigned her life around specific fitness goals. She has had great success with her new routine, and it's a simple routine at that. Her plan involves three things: at least ten thousand steps a day, quality nutritious meals during the week, and strategic cheat meals on the weekend. Her results have been fantastic. They've been so great, in fact, I've decided to make some healthy changes of my own—all because I've seen Co's plan work so well in her life.

This is how we are!

One study in social learning I recently came across compared two groups of chimpanzees given juice boxes:

> "The first group dipped the straw into the juice box, and then sucked on the small amount of juice at the end of the straw. The second group sucked through the straw directly, getting much more juice. When the first group, the 'dippers,' observed the second group, 'the suckers,' what do you think happened? All of the 'dippers' in the first group switched to sucking through the straws directly. By simply observing the other chimps and modeling their behavior, they learned that this was a more efficient method of getting juice."[1]

Again, this is naturally what we do too. When we see behavior in others that works better than our own, we switch to the improved way of living—we stop being "dippers" and become "suckers."

When something looks good on you—when it yields great results in your life—people naturally want to "put that on" in their own lives. That makes you a walking, talking, breathing life-review, informing people about what does and does not work.

The key, then, is wearing the right things. Show people the true benefit of living out the five life-changing conditions. Live them. Rely on them. Display them. Become a living context for the growth and maturity you're pointing people toward.

Begin with Yourself

In common language, I'm simply urging you to model what you hope to see and develop in the people you love and lead. Brené Brown writes about this in the context of parenting, claiming, "the question isn't so much 'Are you parenting the right way?' as it is: 'Are you the adult that you want your child to grow up to be?'"[2] So who are you hoping your loved ones will become? Start becoming that person yourself, and then display that to the people around you.

I'm talking about living toward your picture of maturity, but I'm not talking about perfection. We don't have to live perfectly, but all of us can live out our aspirational life pursuits in front of others. Do that, and you're "wearing it."

Live right in the center of your own growth process, welcoming loved ones into that part of your life. Allow them to see and know your transformational journey—allow them to walk with you as you walk with them. In a sentence, walk intentionally on your journey of growth and invite people to come with you.

Will You Allow Me to Need Us?

In an earlier chapter I wrote about a specific kind of group I've led over the years—I call them turbo groups. A turbo group is an accelerated, need-based group created to equip high-capacity leaders for a specific initiative. Here in San Diego, I live eight miles from the Navy Seal training base. A turbo group is like BUD/S training (i.e., Navy Seal training) for leaders in the church. I'm kind of not kidding.

There are two prerequisites for getting into a turbo group. New members must: (1) Credit us (those of us in the group) with relational safety we haven't earned yet, because we're going to move way faster—relationally—than we would in a typical small group; and (2) Agree to create a life-changing group of their own when the turbo group concludes. Then we all lock arms and step off the cliff into the richest community ever—it's thrilling.

But someone still has to "go first" in the turbo group, so that's what I do. On night one, after we've had a great meal together, shared a little about our lives, and talked about expectations, I tell everyone my life story—because I think they deserve it. I start at the beginning and finish at the end, including much of the pain, struggle, failure, and downside I've lived. I also talk about some of the fun, good, and helpful episodes of my life. Bottom line, I try to provide a brief but unvarnished version of my pathway through life, and then I make a request.

After my story, I look every person in the eyes and ask, "Now . . . will you allow me to need this group?" This is what I wear—what I put on—from the very beginning. Right up front, I ask for their permission to be my normal, authentic self in the group, just like everyone else. I cannot exist in community artificially, so I have to bring both my upside and my downside to the group. I understand I'm the leader of the group, but I lead best from the center of the community—not from a distance. For me, that means bringing some of my own growth areas and hurts to the group as a fully functioning member.

And then I make another request. I look everyone in the eyes again and ask, "And will you allow yourself to need this group, just like me?"

"This is your unique opportunity," I tell them, "to really go for it and push the envelope on change and growth. How often in life will you be in a community like this with a bunch of leaders like all of you?"

I want them to know they don't always have to be strong and put together. I tell them I've accepted both my strengths and my weaknesses, and that my weak parts don't nullify my strong parts. Finally I say, "So if you aren't completely sufficient, strong and competent all the time, we will simply know you're just like the rest of us." What a powerful moment for everyone; I wish you could see the relief on their faces.

Give Your Loved Ones a Gift

All of us wear some behavior or lifestyle—none of us wear nothing. Since you always model something with your life, I'm asking you to be intentional about what you put on. Modeling happens either by default or on purpose. Why not give a gift to your loved ones by starting here, and simply live toward the life you hope they too will live? After all, if you won't wear it, why in the world would they?

2. Ask for It: Get Permission to Influence Loved Ones

Have you ever known someone who smiles when they talk about their painful moments? There are subliminal reasons for smiles like these, but when we experience them with someone it's possible to misjudge what's going on in their heart. I made that misjudgment early on in one of the turbo groups I led.

We were sharing around the circle, each of us responding to one of my riskier get-to-know-you questions. When the conversation came to Diane (not her real name), she briefly shared a recent painful experience, all the while holding a big smile on her face. I misunderstood her response completely and fired off a wisecrack—turning the room to ice.

The rest of the group knew Diane very well, understanding that when she shares hurtful experiences, the bigger her smile, the deeper her pain. I missed that completely and, with one sarcastic comment, flooded the room with mistrust and relational danger. It was so bad, in fact, one of the guys confronted me immediately, essentially telling me what I said was out of line and that I had done real damage to the safety in the group. I was stunned—what did I just do? And what was I going to do next?

I knew there was no reason to keep going with my plans for the evening, because I had decimated the foundation of my influence with the group. All I could think to do was admit my error and start the rebuilding process that very moment. No other option made any sense.

So I turned to Diane and said, "My comment was insensitive and wrong and because of it, I don't deserve your trust. I'm so sorry, will you consider giving me another chance to earn back your trust? Will you give 'us'—this turbo group experience—another chance?" Then I turned to the rest of the group and said, "I've legitimately lost your trust too—will you consider allowing me to re-earn my influence in this group? Will you consider giving me another chance to shepherd?" In a word, I was asking, again, for *permission* to lead.

Over the years I've held this story in my heart as a consummate example of what leaders must have if they are going to shepherd others. Shepherding is an inside job, so it only works when we gain access to the hearts of followers. This is where the whole leadership thing gets tricky, because we only get into someone's life when they allow it—which means we only really get to influence people with their permission. Moreover, our influence can be revoked at any moment if followers close the door on their lives. Either way— influence or exclusion—they get to decide.

Permission Can Be Hard to Swallow

This truism about permission is tough for many leaders to accept. The objection usually goes something like, "Wait a minute, you're telling me I have to *get permission* to sacrifice and give my time, effort, and energy to help someone change and grow?" Yep, that's exactly what I'm saying, because that's how our hearts work.

The hard reality is there are plenty of things you can expect or demand as a leader, but influence isn't one of them. I spend a chapter in my next book breaking down the difference between compliance and growth. The short answer is you can force people to comply—if you have power over them—but you cannot force someone to grow. That's how it works with influence too: you may coerce people into certain behaviors, but you'll never force your way into a single human heart.

Here's how I write about influence and permission:

"All of this is about the current status of our relationships with loved ones. Followers decide if we are safe to follow. They determine if we can be trusted with the truth about their lives. They get to say who is allowed into the private areas of their hearts. *We leaders are entitled to none of this.* We don't simply deserve access, as a function of our existence, even if we carry with us many of the solutions our followers need.

The human heart has an autonomic kill-switch that denies access if we're perceived unsafe, even if the reasons seem irrational. That's the part of the human heart you can't bully. In fact, the harder you push, control, and cajole, if you're barging in, the heart simply squeezes down tighter on itself.

You don't need permission to control anyone you have power over, if power is what you're going for. But you will never influence a single soul without their consent."

Two Kinds of Permission—Ambient and Active

Generally, there are two kinds of permission from followers, and we need them both—usually in a particular order. Before permission can be active it has to be ambient. In other words, our permission exists in the environment before it can show up in our active leadership with people. Let me break this down.

1. Ambient Permission: Permission Always Starts with Relationship

What comes to mind when you think of the word "ambient"? How about the word "ambiance"? Both of these words come from the same Latin root, *ambiens*, which means "to go or be around." That means these words refer to what is all around us—like sound, air temperature, wind, or light and darkness.

Relationship is the ambiance of permission; it is the context for our influence with loved ones. With it, we're free to join them in the details of their lives. Without it, we're left out, walking at a distance, cut off from their joys and concerns, and simply observing as they go about their lives.

What precedes permission is a request. If you have permission from someone, it's because you asked for it. The first ask of shepherding is always relational. In fact, our relationship with followers is not just the environment of our shepherding, it's the very foundation of it.

This means relationship is always the place to start—and stay—with those we lead. It is the essential first request of every parent, teacher, pastor, manager, or coach who desires to help others change and grow. If you take permission seriously, begin right here and never leave. For me, If I'm not creating a relationship, I'm cultivating, deepening, and strengthening the ones I already have. I'm either getting my ambient permission or I'm working to deepen it.

There are all kinds of things you can do to build a relationship, and we don't have the space here to break that all down. In chapter one I wrote at length about relational leadership, and I have more on that coming soon. Feel free to go back and refresh yourself on the difference between "positional" and "relational" leaders. Think, too, about the deeper relationships you already have. How did those begin and deepen? How do you "show up" in those relationships to make them safe and meaningful? What do you do to keep the relationship current and moving toward intimacy? How do relationships start and strengthen? If we we're sitting together, those are some of the questions I'd love to hear you talk about.

But just remember, if you want to become an insider with those you lead, this is absolutely the place to start. In fact, I'm not sure how shepherding works at all without the pulling-power of a safe and truthful relationship.

2. Active Permission: Asking the Right Questions

Questions are the language of permission. Instructions are not. Neither are commands.

Becoming fluent in the language of permission usually requires a shift in the way we understand learning and growth. The most life-changing truths are the ones we tell ourselves. That's simply how human learning and transformation work best. But that's not how it often works in culture today. Our systems are set up to deliver information rather than help people see and speak truth to themselves. Recognizing objective truth—about our own lives and life in general—and then putting that truth into words impacts us in a way we would never understand from being told what to do, or "instructed" on how life works.

Questions create the kinds of conversation that allow people to tell themselves the truth. We help with this by being intentional with our language. Instead of starting with instructions or explaining how life works, we simply begin asking honest, non-manipulative questions. Allow me to offer a few question-asking examples:

- **Ask about their experience:** "How was that for you? How did that make you feel when they said . . . when that happened . . . when you found that out?"

- **Ask about their intentions:** "What do you think you're going to do? What do you want to do now? What were you going for when you said/did that? How is the Holy Spirit weighing in on this? Are you sensing him nudging you?"

- **Ask if they need help:** "Would you like another opinion on that? Would it help to talk about that sometime? Would you like someone to weigh in on your big idea?"

- **Ask about what you think you see:** "Did I offend you when I said/did that the other day? I wonder if you're headed toward burnout; am I seeing that right? If I have a concern, would you want to know?"

- **Ask continuation questions:** "Is this still important to you? Do you want to continue with this idea and strategy, or are you looking for a change? Can I check in with you about what we talked about last week—are you up for that?"

- **Ask for future permission:** (When someone takes a big risk and shares important stuff, I always want back into that conversation again. So I ask for it.) "Would it be okay if we talk about this again? Can I check in with you on this in a few weeks? If I think I see this trend again, can we have another conversation?"

- **Ask for another chance when you make a mistake, like I did with Diane in the turbo group:** "Will you give me another chance? What would another chance look like to you? Can you help me understand where I went wrong with you? What would I have to do to make our relationship safer/better for you?"

I don't carry cue cards with all my best questions, because I'm not looking for techniques to trick people into saying the "right thing." I just know that honest questions, from a curious and intentional heart, help loved ones see the truth in their lives in a powerful way. Asking these questions also strengthens my permission with them. But simply telling them what to do chips away at my influence, one swing of my opinion at a time.

3. See It & Say It: Recognize and Talk About Growth Areas

I used to be a professional tide-pooler. (There's no such thing really—*but there should be!*)

Like many ocean cities, we have hundreds of tidepools along our San Diego beaches, and my sons and I have climbed all around them, looking for crawly creatures.

I became a professional because tide-pooling was an essential part of my paternal job description when my boys were young. I wasn't just one of the thousands of amateur tide-poolers— also called "tourists"—that my sons and I competed with on the weekends. We took it seriously. We got wet. We carried equipment. We got on our bellies and reached into crevices no reasonable person would consider. And if we had to, we even took a little wave-swell over the back from time to time. It's what professionals do.

But I like to give back now and then, so if you want it, I have a tide-pooling pro-tip for you. Here it is: *polarized sunglasses.* No joke, it's as simple as that. This was our secret edge that allowed us to find all the cool critters, and also kept most of the tourists moving along. By switching out our sunglasses, we eliminated the glare on the water—making invisible sea creatures visible. *You're welcome!*

As it turns out, this little recreational life-hack also has a link to the real world. There are things in our lives we can't see until we put on the practices that make them visible. The good news is, anyone can do this—and there's no equipment required. What are those practices? It all comes down to *seeing* and *saying.*

If You Want to See, You're Going to Have to Look

We start seeing the truth about ourselves when we begin looking—though looking is far from automatic. In fact, for many of us, not looking may come way more naturally than looking. It's my experience that—consciously or not—we contrive all sorts of distractions and emotional mechanisms to keep from seeing what's true of our lives. For example, I will never read my bathroom scale if I continue to find reasons not to step on to it. Which means I may also miss signs of something more serious, like a glitchy thyroid or early signs of diabetes. When we choose not to look, that's when the "degree of difficulty" in life becomes a legitimate problem—because not looking does nothing to change reality we hope to avoid.

If you remember, my controlling idea throughout this book is that the Holy Spirit is shining his spotlight on growth areas in our lives. As our internal counselor and guide, he wants to shape and grow our hearts so that we become like Jesus. Simply put, he is always helping us see the truth.

Seeing is the key to growing. You can't transform what you can't see, what you don't know is there, or what you're unwilling to look at. When we help loved ones willingly look up and see what's true of their lives, they take their first active step of transformation.

What Makes the Unseen Seen?

Think of it like this: there is something like a "glare" on the surface of our lives that makes it difficult to see our deeper, more consequential truths. We can be a little "shiny" I guess, a little hard to see because of the way we settle into proper culture—however that culture is defined from day to day. When we simply try to fit in and find our spot in the world, some of our true self often gets pushed out of sight, hidden beneath the reflective surface of our lives. But that won't do if we desire transformation. Growing always comes back to seeing and responding to who we really are, and none of that happens without clarity.

If you want to see loved ones more clearly and help them know what's true of their lives, there are practices you can add to your leadership. These practices are the shepherding version of switching to polarized sunglasses. Here are three of those practices you can put on right away:

1. **Decide to notice what's not obvious in others.**

   Seeing what's not obvious in someone's life is a decision. When you make that decision you activate an "observational" part of your brain stem that otherwise remains dormant (more on that in a moment).

   If you make this decision, you're not deciding *what* you will notice, you're simply deciding *to* notice. This is what we do when we truly want to know who, and how, our loved ones are. It's a decision to focus intentionally and gather the information in front of you—information that requires some effort to collect.

   It's easiest to focus on our own lives; in fact that's the field of view we're born with, but it requires purpose and determination to see others well. So you will have to decide to notice what's true of your loved ones, if you're going to see them at all.

2. **Keep noticing what's not obvious in others. Pay attention.**

   Deciding to notice isn't a one-time deal if you want to shepherd the hearts of others. When we decide to keep noticing over time, it's called "paying attention."

   Quite simply, paying attention is sustained focus and contemplation. It is looking long enough to see what you see and then attaching language and meaning to your observation. After we've paid attention well, we should be able to say, "This is what I think I see, and this is what I think it means." And then we confirm our observations with those we lead.

This practice of paying attention is one of the reasons I love the shepherding metaphor so much. Shepherds never stop paying attention to their sheep. In fact, sheep are so dependent on the focus and care of the shepherd, they would nearly cease to exist without him. Simply put, to shepherd well is to pay attention over time. This is the gift of attention we give loved ones when we keep noticing what's true of their lives.

3. **Focus your attention on what needs noticing most.**
There is a bundle of nerves in your brainstem called the reticular activating system (I said we'd get back to this). The word "reticular" is an adjective describing anything netlike.[3] A spider web is the reticular net a spider uses to catch flies. I pull fish out of the water with a reticular device called a fishing net. And our minds become reticular when we choose to see fundamental truths in the life of a loved one.

Your reticular activating system alerts your mind to the things you want to pick out and notice all around you. It's something like a mental "net" that our minds use to recognize and gather up certain ideas or events we deem important. Since we can't focus on everything with equal intensity, our minds are designed to help us see what we value most.

"Whatever you're looking for is what you see everywhere." I recently heard that on a podcast about how people view culture at large. Another way to say this is, "Whatever's important to you is what you end up noticing all around you."

You may not realize it, but we do this all the time in everyday life. When I started driving my Toyota truck, I began seeing similar trucks everywhere I went. Before that, all those trucks were "invisible" to me. I recently shopped online for a particular computer bag. Guess what I notice everywhere now? Yep, you got it. What we're looking for is what we see everywhere—it's as simple as that.

To shepherd loved ones well, we have to decide what we want to notice in their lives. When we do this, our minds naturally cooperate to help us gather the relevant truths for their growth process. When we skip this, we quite often miss the realities they need to see for significant life change.

The real question, then, is *what are we trying to notice?*

So What Are We Trying to "See"?

To answer this critical question we have to return to our "good buckets" and "bad buckets." Do you remember those? In chapter nine I wrote that we all carry two buckets: a good bucket and a bad bucket. As we live our lives we collect positive and affirming messages in our good bucket and negative and condemning messages in our bad bucket. The messages we collect become our beliefs, and then those beliefs carve out our path through life.

As shepherds, *we're always trying to recognize the messages our loved ones collect*—and, more importantly, the beliefs birthed from those messages. Why? Because our messages and beliefs become the guardrails that determine the direction of our lives. How we respond to those messages determines who we become and what we pursue. Good messages help us change and grow, while the bad messages stand as impassable barriers, halting our forward progress.

A Case Study in "Seeing"

I love the big conversations I have with my son Tim. A few weeks ago we were in one of our bigger chat sessions when he told me, "Mom says you don't know how to let people love you." Whoa . . . hold up there . . . I didn't see that coming.

"Wait . . . what?" I asked, "Mom says I don't know how to *what*?"

He simply repeated himself: "Yeah, she says you have a hard time receiving love from the people who love you."

You know what that's called? It's called "seeing." Someone who knows me well and cares about me sees something in my heart that I don't see on my own. Let's set aside the rest of that conversation and focus more deeply on the observation.

At first I felt exposed by Tim's words, like I was suddenly becoming aware of something embarrassing about myself— something everyone else already sees. But it was a "direct hit" with the truth, and I knew it was accurate the moment I heard it.

Last year I was in Mexico on a big fishing trip with a buddy and our sons. Early on, I had an allergic reaction to something I ate at dinner and woke up in the middle of the night with fat lips, a swollen face and neck, and—in all honesty—a little trouble breathing. It was some of the worst discomfort I've ever felt—a mind-clawing combination of burning and itching, with no relief in sight. That's how I felt, but all I could think was, "How am I not going to wreck everyone's fishing trip? How can I get myself back to California—on my own—without derailing everyone's fun?"

So I concocted a plan to load my fat face onto a Mexican bus the next day for a fifteen-hour ride back to Tijuana, where I could talk someone into picking me up at the border. That way I could avoid being a nuisance and allow the rest of the gang to keep fishing. Kinda crazy, right?

By the next morning I actually felt slightly better and decided to abort my self-rescuing return mission home, but in an unguarded moment I told my older son Joey what I had been planning. He looked at me, tears welling in his eyes, and said, "Dad, you don't have to do something like that. I'll help you. I'll drive you all the way back home. It's what we do."

We believe the messages we've collected, and then we live our lives based on those beliefs. If you're not looking for what's beneath the behavior of those you lead, chances are you will miss the beliefs that distort their truth and hinder them from becoming like Jesus.

Growing up, I collected the message, "You are a burden and a nuisance," which later birthed one of my core beliefs: "You're not worth a big effort." It's saddens me when that message becomes a shield that repels love from important people in my life, but it's altogether tragic when it acts as a barrier keeping me from God himself. Though I collected this message from my biological father, I've been attributing it to my heavenly Father for too long, and now I see how it mutes his approval in my heart and causes me to turn away when I need him most. It also does real damage to my relationships with family and friends.

I couldn't see this message in my own heart until someone who loves me saw it first—and then said something.

And Then We Have to "Say It"

Seeing without saying is like not seeing at all.

My loved ones may see the truth in my life, but that truth has no impact for change unless they say what they see. And that's what Timmy did. He and I have so much safety with each other—our ambient permission is so strong—that he was free to *say what I needed to see.*

Simply put, "saying it" is our verbal response to what we see in others. Until we say what we see, it's almost like we see nothing at all. But saying happens when we reach for the helpful words and questions that allow loved ones to see what we see.

In its most basic form, "saying it" happens best when we *affirm the good messages* and help *refute the bad messages*.

1. Affirming the Good Messages

We affirm the good messages when we notice, celebrate, and feed the life-giving beliefs we see in others. When this becomes our relational habit, strongholds of truth form in hearts all throughout the community.

I don't have the space here to build this out much, but if you want to breathe life into the good messages your loved ones believe, you will devote yourself to this. You will not rest until you become world-class at noticing, celebrating, and feeding their best messages. You will become a "message champion" who keeps the right messages and beliefs alive and well in the hearts of your followers.

Want some criteria for good messages? They are the messages Jesus himself would speak if he were with us physically. How did Jesus speak to people? What messages did he place in buckets all the time? If your loved ones have messages that align with Jesus' own message, be sure those stay out front and obvious. Everything should point back to Jesus' core gospel message of acceptance and truth.

2. Refuting the Bad Messages

Flip that coin now. We refute bad messages when we notice, challenge, and starve the toxic and life-robbing beliefs people carry. Normalize this in your life and chains will fall off hearts all around you.

I take bad messages personally; I'm praying you do too. I see them for what they are—an actual attack on God's plan for the people I love. Think of it like this: for every life-giving truth Jesus wants us to believe, our enemy, Satan, has a corresponding lie. We took a big look at who Satan is and how he behaves in chapter 10, but this is where all his efforts land—right in the hearts of our loved ones.

Someone is out to hurt the people you love, and if he succeeds it won't happen randomly. Our enemy contemplates your loved ones. He schemes. Satan stalks your friends and family like a predator tracking prey, and his weapons are lies, accusations and distorted thoughts.

Long ago, I began picturing myself standing between our enemy and my loved ones. That simple mental picture keeps me alert, scanning for the messages and beliefs that might keep my loved ones from seeing and following Jesus.

Seeing and Saying—Responding to Our Twin Navigators

Our messages and beliefs become our twin navigators in life, determining who we become and what we pursue. They never kick in the door and hijack our hearts, but they still call the shots on where we're headed.

Truth is, we decide for ourselves—intentionally or by default—who gets to hold the compass. Actively or passively, we sign off on the messages we believe and then get busy living our lives under their control and direction. This is why seeing and saying is such a big deal. Knowing whose hands are actually on the steering wheel makes all the difference when we're helping people change and grow.

Jesus often spoke to the messages that motivated the people around him. He looked right past their actual behavior and spoke to the belief beneath the surface. He looked through their "shiny" social facades and said what he saw in people . . . all the time . . . everywhere he went. He "saw it" and then he "said it."

We can do that too for the sake of those we love and lead!

HELP IT AND STICK WITH IT 14

So far, it might seem like this getting started guide has been all about you. *You* have to ask for it. *You* have to wear it. *You* have to see and say it. But what about them? What are the people you lead doing this whole time? That's a good question.

Everything we've focused on so far has been preparation for what we look at right now. So here we go . . . it's time to break out the tools and offer some active help.

1. Help It: Facilitate Next Steps for Loved Ones

Can we have a quick "see it and say it" moment right now?

There is something I've been paying attention to for a long time. Because growth is so important to me, I constantly scan for ways to understand how it happens best. One way I do this is by watching people react to the growth areas they notice in family and friends.

Here's what I think I see: most people—leaders especially—think first about offering information when they see something in someone that needs changing. Let that settle in for a moment. Most often, our relational reflex is to reach for the "right content" when someone needs to change and grow.

Here's how it usually goes. A person is with a friend and shares a struggle he is working through—maybe feeling a bit depressed, fear about losing a relationship, or frustrations with a jerk-boss. Of all the responses available at this point, nearly every single time, the solution offered is content: information, facts, or ideas. Now let that one settle in too.

Isn't that what you see too? Isn't that often our response to people who are stuck and struggling? I don't have hard data on this yet, but my soft data tells me that nearly eight times out of ten, we offer help to people in the form of information. We think "content" first as the solution for growth barriers:

> "If they just read *The Tipping Point* they'd calm down and know it's just a matter of time before all this changes."

> "You know, Daniel Goleman writes that 'framing' is the most helpful way to change how you see your challenges in life. Let me break this down for you ... "

> "I heard a TED Talk about that last week—I'll send you the link."

The vast majority of us believe that giving information so that others know a new truth is the bulk of what it means to help followers grow. It's what I used to believe too. And for the record, *I still believe that the right content plays an essential role in our growth*, it's just the timing on the content I want to clarify.

So let's talk about scurvy for a moment (hang with me here). If you know anything about seventeenth-century mariners, you know that one of the great challenges to exploring the new world was a horrible disease they contracted on long voyages called "scurvy." I mean, just the word "scurvy"—come on, it sounds awful. And it was.

Humans get scurvy from a lack of vitamin C, simple as that. What makes this complicated is you can't effectively grow or store citrus on ships. So sailors routinely suffered from the horrible effects of this disease: bleeding gums, tooth loss, swollen limbs, jaundice, and severe exhaustion. Oh, and you can die from scurvy too.

If you think eating more oranges takes care of the scurvy threat to humans, you'd be mostly right. But . . . did you know your body will struggle to absorb vitamin C if you are deficient in Folate, also called B-9?[1] Okay, that's as far as we're going with the nutrition facts. But it's still true, you can eat fifteen oranges a day and still not have enough vitamin C. Because your body cannot take up what it needs if the biological conditions are out of whack.

Boom! That's how it works with life change too. You can read every book in the Library of Congress and watch all 3,200 TED Talks, but if the conditions aren't right to absorb that information into your heart, it all remains off-limits for your growth process.

Start with People, Not with Content

In a previous chapter I wrote about the explosive growth of the self-help industry. If you dig into the world of self-help—or any kind of help really—it can feel paralyzing. When you need help, where in the world do you start? Which book, podcast, blog, seminar, or video do you choose? And why? What's your rationale for picking one resource over another? This is one of the big challenges of thinking "content first."

But what if you didn't start there? What if, instead, you simply started with questions like: "What does my loved one need most right now?" "What does she need next to move toward her best self?" "What would help him take his next courageous step of growth?" These are process-driven questions, not content-driven questions.

Instead of starting with "information first," what if we simply begin a triage process that allows us to see the kind of help that's most helpful? If our triage points to information, so be it. But if it points to some other growth step, information will have to wait. Cooperating with this triage process is the secret sauce of shepherding well.

Leaders Love Tools . . . Because Tools Are Awesome

I love tools. Mostly, I love what tools do for me—how they make hard jobs doable. Sure, who doesn't love firing up a chop saw now and then, but what good is that saw if you really need a rotary hammer? When you match the tool to the job, that's when everything begins to fall in place.

Tools are essential for personal growth, but just as with building and repairs, the magic happens when you match the tool to the desired outcome. *Think of growth tools as structured responses to the things that need changing and growing in us.* Just as hammers, saws, and drills are good for building a house, so also life-change tools help us cooperate with the Holy Spirit and build out the life Jesus intends for us.

"*But what are the right tools, at the right time?*" That's the question we often fail to ask. Abraham Maslow famously said, "If all you have is a hammer, everything looks like a nail."[2] You need to know a "hammer" isn't your only shepherding option. Having a triage process opens the toolbox and helps us understand which tool to choose for life change.

Let me offer a tool selection process that might help you with this.

Choosing the Right Tool

Below is a series of diagnostic questions I've collected over the years that help me triage next steps for growing. I wish I could tell you where this idea started—if you're reading this and I got it from you, please let me know and I'll eagerly correct my attribution. Anyway, I've added to and refined this list over the years, and it serves me extremely well as I walk with followers on their growth journey. But keep in mind, it all boils down to one guiding question: *"What do they need next to change and grow?"* Let me break this down with five sub-questions, and then I'll offer guidelines afterward.

1. What do they need to *do* to grow?

The big idea: Sometimes our next step is action-based, which means we need to actually do something to change. If you're a kinesthetic learner, you probably perked up a bit just now. And if you love training of any sort, you probably like what you're hearing.

Because there is so much to say about this, allow me to focus a bit. The guiding question here is, "What *active step* will you choose to take in order to grow?" Or you might ask, "What *action* or *behavior* should you choose for your next step of growth?"

The answers to questions like these usually correspond to some character issue the Holy Spirit wants to transform in your follower's life. If he is shining his spotlight on a lack of generosity—or straight up greed—then some form of sacrificial giving or serving might be the ticket. If he's spotlighting pace-of-life issues, the answer might center on spiritual disciplines like solitude, silence, or slowing (yes, slowing is a discipline[3]). You get the idea. If "doing" is a next step, that means there is a practice to live out in order to reshape some part of our character the Holy Spirit is illuminating in us.

This may include: Solitude, study, giving, prayer, liturgy or ritual, a workout plan, confession, serving, spiritual friendship, spiritual practices, spiritual pathways, mowing lawns or painting walls, etc.

2. *Who* do they need to know to grow?

The big idea: Then there are times when our next step is a relationship. It's not what we do or what we know, it's who we get close to that yields our growth. No one grows alone—not for long anyway. At some point we need to add people to our growth process. Who are the people your loved ones need to know in order to grow?

This may include: A mentor (other than you), a counselor, a disciple (i.e., someone to give to and lead), a community, a life "running partner," a "new" parent, a twelve-step group, maybe even a medical doctor, etc.

3. What do they need to *experience* to grow?

The big idea: Some of my greatest moments of growth were birthed in experiences God walked me through. This is true for many of us, because experiences imprint on us in ways nothing else can. So we often need something like Psalm 23 in our lives: the wilderness, green pastures, the presence of enemies, quiet waters, or even the valley of the shadow of death, to become someone new. Experiences like these have a way of reaching to the deeper places in our soul and shaping us profoundly. Maybe a couple of examples will help.

I have lived through nearly tragic episodes of helping a loved one with mental health issues. Those experiences alone have created a vast sea of empathy in my heart for people struggling with similar issues in their families. Also, I have a friend who ran into financial difficulty and nearly ended up homeless at one point in his life. Because of that low point he not only feels deep gratitude for the simpler pleasures in life, but he also feels a profound sense of freedom from always wanting more. In a surprising way, near-homelessness has been his pathway to contentment. No one is signing up for mental health crises or near-homelessness, but if we allow it, God will use those dark valleys to shape us. You can help your loved ones cooperate with God in moments just like these.

Beyond that, there may be times when people need to intentionally step out of the routine of their everyday lives and jump into a new context. Our loved ones don't have to wait for big experiences to show up; we can help them switch things up and walk toward new and life-changing experiences. And you can help get that started—if that's what they need next.

This may include: Poverty or low income (yep, actually living on less, or on very little), intervention (a grace and truth conversation with family and friends), study abroad, become pen pals with an inmate, fast from some part of life, lean into hard consequences, hear someone's story, endure pain or loss, help the homeless, grieve a loss or abuse, receive love from someone in your own love-language, refuse to run from difficulty or discomfort, etc.

4. What do they need to *receive* to grow?

The big idea: There are times we can't take an "active" next step because we're exhausted from a heavy or draining season. Or maybe we're a little beat up by life. When this happens, often the best thing to do is catch our breath, sleep a little more and receive help when it's offered. It's not uncommon, however, for people to resist a step that feels passive like this one. So the point of growth here is simply helping followers become helpable. It's no mistake that Psalm 23 describes God as a shepherd who "*makes me* lie down"—because sometimes lying down is what we need next, yet resist most.

This may include: Schedule a meal train, pay a bill, fix a car or pay for a repair, help them join a small group, invite them for dinner, have unrushed conversations where you just listen, plan a hike or a game of tennis, help create a budget, provide rides to the airport, help find an expert (for a big problem issue), or whatever else best serves their personal needs.

5. What do they need to *know* to grow?

The big idea: Sometimes our next step is, in fact, information-based. There are times when we're stuck behind a knowledge gap that keeps us from recognizing what's next. There may be something we don't understand about ourselves or about the world in general. When this happens, there is often some learning we need to do or a truth we need to discover. That's when we turn to quality information that provides the understanding we need. And to state the obvious, the one source of information we never put down is the Bible. As a primary source from God himself, the Bible is our best guide for living life as Jesus would, if he were us. This is always the first place to point people for the right information.

This may include—Bible reading plans, topical books, theological truth, a conference, a podcast, a blog, a prescribed study project, etc.

Final Guidelines for Using Your Tools

Here are some final thoughts to keep in mind as you break out all your awesome tools.

First, use the tool that works best for your followers, not the tool you like best or the one that helps you most. Keep this process about them, not you; doing so is way harder than it sounds. To do this you will have to look beyond your own pathway and growth challenges and respond precisely to the unique details you see in their lives. More importantly, you have to listen for the leading of the Holy Spirit.

Second, decide which of the tools to use next. I've offered five options:

> They need to **do** something to grow.
> They need to **know someone** to grow.
> They need to **experience** something to grow.

They need to **receive** help to grow.

They need to **acquire information** to grow.

You can't use all these tools at the same time, so you have to decide what to reach for first, and second, and third, etc. This is where the triage process helps you and your loved ones. It's also where our dependence on the Holy Spirit is beyond helpful. What do your followers need right now: an action? A relationship? A life-experience? Help or information? Reaching for that answer helps you narrow which of the five next steps to focus on. Then you simply begin to explore life options aligned on the tool you've selected. If it's information, for example, what information? A Bible passage? A book? A seminar? A blog post? A sermon?

And keep in mind, after deciding on a next step, you may realize there's a more helpful tool you overlooked. So switch out your tools—it's as simple as that. If, together, you decide to make a change and focus in a different area, no harm and no foul.

Third, "helping it" stands on the shoulders of all the other practices I've mentioned so far. Without permission, for example, people often feel pushed around by all the "help" you want to give them, or they simply feel like your project. And if you're not "wearing" some of the practices you're offering, why would they? This is why I've waited nearly to the end of this book to start talking about all the practical tools we leaders love to break out.

Finally, always remember that choosing next steps is a collaborative effort, not a decree we hand down to our "subjects." If they aren't fully participating members of the decision-making process, you've slipped out of "permission" and relational leadership and into "compliance" and positional leadership. Asking, guiding, suggesting, and challenging are all legit practices of shepherding. But no one will put up with feeling pushed around for long. Dallas Willard writes, "In life, some things that can be pulled cannot be pushed, and some things that can be pushed cannot be pulled. Making disciples is a matter of pulling people, of drawing them through who we are and what we say."[4] Enough said.

5. Stick with It—Give Growth the Time It Needs to Work

I'm pretty sure I don't need to make a big argument against the out-of-control pace of our twenty-first century lives. Right? Far too many of us live too fast and do too much—and then pay for it in anxiety, poor health, and shallow relationships. When we get pace-of-life wrong, it always seems to come back to *speed* and *volume*.

These twin demons will wreck your life and destroy your influence with people, if you allow it. In fact, you can get all the other practices right and if you get this one wrong, chances are quite high that it will derail the entire growth process with your loved ones. Because the human heart refuses to be rushed.

"Ruthlessly Eliminate Hurry"

A couple decades ago, Dallas Willard famously counseled John Ortberg to, "*ruthlessly eliminate* hurry from your life." Dallas did not tell John to "be a little rude to hurry" or to "ignore hurry" from time to time. He went big—with absolute language—to describe the permanent exile of hurry from John's life.

Think of what it means to be ruthless. By definition, to act ruthlessly requires no pity, no mercy. You could even say ruthless behavior is heartless and savage, completely detached from sympathy or kindness. Many believe that "ruthless" comes from the Germanic verb "rue," which means to, "affect with sorrow or to grieve."[5] Tack on a few suffixes and we get "rue-less-ness," or the absence of sorrow and grief for someone or something.

Others speculate that "ruthless" might be influenced by the German cognate *rucksicht*, which carries the idea of "back sight," or "looking back."[6] In this sense, ruthless behavior is charging ahead without regard for what happens behind you. It's the idea that whatever the consequences may be, the present circumstances are so bad—so unpreferable—that you do whatever it takes to smash through the conditions without so much as a backward glance.

At the time of this writing, California is burning down—or so it seems. Something like three million acres of the state are on fire at this moment. In 2019 we had a fire that consumed the entire town of Paradise—population 26,800. Some of the residents, trapped by that fire, were forced to act without regard for the consequences and drive through massive walls of fire to escape. That, my friends, is ruthless behavior.

Now think about what it would take to drive you to *holy ruthlessness*? What would have to happen for you to treat someone, or some set of circumstances, without sympathy or regard? It's been said that a good father would die for his children, but a mother—oh a mother now—she would kill for her kids if they were in danger. That kind of protection is nothing less than ethically ruthless behavior. It's also the kind of righteous ruthlessness we need when the threat of hurry shows up in our lives, or in the way we shepherd.

The solution to sped-up living is the forcible ejection of hurry from your life. Bum-rush the miscreant hurry, not just from your own life, but from the way you do life with others—especially with those you love and lead. One use of the Latin word for eliminate—*eliminatus*—means "to throw across the threshold of a door."[7] It's the idea of tossing something out of your house for good, or even driving it away. Bottom line, whatever you're getting rid of, you consider it so abhorrent you want it gone for good.

I don't ever want to imply more than Dallas Willard intends to say, but this is how I think about the impact of hurry on people: hurry must never be accommodated or treated kindly, because it's not just a bad habit or misguided living. Unchecked, hurry will bind you, and then take from you the values you hold dear and the relationships you treasure. It will also hobble the entire growth process, much like what happens when a jogger falls-out trying to keep pace with a world-class runner. The human heart was never intended to keep up with a runaway culture like ours.

Healthy Growth Has Its Own Speed

Nothing healthy grows faster than it is intended to grow. That means there is healthy growth and unhealthy growth.

When we see a child again after some time has passed, we often gush, "Look how big you are! Did you become a giant, or what?" This is healthy growth: their young bodies are doing what they're supposed to do at the right pace. But when we sit with a friend whose cancer has metastasized, there is no joy. There is only the uncertainty and fear of sudden, unwanted growth that's threatening their very life.

Rushed change rarely stays changed. When I talk to leaders about this, I often speak in terms of "shallow" and "deep." "Shallow" is about your hands—what you do, while "deep" is about your heart—who you are and what you love.

Our culture is addicted to the shallow version of change—mostly because we're obsessed with ever-quicker results. This explains why the "go faster, do more" mantra feels so good to us, because it feels like healthy progress—maybe the way fast food might feel like a real meal. The problem with eating fast food on the run is lack of long-term fuel and staying power. When life becomes difficult and grinding—and it always becomes difficult and grinding at times—that's when our shallow changes fail us.

Just like hard labor after a sugary breakfast breaks down your body, difficulty in life breaks down your soul if you're relying on behavior modification as the foundation of your character.

Intentional heart change, on the other hand, has staying power. The problem is, you just can't rush that kind of change—which is why *sticking with it* is so essential for shepherding.

Alan Fadling, in his book *An Unhurried Life*, tells the story of visiting a vineyard in northern California.[8] The owner of the vineyard explained to Alan his practice of "dry farming," in which his vines rely solely on water provided by natural conditions. He contrasted that to grape vines that are "addicted" to artificial drip irrigation.

The big difference between irrigated and non-irrigated vines shows up mostly underground. Artificially watered vines have a small onion-shaped root ball at the surface, since they have no need to plunge deeper than a few inches of soil for water. Unwatered vines, however, grow a mass of roots equal to the size of the plant above ground as they stretch deeply for the water table.

There is both an easy and a hard source of water for these grapevines. The easy source is always at the surface, so there's no reason for the vines to send their roots deep into the nutrient-rich soil. But when the easy source is removed, the vines struggle and plunge their roots into the earth to get what they need. Early on, this change from easy to hard means a big drop-off in grape yield— sometimes as much as forty-five percent. But before long—usually just a couple of years—the vines return to near 100% yield . . . without a drop of artificial irrigation.

The big transformation, however, is the quality of the grape. When a vine has the time to struggle through soil for the water it needs, the transformation produces a kind of life it can't get otherwise. In this case, deep change makes all the difference.

Deep change—the kind we have to reach for, the kind that takes longer and requires more—that kind of change makes all the difference in our lives too. Unfortunately, far too many won't know that kind of change, because it's just not available at the speed of culture.

The Solution: Living at the Speed of Jesus

When we read about Jesus in the Gospels, we see that he lives free from anything like the internal game clock that drives most of us. He refuses to cooperate with outside pressure to pick up his pace, opting instead to simply love his father—and people—from the deep center of his life.

Jesus never outran his love. He never lived faster than his ability to intentionally care for people around him. Motivated by that love, he consistently said "no" to the expectations others demanded of him to speed up and deliver more. Have you ever thought about the vast social pressure Jesus did not allow to determine his speed and direction through life? Here are some of the pressures Jesus pushed back on: his own family (Luke 2:42-52, 3:31-35), systemic cultural values (Luke 19:5-7; John 4:7-9), a dying friend (John 11), urgent tasks (Luke 10:38-42), healing a dying daughter (Mark 5:21-35), expectations of the crowds (Matthew 14:22-23; Mark 6:30-32; Luke 5:15-16), the religious leaders (Mark 8:11-13, 14:53-61; Luke 13:10-17; Luke 19:39-40; John 8:1-11), the disciples (Mark 8:31-33, 10:13-16; Luke 18:15-17), the weather (Mark 4:35-39), the Roman government (Mark 15:1-5), Satan (Matthew 4, Mark 1, Luke 4), and death itself (Matthew 28; Mark 16; Luke 24; John 20). Any one of these pressures would spell real trouble for me—maybe for you too. But Jesus allowed none of these to accelerate his care for and influence with people.

Sometimes we long for slowing down as a way to improve our quality of life. The greatest quality of life for Jesus was living at the speed of love—love for his Father and for all of us. As it turns out, it's that same love that led him to save the world.

Give Life-Changing Conditions Time to Work

All I'm asking is that you *give life-changing conditions the time they need* to transform your loved ones. It's hard to do just about anything in a hurry, but creating life-changing conditions is impossible in a rush. What we *can* rush are quick fixes, barked orders, instructions on the fly, a short text, a brief phone call, or a hurried recommendation. But none of that will do if caring for loved ones is what we have in mind. Why spend the effort to create life-changing conditions and then abbreviate their impact? Stick with it, and before you know it, deep and lasting change will emerge.

Hurry is to be man-handled, roughed up and tossed out of our lives—never to be allowed back. In its place, we can become intentional shepherds who create an environment for growth, and then protect that environment for as long as it takes to yield the deep version of change in others. We can choose to *stick with it* over the long haul, because only deep, hard-fought, time-tested heart-change is good enough for the ones we love.

Finally . . . One Last Time . . .
"Who Do You Love?"

This is where we started, and it's the right place to finish up. It's amazing what we figure out and accomplish when our hearts are fully awake.

You can absolutely do this! You can help the people you love move along in their growth journey. If you will wear it, ask for it, see it & say it, help it, and stick with it, you can create the conditions—safety, truth, vulnerability, affirmation, and caregiving—your loved ones need to change and grow. The human heart may complicated, but our shepherding doesn't have to be.

Count on my prayers as you build out a life-changing environment for the people you love. They are worth your biggest, best effort!

SPECIAL THANKS

"He loved her most." Sweetheart, you and I both know none of this gets written if not for you. I love our life. I love you more!

Thank you Joey, Zach, and Timmy. There's no ranking there, just the order in which you arrived. You three motivate much of what I do. Creating these life-changing conditions for you has been my preoccupation your whole lives. I love you sons!

Thank you Tim Halgat. I'm most certain if the building is on fire, you're the one coming in after me. Thanks for keeping your eye on me, for chasing me down when I wandered into trouble and for pulling me off the ledge when I got stuck. Jesus has used you to save me more times than I can count, which means I've needed a brother who would love me like you. I love you back.

Thank you Chris Jones. It terrifies me to think who I'd be if we were never friends. I wonder what it feels like for you, knowing that you've changed my family for generations to come. Thank you for including us in your adventures and for helping us Dehnert boys become the men we are. We love you Jonesy.

Thank you John Ortberg. Jesus got all this started through you. I often hear your words in my head. Weird, huh? Not really, I guess, if those words lead to life and blessing the way yours do for me. I can't imagine how broken and crushed I'd be without your love and influence . . . at just the right time.

Thank you Mike Yearley. Thank you for the eighty hours of interviews and process we went through before you hired me. It made me feel paid attention to and known . . . and legitimately wanted after you offered me the job. Thank you most for being such an agent of healing and change in my life. I can't remember a time I felt more cared for than when we were teammates. I'm a "bigger" leader because of you.

I'm grateful to my mother and father. In the end, you gave me enough and I miss you both. Life will toss you into a fist fight from time to time, so it's good to have a little experience when that happens. Thank you for the gifts of toughness, hard work and aggression—they've come in handy my whole life. I think you may be okay with how I turned out.

ENDNOTES

Chapter 1

1   John 14:16-17, 26; 16:7, 12-15

2   1 Corinthians 2:2

3   1 Corinthians 1:25

4   1 Corinthians 2:1-5

5   John Maxwell contrasts positional and relational leadership in his helpful book, *The 5 Levels of Leadership* (New York, NY: Center Street, 2011).

6   Some actually attribute this quote to Theodore Roosevelt, in case you were wondering.

7   Maxwell, John. Leadership seminar, Skyline Wesleyan Church, 1993.

8   Galatians 4:19

9   The authenticity of the origin of this quote is uncertain, but the idea it communicates is beyond helpful. In the source cited below, the author writes of a group of people who, from their love of sailing, divided their labor to build a sailboat. Saint-Exupery, Antoine de. Oeuvres (Paris, France: Gallimard, 1959), p. 687.

10   Smith, James K. A. *You Are What You Love* (Grand Rapids, MI: Brazos Press, 2016), p. 12.

11   Ibid. Smith, p. 10.

12   Colossians 1:3-6

Chapter 2

1   1 Peter 2:25

2   1 Peter 5:2-4

3   Mark 3:13-19; Luke 6:12-16

4   Scazzero, Peter. *The Emotionally Healthy Church* (Grand Rapids, MI: Zondervan, 2003).

5   George, Carl F. *Prepare Your Church for the Future* (Grand Rapids, MI: Baker Books, 1992).

6   Exodus 18:13-26

7   Goleman, Daniel; Boyatzis, Richard; and McKee, Annie. *Primal Leadership* (Boston, MA: Harvard Business School Press, 2002), p. 118.

8   The New Testament unanimously declares Jesus as the ultimate and final goal of our maturity process: Romans 13:14; 1 Corinthians 11:1; 2 Corinthians 3:16-18; Galatians 4:19; Ephesians 4:11-15, 5:1-2; Philippians 2:3-5; 1 Peter 2:21, 4:1; 1 John 2:6

9   1 Peter 2:22

10   1 John 3:5

11   Hebrews 4:15

12   Matthew 3:17; Mark 1:11; Luke 3:22

13   The practice of imitation is a dominant New Testament theme for following Jesus: 1 Corinthians 4:16-17, 11:1; Ephesians 5:1-2; Philippians 3:17; Hebrews 6:12, 13:7; 1 Peter 2:21; 3 John 11.

14   For the record, part of any answer, regarding any life-situation we encounter, will always include Jesus' core values; among them, loving God and loving people (Matthew 22:34-40), radical acceptance and inclusivity (Matthew 9:9-13; Luke 7:36-50, 19:1-10; John 4, 8:1-11), grace & truth (John 1:14, 16-17; 2 John 3), humility, sacrifice, and generosity. Beyond those core values, the direction we receive will be as specific as the details of our own lives.

15   How else do you explain verses like 1 Thessalonians 5:17: "pray continually…"; Ephesians 6:18: "And pray in the Spirit on all occasions with all kinds of prayers and requests"?

16   Dryer, Elizabeth A. *Earth Crammed with Heaven* (Mahwah, NJ; Paulist Press, 1994).

17 Barton, Ruth Haley. *Strengthening the Soul of Your Leadership*, (Downers Grove, IL: InterVarsity Press, 2008), p. 62.

18 Ibid. Barton, p. 62.

19 I first heard of the practice of *statio* from Peter Scazzero: Scazzero, Peter. *The Emotionally Healthy Leader* (Grand Rapids, MI: Zondervan, 2015), p. 194.

20 Chittister, Joan. *Wisdom Distilled from the Daily: Living the Rule of St. Benedict Today* (New York: HarperCollins, 2013).

21 Stanley, Andy. *The Principle of the Path* (Nashville, TN: Thomas Nelson, 2008), pp. 11-12.

Chapter 3

1   Genesis 3:17

2   Genesis 2:25

3   Genesis 2:18

4   Ortberg, John. *Everybody's Normal Till You Get to Know Them* (Grand Rapids, MI: Zondervan, 2003), p. 31.

5   Ibid. Ortberg, pp. 31-32.

6   Genesis 3:6

7   See Genesis 3:1-5

8   Bauby, Jean-Dominique. *The Diving Bell and the Butterfly* (New York, NY: Random House, 1997). Also an Oscar-nominated motion picture of the same title, 2007.

9   Ibid. Ortberg, p. 82.

Chapter 4

1   "Circles of safety" is also one of the controlling metaphors of Simon Sinek's invaluable book Leaders Eat Last (Sinek, Simon. *Leaders Eat Last* [New York, NY: Penguin, 2014]). I depended heavily on his work as it relates to the value of leaders who create those circles. This is a must-read for anyone who wants to create safe conditions for others.

2   Meyers, Stephanie (2013, July 31). "Simon Sinek: How Extraordinary Leaders Evolve." Retrieved from https://www.inc.com/stephanie-meyers/simon-sinek-evolution-leadership.html

3   Sinek, Simon (2014, March). "Why good leaders make you feel safe." Retrieved from https://www.ted.com/talks/simon_sinek_why_good_leaders_make_you_feel_safe

4   Ibid. Sinek.

5   Smalley, Gary. *The DNA of Relationships* (Carol Stream, IL: Tyndale), p. 86.

6   Friedland-Kays, Eric and Dana, Deb (2017, December 8). "Being Polyvagal: The Polyvagal Theory Explained." Retrieved from https://www.windhorseimh.org/mental-health-education/polyvagal-theory-explained/

     Neuroception is, "our innate unconscious awareness through the autonomic nervous system to influences in the body, in the environment, and in interactions between people."

7   Boeder, Ellen (2017, August). "Emotional Safety is Necessary for Emotional Connection." Retrieved from https://www.gottman.com/blog/emotional-safety-is-necessary-for-emotional-connection/

     "Social Engagement System" is a phrase coined by Stephen Porges to describe the part of the vagus nerve that helps us connect with people and communicate. Ellen Boeder explains that the autonomic nervous system, "mediates safety, trust and intimacy through a subsystem (called) the social engagement system."

8   Sinek, Simon. *Leaders Eat Last* (New York, NY: Penguin, 2014), pp. 49ff.

9   Ibid. Sinek.

10   Ibid. Boeder.

11   Ibid. Boeder.

12   Ibid. Boeder.

13   *"I exist for you, and not the other way around,"* is a profoundly Jesus-like orientation toward leading others. Matthew 20:25-28, John 10:11-15 and Philippians 2:3-8 make it clear that Jesus' entering our world and dying on the cross were the ultimate acts of love, selflessness, and generosity.

14   I came upon this question from the father/daughter team, Arch Hart and Sharon Hart-Morris. They write about the marriage relationship, but their question applies to all of our important relationships.

Hart, Archibald and Hart-Morris, Sharon. *Safe Haven Marriage* (Nashville, TN: W Publishing Group, 2003), p. 28.

15 Philippians 2:12

16 Philippians 2:5

17 Philippians 2:13

18 Genesis 1:28

19 Galatians 1:4 (NLT)

20 Galatians 4:4-7

21 Isaiah 53:4-6; Romans 4:23-25; 2 Corinthians 5:21; Philippians 3:8-9; 1 Peter 3:18

22 Philippians 2:3-8

23 John 10:11, 14-15

24 John 15:12-13

25 Matthew 20:25-28

26 Sinek, Simon. *Leaders Eat Last* (New York, NY: Penguin, 2014), p. 66

27 Ibid. Sinek, p. 66

28 Sinek, Simon (2014, March). "Why good leaders make you feel safe."

29 Sinek, Simon (2013, November 26). "What 'Leaders Eat Last' means." Retrieved from https://www.youtube.com/watch?v=YMeuk0ZtLM0

30 John 10:11

31 Ibid. Sinek, *Leaders Eat Last*. I depend heavily on the numerous ways that Sinek explains, throughout his book, how "real leaders" establish and maintain safety. The following is adapted from his work.

32 Ibid. Sinek, p. 65.

Chapter 5

1 The name and details of this story have been changed to protect the privacy of my little friends.

2 Unknown Director (2018). "Hard Knocks: Training Camp with the Cleveland Browns" [Television Series]. New York, NY; HBO.

3 "Self-esteem." 2019. In Merriam-Webster.com. Retrieved January 29, 2019, from https://www.merriam-webster.com/dictionary/self-esteem

4 Willard, Dallas. *Renovation of the Heart* (Colorado Springs, CO: NavPress, 2002), p. 49.

5   Ibid. Willard.

6   Ibid. Willard.

7   James 1:22-24

8   Ortberg. John. *Everybody's Normal Till You Get to Know Them* (Grand Rapids, MI: Zondervan, 2003), p. 74.

9   Allender, Dan. *To Be Told* (Colorado Springs, CO: Waterbrook Press, 2005).

10   Cloud, Henry and Townsend, John. *How People Grow* (Grand Rapids, MI: Zondervan), pp. 105-106.

11   2 Timothy 3:1-8

Chapter 6

1   Scazzero, Peter. *The Emotionally Healthy Church* (Grand Rapids, MI: Zondervan, 2003), pp. 69-70.

2   John 4:6-26

3   Later in John 7:37-39 Jesus circles back on his offer of water for thirsty people. The Holy Spirit is the one who quenches our deepest thirst; he comes in and becomes a stream of life within followers of Jesus.

4   John 14:6

5   John 8:12, 31-32

6   Just a few passages on our lack of goodness. "Total depravity" is the phrase the reformers use to describe this: Psalm 51:5; Jeremiah 17:9; Romans 1:18-32, 3:23, 7:18; Galatians 5:19-21; Ephesians 2:1; 2 Timothy 3:1-5

7   Jesus is sinless: 2 Corinthians 5:21; Hebrews 4:15, 7:23-26; 1 Peter 2:22; 1 John 3:5

8   Greer, J.D. *Gospel* (Nashville, TN: B & H Publishing, 2011), p. 46. Greer attributes this quote to Saint Athanasius.

9   Romans 3:21-22, 4:3, 22-24; 2 Corinthians 5:21; Galatians 3:13; Philippians 3:7-9; Colossians 2:13-14; Titus 3:3-5

10   Undeclared contributor (2017, October 23). "Luther on Righteousness." Retrieved from https://www.crosslands.training/blog/2017/10/16/luther-on-righteousness (from Martin Luther, Galatians, eds. McGrath, Alister, and Packer, J. I., Crossway, 1998, xvii-xxiii.)

"Therefore, the afflicted and troubled conscience has no remedy against desperation and eternal death unless it takes hold of the forgiveness of sins by grace, freely offered in Christ Jesus – that is to say, this passive faith or Christian righteousness . . . Just as the earth does not generate rain and cannot of itself work to produce it, but receives it by the mere gift of God from above, so this heavenly righteousness is given us by God without our working for or deserving it . . ."

11   Ibid. Greer, p. 44.

12   Miller, Jack. "Received Righteousness" lecture. Serge, 2013. MP3 file.

13   Ibid. Miller.

14   Willard, Dallas. *Renovation of the Heart* (Colorado Springs, CO: NavPress, 2002), p. 13.

15   Matthew 4:17 is the context for Jesus' Sermon on the Mount: "From that time on Jesus began to preach, 'Repent, for the kingdom of heaven is near.'"

16   Matthew 7:24 (New Living Translation)

17   Matthew 7:26 (New Living Translation)

18   2 Timothy 3:16; 2 Peter 1:20-21

19   Luke 22:44-45; Acts 17:2-4; 18:27-28; 26:22; 28:23; Romans 3:21-22; 16:25-27

20   Matthew 7:16-18 (New Living Translation)

21   Kalinowski, Caesar. *The Gospel Primer* (China: Missio Publishing, 2013), p. 115.

22   Just a few examples: Mark 10:17-22, the rich young man; Luke 7:36-50, the woman wiping Jesus' feet; Luke 19:1-9, Zacchaeus; John 8:1-11, the woman caught in adultery.

Chapter 7

1   Brown, Brené. *Daring Greatly* (New York, NY: Gotham Books, 2012), p. 87.

2   Ibid. Brown, *Daring Greatly*, pp. 91-92.

3   Willard, Dallas. *Renovation of the Heart* (Colorado Springs, CO: NavPress, 2002), p. 53.

4   Ibid. Willard, p. 33.

5   Jeremiah 17:9, New Living Translation

6   Mark 7:20-23, New Living Translation

7   For further reading on the condition of the human heart, see Psalm 14:2-3, 51:5, 58:3; Ecclesiastes 9:3; John 3:19; Romans 1:18-25, 3:9-23, 7:18; Ephesians 2:1-5, 4:17-19; 1 John 1:8-10

8   Stanton, Liz (Writer) and Carvell, Tim (Director). (2019). "Public Shaming" [Television series episode]. In Oliver, John & Thoday, Jon (Executive Producer). *Last Week Tonight with John Oliver*. Los Angeles, CA: HBO.

9   Ibid, Oliver.

10   Brooks, Arthur C. (2019, March). "Our Culture of Contempt." Retrieved from https://www.aei.org/articles/our-culture-of-contempt/

11   Ibid. Brooks. He quotes the German philosopher Arthur Schopenhauer.

12   Senge, Peter; Kleiner, Art; Roberts, Charlotte; Ross, Richard B.; Smith, Bryan J. *The Fifth Discipline Fieldbook* (New York, NY: Doubleday, 1994), p. 3.

13   Ibid. Senge, Kleiner, Roberts, Ross, Smith.

14   Ibid. Brown, Daring Greatly, p. 8.

15   Lencioni, Patrick. Getting Naked (San Francisco, CA: Jossey-Bass, 2010), p. vii.

16   Ibid. Brown, Daring Greatly, p. 41.

17   That may be the shortest, most over-simplified summary of Romans 1-4 ever. So don't require too much of it.

18   To this point, first person language—I, us and we—is nearly absent in Paul's letter. In chapter one Paul uses third person language—they, them, those—to describe our ruined world. In chapter two he uses the impersonal, or hypothetical "you" in the sense of "one" or "oneself." In chapter three, we see a lot of distant language like "all" and "no one" along with more third-person references. In chapter four we do, in fact, read first-person language, but he uses it specifically in regard to justification by faith, not in terms of personal accountability or responsibility.

Chapter 8

1   Lewis Smedes and John Bradshaw distinguish between "healthy" shame and "toxic" or unhealthy shame. I don't intend to make that distinction here, though I agree fully with their contrast. For more information, see *Shame & Grace*, (Smedes), chapters two and four, and Healing the Shame that Binds You (Bradshaw), chapter one.

2   Smedes, Lewis. *Shame & Grace* (New York, NY: HarperCollins, 1993), p. 32. Lewis Smedes masterfully contrasts three versions of ourselves: The Actual Self, the False Self, and the True Self.

3   Ibid. Brown, *Daring Greatly*, pp. 28ff. Brené Brown writes extensively about shame as "scarcity." This is the idea that one is never enough. You can add any desired trait to the front of that word: never smart, small, tall, rich, fit, maternal (etc.) enough.

4   Ibid. Smedes, p. 6.

5   Ibid. Smedes, pp. 63-64.

6   This is the recurring line from the children's book, *Love You Forever*, by Robert Munsch, (Ontario, Canada: Firefly Books,1995).

7   Brown, Brené. *Daring Greatly* (New York, NY: Gotham Books, 2012), pp. 68-69. This is adapted from Brown's work.

8   Genesis 3:9

9   Bradshaw, John. *Healing the Shame that Binds You* (Deerfield Beach, FL: Health Communications Inc, 1988), p. 121.

10   Ibid. Brown, p. 45.

11   Ibid. Brown, p. 67.

12   Ibid. Bradshaw, p. 120.

13   Brown, Brené. *I Thought It Was Me (But it Isn't)* (New York, NY: Avery, 2007), p. 32.

14   2 Corinthians 1:3-11, 6:4-10, 11:24-28; 2 Timothy 4:6

15   Ibid. As quoted in Bradshaw, p. 183.

Chapter 9

1   Hendrie, Shifra (2008, December). "The Kabbalah of Speech." Retrieved from https://www.chabad.org/library/article_cdo/aid/327516/jewish/The-Kabbalah-of-Speech.htm

2   Ibid. Shifra.

3   Genesis 27:33-34, 41: "The days of mourning for my father are near; then I will kill my brother Jacob."

4   Genesis 27:33. Discovering he had been deceived, and not knowing who he had blessed, Isaac declares that whoever the recipient was, that man will indeed be blessed. His words had been spoken.

5   Heschel, Susannah. *God in Search of Man* (Lanham, MD: Aronson, 1987), p. ix.

6   Numbers 6:24-26

7   Unknown source. Adapted from a Michael Eisner quote on branding.

8   Willard, Dallas. *Renovation of the Heart* (Colorado Springs, CO: Navpress, 2002), p. 111.

9   Smedes, Lewis. *Shame & Grace* (New York, NY: HarperCollins, 1993), p. 53.

10   Smith, Mandy (2016, September). "The Pastoral Work of Reshaping Imaginations." Retrieved from https://www.christianitytoday.com/pastors/2016/september-web-exclusives/pastoral-work-of-reshaping-imaginations.html

Chapter 10

1   Smedes, Lewis. *Shame & Grace* (New York, NY: HarperCollins, 1993), p. 115.

2   Genesis 3:1

3   Allen, R. B; 1698 עָרַם; Harris, R. L.; Archer, G. L. Jr. and Waltke, B. K. (Editors). *Theological Wordbook of the Old Testament*, electronic edition, (Chicago, IL: Moody Press, 1999) p. 697.

4   Genesis 3; Matthew 4

5   John 8:44a

6   John 8:44b

7   Ephesians 6:11; 2 Corinthians 2:11

8   1 Peter 5:8

9   Romans 8:28-30

10   Romans 8:31-34

11   Zechariah 3:1; Job 1:6-11, 2:1-4; Revelation 12:10. In these passages, we see Satan in God's presence, accusing God's people. The Revelation passage indicates that his accusations are non-stop.

12   Romans 8:34. We also read this theme of "Jesus as defender" in Hebrews 7:25, 9:24 and 1 John 2:1-2.

13   Romans 8:35, 37, 39

14   Pentecost, J. Dwight. *Your Adversary the Devil* (Grand Rapids, MI: Zondervan, 1969), p. 102.

15   Ibid. Smedes. p. 32.

16   Ibid. Smedes. p. 38.

17   Snyder, Morgan (2015, February). "Wild at Heart Bootcamp Message." In his message, he describes the effect of perceived identity on personal authenticity and spiritual growth.

18   Ortberg, John. *The Me I Want to Be* (Grand Rapids, MI: Zondervan, 2010), p. 15.

19   Ibid. Ortberg, p. 16.

20   1 Peter 5:9

Chapter 11

1   Prensky, Marc (2001, October 5). "Digital Natives, Digital Immigrants Part 1." On the Horizon, Vol. 9 No. 5, pp. 1-6. Retrieved from https://www.marcprensky.com/writing/Prensky%20-%20Digital%20Natives,%20Digital%20Immigrants%20-%20Part1.pdf

2   Ni, Preston (2016, November 6). "8 Keys to Handling Adult Bullies." Retrieved from https://www.psychologytoday.com/us/blog/communication-success/201611/8-keys-handling-adult-bullies.

3   Brown, Brené. *Daring Greatly* (New York, NY: Gotham Books, 2012), pp. 106-107.

4   Sinclair, Marshall (2019, February 24). "Why the Self-help Industry is Dominating the U.S." Retrieved from https://medium.com/s/story/no-please-help-yourself-981058f3b7cf

5   Lamb-Shapiro, Jessica (2013, November 29). "A Short History of Self-help, the World's Bestselling Genre." Retrieved from https://

publishingperspectives.com/2013/11/a-short-history-of-self-help-the-worlds-bestselling-genre/

6   Ibid. Lamb-Shapiro.

7   Ince, Robin (2014, October 21). "The Ancient Roots of Self-help." Retrieved from http://www.bbc.com/culture/story/20140805-the-ancient-roots-of-self-help

8   Ibid. Ince.

9   Apparently the self-help industry isn't exactly coming through with the help it offers. Lamb-Shapiro quotes publishing statistics that cast doubt on the effectiveness of the genre. She points out publishing statistics that claim 80% of self-help customers are repeat buyers, suggesting that what they've already purchased isn't really working. Some statistics, per Lamb-Shapiro, also suggest that, on average, most buyers only read the first twenty pages of self-help books. Apparently, it's the practice of buying self-help books that customers like most.

10   Ibid. As quoted by Sinclair.

11   For the record, "Heaven helps those who help themselves" is an adaptation of "God helps those who help themselves," attributed to Algernon Sidney, who is credited with this current wording, and to Benjamin Franklin, who popularized it in his *Poor Richard's Almanac*. Retrievedfromhttps://en.wikipedia.org/wiki/God_helps_those_who_help_themselves

12   Willard, Dallas. *Renovation of the Heart* (Colorado Springs, CO: NavPress), p. 179.

13   Ibid, Willard.

14   For more on God's imperatives for social care and justice, see Exodus 22:21-24, 23:2, 6-9; Leviticus 19:15, 25:35; Deuteronomy 10:17-19, 16:18-20, 24:17-22, 25:13-16, 27:19; Psalm 9:7-9, 106:3, 140:12; Proverbs 22:22-23; Isaiah 1:16-7, 10:1-2; Jeremiah 22:3; Micah 2:1-2, 6:8; Zechariah 7:9-10

15   Acts 2:42-47, 4:32-35; 2 Corinthians 8:1-15

16   John 13:34 (NLT)

17   Isaiah 25:4 (NASB)

18   Romans 5:6, 8 (NLT)

19 John 4:14, 7:38-39

20 Cloud, Henry. *Integrity* (New York, NY: HarperCollins, 2006), pp. 76-77.

21 Oswalt, J. N.; Harris, R. L.; Archer, G. L. Jr. and Waltke, B. K. (Eds.). *Theological Wordbook of the Old Testament* (electronic ed.), (Chicago, IL: Moody Press, 1999), p. 101.

22 Matthew 20:25-28; John 10:15, 17-18; 1 John 3:16

23 Do you know about meal trains? I didn't until recently. What an amazing gift for people going through a high-need, high-demand time in their lives. For more info, see https://www.mealtrain.com/.

24 Keller, T. J. (2010, January 25) [Video file]. Retrieved from https://vimeo.com/8977644

25 Ibid. Keller.

26 Stott, John R. W. *The Cross of Christ* (Downers Grove, IL: 2006), p. 159.

27 Hebrews 2:9; Revelation 1:17-18

28 John 14:1-4; Romans 2:16; Revelation 11:5, 19:11-16

29 Acts 2:32-33; 1 John 2:1

Chapter 12

1 Leonard, Barry (2019, January 13). "How surviving the 'Miracle on the Hudson' changed my life: COLUMN." Retrieved from https://abcnews.go.com/US/column-surviving-miracle-hudson-plane-crash-changed-life/story?id=60316724

2 Ibid. Leonard.

3 John 3:3, 5-6, 16-18

4 Greer, J.D. Gospel (Nashville, TN: B&H Publishing, 2011), p. 46.

5 Anonymous Serge Authors. *Sonship—3rd Edition* (Greensboro, NC: New Growth Press, 2013), p. 169. I first read about "The Propulsion of Grace" in the Sonship training manual from Serge, formerly World Harvest Mission.

6 Galatians 4:1-7

7 Ibid. Sonship, p. 169

8 Ibid. Greer, p. 44

9 John 10:10

10 Galatians 6:2

11 Galatians 6:5

12 Paul uses it here in Galatians 6:2 and one other time in 1 Corinthians 9:21, parenthetically.

13 Matthew 22:37-40

14 There is only one speaking illustration that I made up all on my own; the one you're about to read. One time I actually saw this story—my story—on a preaching website, and thought, "Yes, I've made it. Someone is using my story." A few minutes later I found "Allegory of the long spoons" on Wikipedia—https://en.wikipedia.org/wiki/Allegory_of_the_long_spoons. Uuugghh!! I've never created a new thing in my life.

Chapter 13

1 Pelz, William (Curator) (Date unknown). *Observational Learning (Modeling)*. Retrieved from https://courses.lumenlearning.com/suny-hccc-ss-151-1/chapter/observational-learning-modeling/

2 Brown, Brené. *Daring Greatly* (New York, NY: Gotham Books, 2012), p. 217.

3 "Reticular." 2020. In Vocabulary.com. Retrieved from https://www.vocabulary.com/dictionary/reticular

Chapter 14

1 Crosta, Peter (2017, December). "Everything you need to know about scurvy." Retrieved from https://www.medicalnewstoday.com/articles/155758

2 There is some dispute about who said this—or a version of this—first. You get the idea though, right? If you've got a single tool, it will create a bias of over-reliance on that tool. The single tool we rely on creates tunnel vision only for the problem that tool fixes. If you've got a tool that "fixes" depression, everyone around you looks depressed. Same with single tools for anxiety, conflict, addiction, grief, greed . . . or whatever.

3   John Ortberg writes about the discipline of "slowing" in his book, *The Life You've Always Wanted*, pp. 81-96. Grab a coffee, relax in a soft chair and check out what he has to say. You'll be happy you did.

4   Willard, Dallas. *Living in Christ's Presence* (Downers Grove, IL: InterVarsity Press, 2014), p. 17.

5   Kruth, Rebecca and Curzan, Anne (2017, September). "Here's some 'ruth' for the 'ruthless.'" Retrieved from https://www.michiganradio. org/post/heres-some-ruth-ruthless

6   Au, Tom (2011, August). "What is the meaning and etymology of 'ruthless'?" Retrieved from https://english.stackexchange.com/ questions/36933/what-is-the-meaning-and-etymology-of-ruthless

7   "Eliminate." 2020. In etymonline.com. Retrieved September 9, 2020, from https://www.etymonline.com/word/eliminate

8   Fadling, Alan. *An Unhurried Life* (Downers Grove, IL: InterVarsity Press, 2013), p. 150.